SEVEN
PROMISES
OF A
PROMISE
KEEPER

SEVEN PROMISES OF A PROMISE KEEPER

WORD PUBLISHING

NASHVILLE

A Thomas Nelson Company

Published in association with Sealy M. Yates, Literary Agent, Orange, California.

Library of Congress Cataloging-in-Publication Data

Seven promises of a promise keeper / [compiled] by Bill McCartney, Greg Laurie, Jack Hayford.
— Rev. and expanded.
    p.   cm.
  ISBN 0-8499-3730-2 (trade paper)
  1. Christian men—Religious life. 2. Promise Keepers (Organization). I. McCartney, Bill.
II. Laurie, Greg. III. Hayford, Jack W.
  BV4528.2.S48   1999
  248.8'42—dc21   99-11090
                                                                                          CIP

Printed in the United States of America
99 00 01 02 03 04 QPV 8 7 6 5 4 3 2 1

Contents

Foreword:

Seeking God's Favor

by Bill McCartney

There's tremendous power in the spoken word. When a man gives you his word, if he's worth his salt, he'll deliver on all his promises. Let me illustrate what I mean.

When I was coaching the Colorado University football team in 1987, we were preparing to go to Norman, Oklahoma, to play the Sooners. The Sooners were the top-ranked team in the country and coming home to play after being on the road. In addition, our Colorado team was extremely young. For as long as anyone could remember, the Sooners had intimidated Colorado not only with their talent, but also with their downright offensive demeanor. Colorado had become a cakewalk for them. They had won thirteen of the previous fourteen head-to-head match-ups and had averaged more than forty points a game in doing it. Colorado was one of the big reasons Oklahoma was turning out All-Americans and Heisman Trophy winners!

Clearly, we needed to try a new approach. I had to find some way to motivate my players to give the performance of their lives. I finally decided to issue a challenge based on their word as young men. On the Thursday night before the game, I laid this on them: "Men," I said, "no one is getting on that plane for the trip to Norman until he has looked me in the eye and told me what I can expect of him in Saturday's game." The next morning, I set aside three hours and met individually in my office with the sixty players who would be making the trip. Three minutes each; that's all it took.

As I summoned each young man into my office and had him sit down across from me, I looked at him and said, "Now, son, I want to know what I can expect from you when we go to Norman to play Oklahoma."

Each one looked me squarely in the eye and said something like, "Coach, you can count on me to play every down to the best of my ability. I'll play my heart out against Oklahoma." Then, depending on his position, each player added, "I'll block better than I've ever blocked before." "I'll tackle with more authority." Or "I'll run with precision and strength."

I told each man, "I'm going to hold you to your word," then I added that I wanted him to be positive and excited so his teammates would pick up on that attitude.

Having set the tone with those meetings, the team that boarded that plane was on a mission. I knew that collectively, those sixty players would spend themselves in a valiant effort. I didn't know if we could win, but I knew we wouldn't lose because of a lack of effort. Those young men would play their hearts out.

The game was scheduled at night and televised nationally on ESPN, so I realized that a lot of the high-school players we were trying to recruit around the country would be watching. And what they saw, before the night was over, was that we would no longer lie down for Oklahoma! We did, indeed, spend ourselves, trailing by just four points at halftime, though we eventually lost 24–6. But the good news was that each of us knew he had given himself for the team. Each player kept his promise and extended himself. We had taken a significant step forward as a team.

If that kind of dynamic exists in a man's word to a football coach, how much more is it at work when men gather in Jesus' name, look each other squarely in the eyes, and declare what can be expected of them? When that happens, there's an unleashing of God's Spirit, an outpouring of His grace and strength that enables us to become Promise Keepers, men who are willing to contend for God's truth.

Now, bear in mind that our ultimate goal—being "conformed to the likeness of his Son" (Rom. 8:29)—is a lifelong process. Just as the Colorado football teams didn't become national contenders overnight, so we won't instantly become perfectly godly men. But as Colorado football began its transformation into a championship program to a large extent with that one game, we Christians also begin by committing our lives to Jesus Christ and becoming a new creation (see 2 Cor. 5:17). Then we make the kinds of commitments to growth embodied in the seven promises covered in this book. We make them to other men who will hold us accountable and give us the benefit of their experience and wisdom. As we do this, our thoughts, words, decisions, and actions will change over time. And our families, friends, coworkers, churches, and communities will receive the blessing of God's work in us.

There's a lot to chew on in this book: seven areas of commitment, each of them big and potentially life-changing. The task may seem overwhelming. So where do you start? Let me suggest that you pray, fully reflect on what you've read, and then identify the one thing that God's Spirit has most impressed upon your heart as something you need to do.

Next, take that one thing to a Christian brother, look him in the eyes, and tell him what he can expect from you. When he does the same with you, again look him squarely in the eyes and say, "As your brother in Christ, I'm going to hold you to it." Then encourage each other along the way. Pray for each other; call one another regularly; rally your brother when he's weak. Catch your brother when he falls, and be his biggest fan when he succeeds.

You see, when you make a promise to a brother, you declare your intentions and obligate yourself to follow through. You bind yourself to that person, too. You actually look into the future and determine, by your deliberate choice, that part of it relates to your promise.

Jesus said, "Enter through the narrow gate. For wide is the gate and broad is the road that leads to destruction, and many enter through it. But small is the gate and narrow the road that leads to life, and only a few find it" (Matt. 7:13–14). Most men are on the broad road. Which one will you walk?

We're in a war, men, whether we acknowledge it or not. The enemy is real, and he doesn't like to see men of God take a stand for Jesus Christ and contest his lies (see 2 Cor. 10:3–5). But Almighty God is for us, and we know that if we walk the narrow road that leads to life, we have an extremely capable leader in Jesus, the King of kings and Lord of lords. And He is faithful to provide the grace and strength we need along the way.

You and I serve royalty, and we have a costly responsibility. But listen to this promise in John 12:26: "My Father will honor the one who serves me." Accordingly, there's nothing I want more in life than to serve Jesus Christ, because I want Almighty God's favor on me. How about you?

Reconciling with Your Heavenly Father

by Greg Laurie

We have all heard the saying that there is nothing new under the sun. In the twentieth century we believe this is true. We've "seen it all, heard everything, been there, done that." At times, we're convinced that we have nothing left to learn. Yet our attitude is not unique. In some ways, this attitude has existed throughout history—it is called pride.

You may have been raised in the Christian church since your childhood—and that's a wonderful thing—or you may be entertaining the idea of becoming a Christian for the first time in your life. In either case, there is always more to learn of God. We find this reality confirmed in a conversation that took place more than two thousand years ago—a conversation between a man named Nicodemus and Jesus, recorded in the Book of John (John 3:1–21).

Now, you might ask, what does a conversation between some religious guy named Nicodemus and a Jewish carpenter from Nazareth have to do with us today? The answer is *everything*! For this is not merely a conversation between two men. It is a conversation between God and man. And if we were given the opportunity to choose a candidate to speak to God on behalf of the human race, we couldn't find anyone better suited than Nicodemus.

Nicodemus was an impressive man. He was famous, wealthy, respected, devout, and moral. He was an intellectual—a man at the top of his profession. Yet, in spite of all of his success, there was an emptiness deep inside of him. So, when he began to hear about a man named Jesus who was performing miracles, Nicodemus decided to seek Jesus out. He had questions he hoped Jesus could answer.

CIRCUMSTANCES CANNOT GIVE LIFE MEANING

Nicodemus had everything that one could want in life, but something was still missing. You know, as long as you are chasing your dreams, you can put up with many of the disappointments of life. You reason, "One of these days things are going to work out for me. One of these days my ship will come in. I'm going to get that education. I'll make that first million. I'll get that promotion. I'll find that perfect woman." When you're single, you say, "If I could get married, then I would be happy." Then you get married and you say, "If I could get divorced, I would be happy." After you're divorced, you say, "If I could get remarried, then I would be happy."

Then you say, "I know what it is, I need kids. If I had children, then I would be happy." Then you have children and say, "If I could get these kids out of my house, then I would be happy." Then you say, "Maybe I need a bigger house." So you build a bigger house, but then you say, "No, I need to downsize. If I had a smaller house . . ." *et cetera, et cetera, et cetera.*

WEALTH DOES NOT BUY HAPPINESS

The Bible says, "Death and Destruction are never satisfied, and neither are the eyes of man" (Prov. 27:20). When you attain everything that you have ever wanted to find fulfillment, yet you are empty, you begin to search even more. That's why we read of celebrities with great personal wealth joining the "flavor-of-the-month" religion or turning to drugs and alcohol. We ask, "How could that be? They have everything, so why are they so empty?" It's because when you get it all, you realize that the things you can buy in this world will not fill the void in your life that was created to be filled by God and God alone. Money can buy you a therapist. It can buy you a marriage counselor. But it can't make you happy.

EDUCATION DOES NOT ANSWER OUR DEEPEST QUESTS

The Bible tells us that Nicodemus was a Pharisee. Pharisees were a small, select group of Jews. Each had taken a solemn vow before three witnesses they would devote every moment of their life to keeping the Ten Commandments. Even more than that, Nicodemus was one of their primary leaders, a member of the Jewish Sanhedrin. This body was the chief ruling authority in all of Israel. They wrote laws and conducted trials—the equivalent of the Supreme Court today.

Nicodemus was well educated. When he came to Jesus at night seeking spiritual answers Jesus says "You are the teacher in Israel. Don't *you* know these things? Nicodemus, your name is a household word. Everybody knows about you. You're known to be a man of the Scripture, a man of wisdom. You're supposed to have all the answers. And you come to Me asking these questions?" You see, behind the charade, behind the mask, Nicodemus was a man who was empty. He was hungry for true spiritual life.

Does that describe you right now? Maybe you think you have it all together, but you're falling apart on the inside. You're in church every Sunday, Bible under your arm; you know the words to the hymns, but are you still empty inside and lonely? Do you wonder if God has truly forgiven you of your sins? Do you wonder if Jesus Christ really lives in your heart?

A PERSONAL CHOICE TO BEGIN ANEW

God has no grandchildren. He only has sons and daughters. Every one of us has to come to a moment in our life when we realize that we're sinners, that we're separated from God, and that we must ask Him to forgive us. Our parents can't do that for us. Our friends can't do that for us. *We* need to decide.

Nicodemus came by night, the Bible says (see John 3:2; 19:39). This is mentioned more than once in Scripture, so it's certainly worth noting. Perhaps he was afraid of being seen. After all, he was well known, even famous. If he were alive today, the press would have been following him, taking pictures of him. Possibly, Nicodemus didn't want to be seen. Or perhaps he was afraid of the criticism of others, afraid of what they might think.

I wonder how many have been kept from Christ because they were afraid of what others might think. Yes, it's true, Nicodemus came by night, but at least he came. He may have lacked boldness to identify himself with Christ at first, but, in the end, Nicodemus became one of Jesus' bravest followers.

Some have great beginnings with Jesus, only to deny Him later. While Nicodemus was still groping his way, Judas was a full-fledged disciple, intimately connected to Jesus. Later, Judas betrayed Jesus and hanged himself, while Nicodemus came to the cross, along with his friend Joseph, to get the broken body of Jesus and to bury it. He took a stand for the Lord in the end.

Maybe you haven't been so strong up to this point. But you can make a commitment or a recommitment *now* that will last you the rest of your life. Maybe you did not have a strong beginning, but you can have a great ending—finishing well, following Christ. And the end counts the most.

AGE IS NOT AN ISSUE

Nicodemus was probably an elderly man, getting on in years—which may account for some of his slowness and caution. He asked Jesus, "How can a man be born when he is old? Can he enter a second time into his mother's womb?" (John 3:4, NKJV).

Possibly you, too, are getting on in years. But even if you're older and set in your ways, Christ can change you. You may think it's too late for you—you can't teach an old dog new tricks. But you're not a dog, and these aren't tricks. We're talking about what God can do. He can change you.

I come from a broken home. I had many men who claimed to be a father to me, many men I had to call "Dad." I became disillusioned and cynical at an early age. But one man that my mom married, Oscar Laurie, adopted me and gave me his last name. He was a good man, a moral man, an attorney by profession. When my mom left him, it was one of the hardest things I ever faced.

I remember getting out of school one day, and our car was parked out front, filled with all of our belongings. My mom told me to get in the car. She told me that we were going to Hawaii—

but Dad wasn't coming. It would be many years before I saw him again.

After I became a Christian, it was important to me to reconnect with Dad. So I called his home—he was still in New Jersey. He had remarried and had other children, and I felt awkward trying to break the ice that had accumulated during our long separation. But I persevered. As we talked about our lives, his wife at one point asked me how I came to be a Christian and a pastor. I told her my story while my father just sat staring, his face in his hands. I felt as if I were on trial, and he was weighing the case.

As I shared what Christ had done for me, Dad did not say a word. Finally, he said to me, "Greg, would you like to walk with me in the morning? I need to walk to help my circulation." Surviving a recent heart attack that almost ended his life, Dad now was taking steps to improve his health. I agreed to join him.

Early the next morning, while we walked in the cold New Jersey air, Dad shared that he had been thinking about what I had said the night before. "I want to know what I need to do to become a Christian," he said. I could hardly believe my ears. I thought maybe he hadn't understood, so I told him the whole story again. He said, "I want to do it right now." We stopped walking, and Dad gave his life to Jesus in a park—right then.

In another instance, at a Billy Graham crusade, I overheard an interesting conversation. Billy had just invited people to come forward and give their lives to Christ. In the row behind me, a little boy about nine years old turned to his father and said, "Daddy, I want to go down there right now." But his father said no.

So the boy repeated, "Daddy, I want to go down there right now and become a Christian." His father said no again. (I almost turned around and said, "Dad, let him go!" But I decided to stay out of it and see what happened.)

The father then said, "Son, you don't realize what he's asking. He's asking for people to go down there to become Christians."

The little boy countered, "Daddy, I want to be a Christian. I'm going down there whether you let me or not. I'm going!" (I liked that!) With that, the father relented and asked his son if he wanted him to go with him. So, they got up and walked forward—father and son—

to make a commitment to Christ. That little boy knew what he wanted to do. No one else could do it for him.

COME AS YOU ARE

God demonstrated His love for us while we were yet sinners. Jesus said, "Greater love has no one than this, that he lay down his life for his friends" (John 15:13). Christ showed His love for us by dying on the cross in our place. Why did He die on that cross? We are *all* separated from God because of sin. Our hearts are dark. In the light of God's perfect justice, we deserve to die. Jesus knew that we could not save ourselves or change our situation, so He offered Himself in our place.

God says in Jeremiah, "I know the thoughts I think toward you, says the LORD, thoughts of peace not of evil, to give you a future and a hope" (Jer. 29:11, NKJV). God is thinking about you; He loves you. And He can forgive you, no matter what you have done. It was not nails that held Jesus to the cross, it was love. For you! And for me.

The question is, What are we going to do with this wonderful gift? Jesus said that if you believe, you will not perish (see John 3:16). The word *believe* does not just mean to accept intellectually that a man named Jesus lived and died. It means "to cling to, rely on." Have you put your faith in Jesus and Jesus alone? This doesn't mean just going to church or reading your Bible. God wants much more than for us to *say* we believe. He wants us to place our whole life in His hands.

WHAT MUST YOU DO?

On that night so long ago, Nicodemus posed the question for all mankind: How can a man be born again?

You need to believe. Jesus told Nicodemus, "For God so loved the world that he gave his one and only Son, that whoever believes in him shall not perish but have eternal life" (John 3:16).

You need to confess that you're a sinner. Romans 3:23 says, "For all have sinned and fall short of the glory of God." We have all broken His commandments in our actions and in our hearts—every single one. Realize Christ died for *your* sins. He shed his blood for *you*.

You need to repent. What does the word *repent* mean? It means to change your direction, to hang a U-turn in the road of life. You've been running away from God. It's time to turn around and run *to* God.

You need to receive Christ into your life. Scripture says, "To all who received him, to those who believed in his name, he gave them the right to become children of God" (John 1:12). Christianity is not merely believing a creed or living by a list of rules; it's having Christ in your heart to direct and empower you.

You need to do it now. The Bible says, "Now is the day of salvation" (2 Cor. 6:2). The devil will whisper in your ear tomorrow, but God's Spirit is saying, "Today, tonight." Make your decision *now*.

You know you want to get right with God. You know you want to change. You know you want your sins forgiven. You know that you want to go to heaven. God loves you and wants to forgive you. He wants to welcome you into His kingdom, but you must respond to His invitation.

All you have to lose is emptiness, loneliness, guilt, and the fear of death. In their place, God will give you fulfillment, purpose, forgiveness, and the hope of heaven. It's God's trade-in deal: You come with your sins to Christ, and He'll clean up your life.

PRAYER OF COMMITMENT

Father, I'm coming home. Please make me Your son. I turn from my sin. I accept Your forgiveness, made possible through Jesus Christ by His death on the cross. I place my faith in Jesus alone. I receive Him as my Savior and Lord. I want to follow and serve Him. Let today be the beginning of my new journey as Your son and a member of Your family. You've always kept Your promises. Help me to keep my promises, too. In Jesus' name I pray. Amen.

In the Life
of One Man

David had a good thing going—or so he thought. He was driving with a group of men from North Dakota to Minneapolis for an August 1997 Promise Keepers conference. By simply agreeing to attend such an event, he hoped to persuade his wife, Sara, that he was serious about making some monumental changes.

In six short years, he had made a mockery of their marriage. Only weeks earlier—after hours of fighting—Sara had pried out a confession. After chronic lying about everything from his golf score to his after-hours roving, David finally came clean. He had cheated on Sara—twice. Divorce seemed inevitable.

But David's confession had an unforeseen effect. To Sara's embattled heart, it brought an inexplicable sense of relief. The news was bad, but she was heartened that her husband had at last told the truth. And David, shamed and humiliated to divulge his breach, found the disclosure had surprisingly improved communication between them. For reasons unknown, Sara seemed to be softening. After years of bickering, they were actually talking. *Is there hope after all?* David wondered.

The invitation to Minneapolis was timely. Their neighbors, Bill and Heather, were well acquainted with the couple's struggles. As a regular

Promise Keepers attendee, Bill had witnessed miracles unfolding in men's hearts. He invited David to the event, hoping to kindle a spark of faith—and possibly to avert a marital catastrophe. David thought it was an opportunity to "prove" his willingness to turn over a new leaf. He might have to endure an interminably boring conference, but, with luck, he'd earn some brownie points with Sara and buy some time to sort out the mess.

The plan soon went awry. The first challenge occurred a few miles outside town, when Bill nonchalantly popped a Promise Keepers tape into the deck. As the first sobering organ strains filled the car, David paled. He thought, *Oh man, I'm in for a whole weekend of this?* While Bill talked about God with his father and brother, David sat back and braced himself to do whatever it took to get through the weekend.

He faced his second crisis when their car pulled into downtown Minneapolis. The streets were filled with men walking to the Metrodome. David shuddered when he saw thousands of men carrying Bibles, wearing PK T-shirts and hats, hugging each other, and—*crying!* "I couldn't believe my eyes. And the conference hadn't even started," he recalled.

He began to wonder if he had made a huge mistake when his group settled into the highest reaches of the stadium. David listened halfheartedly as the first speaker that evening closed with an invitation for men to accept Jesus Christ as their Lord and Savior. How could he base his whole life on blind faith when he really needed the "cold, hard facts"? A newsreel of memories flooded his mind: the arrogant bully he became as a military policeman, his reckless fights and drinking binges, drifting from job to job, rowdy and aimless years as a long-haul trucker, a stormy marriage, and two beautiful children.

The words from the platform snapped David back to the Metrodome. "Get out of your seats, men!" A small voice from somewhere began to whisper, "You're doing all that sinning. It won't look good for you if you die and end up before God." It made him start to wonder if all this stuff about God was true. Was he going to end up in hell?

Men streamed into the aisles. Watching the startling pageant, David thought, *If I had any brains, I'd go down there. It would look good. Bill will tell his wife, and she will tell Sara.*

Against every natural impulse, David finally stood, shuffled to an aisle, and began the long descent to the stadium floor. Within minutes, he was stuck in the gridlock on the stairs while the words to a song poured over the crowd: *Jesus . . . You are my life . . . I come to You . . . I run to You . . . There's no greater joy than knowing You . . . You are my life. . . .*

When David reached the mezzanine, several flights above the stadium floor, he began to sob. In that instant, the message of the song snapped into focus. He suddenly realized he did believe in God and that he wanted to give his life to Jesus.

David was encircled by men, hugging and encouraging him. "The next thing I remember, I was on my knees in front of the stage. Bill somehow appeared and prayed with me as I asked for forgiveness for hurting my wife, for the lying, the adultery. I asked the Lord to take over my life."

David now understood why he had come to Minneapolis. A life of deception and futility died in the spot where he knelt. He called Sara when he returned to the hotel.

"I just poured my heart out to her, crying and pleading for forgiveness. I told her I was ready to commit myself to the Lord. She didn't have a lot to say because she couldn't stop crying."

Back home, David understood that in spite of his new faith, he faced a long, uphill road to regain Sara's trust, to prove his words to her on the phone were *real*. It would be the challenge of his life, yet Sara sensed something that gave her hope. She could tell he was trying.

David entertains no illusions. Each day he faces the gaping wounds he has inflicted on their relationship. "All I know is, I'm in this for the duration. I'm going to keep moving—try to keep growing. God has given me another chance. He showed me what I need to do to be a better man."

A MAN AND HIS GOD

A Promise Keeper is committed to
honoring Jesus Christ through worship,
prayer, and obedience to God's Word in
the power of the Holy Spirit.

Setting a Sure Foundation

by Jack Hayford

A teary-eyed blonde and crumbled buildings.

They seemed to have no relationship, but I couldn't escape the parallels they represented.

The first was a young woman, a sweet and lovely wife who had come to my office for counsel that morning. The second was the news report regarding thousands who were instantly crushed as buildings toppled from an earthquake in Mexico. The weeping wife poured out her heart that morning in my office. As she talked, I thought of the images I'd seen on television of mourning multitudes digging through rubble. The two disasters had the same root cause—negligence in building standards. Lousy foundations make for temporary homes.

The woman wasn't whiny or complaining. In fact, she hadn't volunteered any information that would pin the fault on her husband. I appreciated that: She was entirely ready to accept full responsibility for her situation. But the more I inquired, the clearer it became that, whatever her shortcomings, there was a sad, underlying reason for the lack of development in her marriage. The man of the house believed in God but had no pattern whatsoever for worshiping Him.

Oh, the husband had some half-baked notions he would conveniently throw up, like a "Hail Mary" football pass when faced with a desperate, need-an-answer situation. You know what I mean; it goes like this: "I believe in worshiping God according to the dictates of my own conscience. I don't think you need to be in a church—I simply worship God from my heart, wherever I am. I think you can worship God as much in the mountains as in town at church. I want to be honest and sincere about worship, and I don't think people who try to prove their superiority over others by going to church are any better than me."

And the drone goes on. It's an empty argument concocted by a mind that has rarely, if ever, taken time to assess the shallowness of its foundational thought. Whatever may be correct in the "straw man" propositions, the basic goal isn't to assure sincere worship but to avoid commitment.

THE FOUNDATIONAL COMMITMENT

Who, how, and when a man worships determine everything about his life. That's the reason the first promise a man needs to keep is that he'll be honest with God. And honesty with Almighty God—the Creator of all things, including us; the Giver of all life, including ours; the Savior of all sinners, including us; and the Master of human destiny, including ours—this God—above and beyond all pretenders to His throne—demands attention to His ways of worship. The whimsy and flimsy of human reason, the puff and pride of human arrogance, only need to pass once through the flame of His presence to be shown for what they are: nothing. And a life built with nothing at its center results in homes and relationships with nothing underneath them. Like the frustrated wife in my office, like the pancaked houses in Mexico, groundless "faith" and lack of commitment to worship result in homes without foundations and relationships without roots. When stress comes, they can't stand the test.

How can a man find the path to worship that pours substance into him, strength into his life's foundations, unshakable stability into his marriage, steadfastness into his relationships, and trustworthiness into his work and business practices? The answer is found by beginning where God has always started with men—at worship!

A TIMELESS PATTERN

It's not as if the picture and principles aren't clear.

See God introducing Adam to *redeeming worship* in the garden, after sin had marred that setting and the promise of a Savior was given (see Gen. 3:15).

See God calling Abraham to *faith-filled worship* and promising to thereby make him an instrument of blessing to all the families of mankind (see Gen. 12:1–3).

See God calling Moses to *delivering worship*, showing how the sacrifice of the lamb would save enslaved households from death and open a future with meaning (see Exod. 12:1–28).

See God calling Isaiah to *purifying worship* as the young man stood in the presence of the Lord, stunned by God's greatness and humbled by his own sinfulness (see Isa. 6:1–5).

See the church born in *empowering worship* as God's Spirit began the era of our witness as believers in Jesus Christ—the church praising God and seeing supernatural grace bringing multitudes to Christ (see Acts 2).

Each of those expressions of worship has a counterpart in a man's life today. Each has an application that can forge solid "stuff" into the foundation of a Promise Keeper's life.

1. Redeeming Worship

Redeeming worship centers on the Lord's Table. However your tradition chooses to celebrate the Lord's Supper, we are all called to this centerpiece of Christian worship.

Jesus, the builder of the church, commanded that this regular practice be laid in the foundations of our observance as worshipers (see 1 Cor. 11:23–26). The power of the redeeming blood of Christ not only saves our souls, but it is also the foundation of all redemptive, recovering, renewing works of God.

2. Faith-filled Worship

Faith-filled worship calls for action. When Abraham heard God's voice, he broke with convenience, got up, and went where God said to go (see Gen. 12).

It isn't difficult to draw this analogy to one of the most fundamental calls you and I face every week: the wake-up call to gather with the people of God to worship Him. Listen to the call: "Let us not give up meeting together, as some are in the habit of doing, but let us encourage one another—and all the more as you see the Day approaching" (Heb. 10:25).

There's no escaping the fact that worship gets intensely practical at this point. It takes place (1) at a certain time, (2) at a certain place, (3) with a certain group, and (4) for very certain reasons. Try to spiritualize it any way you please—or try to scorn "church" as traditional, ritualistic, passé, or boring—still the Bible lays down a mandate: Don't forsake it!

Yes, it costs inconvenience of schedule, preparation, tolerance, and grace, plus the humbling of ourselves. We need to get up, get going, get there on time, get a right attitude, get with the program, and get ready to receive from the input of others (who sometimes don't fascinate us all that much). The fruit of this commitment is the laying of strong foundations of practical faith—the real faith that follows God and affects others around us, as Abraham's did.

3. Delivering Worship

Delivering worship is that which frees a man from bondage, liberates his family to its greatest possibilities, and opens the way to the future without the entanglements of the past. That's what happened when Moses submitted to worship.

This type of worship was revealed most dramatically in two events that occurred within days of one another: the Passover in Egypt and Israel's passage through the Red Sea. The story that unfolds in the first fifteen chapters of Exodus hinged on a private encounter between Moses and God Himself. What resulted was a man's household being set free and his own life finding its intended destiny. Walk through it with him.

1. *God calls a man into His fiery presence* (see Exod. 3:1–4). We should put away idle notions that worship can be tamed to our own tastes. The man who fears drawing near to the flame of God's Spirit at work will never experience a complete burning away of fear and pride.

2. *God calls a man to remove his shoes* (see Exod. 3:5). The issue wasn't

bare feet but the removal of one's own self-fashioned support. In other words, God wanted of Moses and desires of us a will to put nothing of our own creation between ourselves and Him. And standing barefoot in the rocky terrain of a desert, as Moses did, will cause a man to walk more cautiously before God.

3. *God calls a man to know His heart* (see Exod. 3:7–8). Notice how it was in God's presence that Moses learned of God's gentle heart, loving concern, compassionate nature, and desire to heal and deliver. You and I need to be in His presence for the same reason. My family—yours, too—needs a husband and dad who is regularly being imbued with God's love, understanding, and gentleness.

4. *God calls a man to leadership* (see Exod. 3:9–10). For Moses, the call was to lead a nation, whereas your call and mine will likely be less visible. But make no mistake, we are leaders! And there is no avoiding the fact that people around us will be affected by whether or not we accept our call to God's purpose in our lives.

The bottom line of this whole encounter is *how* God showed Moses the way His purposes would be fulfilled in him. We read it in Exodus 3:11–12: "But Moses said to God, 'Who am I, that I should go to Pharaoh and bring the Israelites out of Egypt?' And God said, 'I will be with you. And this will be the sign to you that it is I who have sent you: When you have brought the people out of Egypt, you will worship God on this mountain.'"

Moses' response was as incredulous as yours or mine would be: "Who am I?" In short, the man was saying, "Hey, God, I know *You're* mighty, but I don't think I could ever become what You're saying I'm to become." God's answer was terse and direct: "You shall worship God on this mountain!" It was stated so briefly as to pass notice and put so simply as to defy belief. God was saying, "The answer to your question 'Who am I?' is in your *worshiping Me*. You will find who you are when you know who I am!"

Chuck was a hard-nosed guy, a tough, hard-hat type to whom worship seemed more suited for women and children. Sam was a business executive—in many ways the precise opposite of Chuck except for his conclusions about worship. They exemplified what I've found to be the most common presumptions by men who think worship too mystical, too holy, too "beyond" for them.

Both Chuck and Sam became part of our monthly men's gatherings where I had prioritized three things: (1) forthright, no-games-played *worship*, (2) honest, say-it-out-loud-to-someone sharing in *prayer*, and (3) straight-from-the-shoulder, Bible-centered, practical *teaching*. I watched them, just as I've watched hundreds of others, break free through delivering worship. *Guys* who break the sound barrier and sing from the heart (no matter how bad their voices); *guys* who kneel humbly with a group of men, lifting their voices in concerted prayer; *guys* who express their surrender to the Almighty as Paul called men to do with upraised hands (see 1 Tim. 2:8)—*these guys change!*

4. Purifying Worship

Purifying worship comes from a man's *waiting* in the presence of God. Whatever may be said for the essential place of *corporate* worship in the church, there is still no substitute for *private* worship—meeting God alone.

Isaiah's record of his face-to-face meeting with the living God relates how ashamed he became of his impurity: " 'Woe to me!' I cried. 'I am ruined! For I am a man of unclean lips, and I live among a people of unclean lips'" (Isa. 6:5). In short, "God, I'm stained, and I work in an atmosphere cluttered with foul mouths and ungodliness." Sound familiar?

However, I've met thousands of men who have surmounted the power of personal and societal uncleanness, of profanity, of mental impurity or foul habits. And they didn't accomplish it by the grit of self-imposed efforts at stringent discipline. They found purity through the power of being in God's presence!

Listen to Jesus' words: "Blessed are the pure in heart, for they will see God" (Matt. 5:8). Check this closely, because too many read this text to mean, "Everybody who's perfect will arrive in heaven some day." But Jesus wasn't talking about purity in ritual terms. He was talking about the fundamental definition: Purity is "that which is undiluted by other substances." Now, join that to the place Jesus pointed at, to the heart of a man—that's where God seeks undiluted commitment.

So what does it all mean? The answer is in what Jesus did and didn't say. He *didn't* say, "Blessed are the pure in mouth . . . hands . . . mind . . . feet." No. Christ calls you and me to come, candidly and with a *heart fully opened* in worship, into the privacy of His presence. Then something will happen: If we bring our whole heart, without restriction or reservation, we will see God!

That, my brother, doesn't mean you or I will have a phantasmic vision of heaven or see fleecy clouds with flying angels. It means we will become candidates for seeing God's *nature* take over our lives, God's *hand* provide for our needs, and God's *grace* work through our touch, words, and witness. *We will see God.* It's the privilege of the purified, not earned by accomplished holiness but realized through the total devotion of a man's heart at worship.

5. Empowering Worship

Empowering worship emerges from that quest for God that receptively opens to the fullness of His Holy Spirit. Acts 2 is a case study of men who had *walked* with Christ coming to the moment when they were *filled* with His Spirit and power. It happened in an atmosphere of worship.

The record of Scripture is expanded by the record of history; men who worship become men of spiritual power. It isn't because they have a mystical experience but because they are filled with the mightiness of Jesus. Their power isn't in self-gratifying displays of personal accomplishment but in humble service, faith-filled prayer, and their availability to allow the Holy Spirit to deliver His gifts through their lives.

Worship also sustains this divine empowering. Being filled doesn't guarantee being full today. That's why the apostle Paul commanded, "Keep on being filled with the Holy Spirit" (Eph. 5:18, my literal translation). Then he prescribed the way to such sustained fullness: "Speak to one another with psalms, hymns, and spiritual songs. Sing and make music in your heart to the Lord" (Eph. 5:19). There it is, put as clearly as possible: *Worship sustains Holy Spirit fullness.* A life of power is maintained by a man's spending time daily in God's presence—praising Him.

PRESENT YOURSELF TO GOD

No text in the Bible makes it more clear:

> Therefore, I urge you, brothers, in view of God's mercy, to offer your
> bodies as living sacrifices, holy and pleasing to God—this is your
> spiritual act of worship. Do not conform any longer to the pattern of
> this world, but be transformed by the renewing of your mind. Then
> you will be able to test and approve what God's will is—his good,
> pleasing and perfect will. (Rom. 12:1–2)

Those pointed words call for a man's entire being—body, mind,
emotions, spirit—to be presented to God in worship. The result is
transformation from world-mindedness to Christ-mindedness, and
proof of the will of God—which is demonstrated and verified in his
life.

The infusion of this kind of "stuff" into a man puts substance in his
character, concrete in his family's foundation, holy steel in his soul's
strength, and weight in his person and presence. The Promise
Keeper's first priority is *worship*. For in meeting the Almighty, the
foundation for all of life's "promises yet to keep" is laid in the unshak-
ableness of His being. It's the strongest place any of us can stand.

And we stand best when we've first learned to kneel in worship.

 # Why Men

Must Pray

by Wellington Boone

Today, we are faced with a culture in steady decline. The number of violent crimes in the United States, for example, has increased 570 percent since 1960, while the population increased only 43 percent. Over the same period, illegitimate births increased more than 400 percent. The U.S. has the highest rates of teen pregnancy, abortion, and childbirth in the industrialized world. From 1960 to 1993, SAT scores dropped 67 points. I could go on and on, but you get the picture. There's no doubt that the situation is grim. What can we men possibly do to make a difference?

Well, for one thing, we can pray for revival.

Before you dismiss that idea as simplistic, consider that this isn't the first time a country has faced such a crisis. In 1735, Wales was in decline politically and spiritually. There was an upsurge of the occult and the renewed practice of divination and black magic.

In that same year, a young man named Howell Harris was converted to Christianity. Soon after, Harris was praying in the village where he was a teacher, and God met him in a powerful way. Nothing seemed impossible to him. He began to travel everywhere, preaching, until all of South Wales was awakened. Even notorious criminals were converted and changed their ways.

The secret of Harris's influence on the masses was prayer. He understood that nothing would be accomplished, either in himself or in his troubled nation, without prayer—personal, private communion with God.

In every generation, revival has come as the result of prayer. For example, powerful prayer preceded America's First Great Awakening, which gave the colonists a unified biblical view of the principles of freedom and helped pave the way for the American Revolution. The Second Great Awakening, which preceded the Civil War, brought a conviction from God that slavery was a sin. It was led by men like Charles Finney, who prayed for hours upon hours and days upon days.

God still needs men who, like Howell Harris and Charles Finney, will give themselves to prayer and then go and do whatever the Holy Spirit tells them.

Revival is the movement of the Holy Spirit in an extraordinary way that causes multitudes to be drawn to Christ. That's what we need today. America needs revival. The church needs revival. Families need revival. Men need revival.

The prayer that sparks revival begins long before the countryside seems to awaken from its slumber in sin. It starts when men fall on their knees and cry out to God. That's where true intimacy with God takes place and we begin the journey of being transformed into the image of Christ. And as men are transformed, the course of a nation can be changed.

The need for revival to start within the praying individual was brought home to me powerfully a few years ago. I was driving across the country from my home in Virginia on what I call a prayer sabbatical, something I do every year to get alone with God. As I drove along, praying, I asked God to change hearts in the inner city and bring another Great Awakening. Suddenly, the biblical story of blind Bartimaeus flashed through my mind. He hated being blind, and I was stirred by his zeal. When he heard Jesus approaching, he cried out, "Jesus, Son of David, have mercy on me!" (Mark 10:47).

Then I thought, *I'm blind, too, because I don't know my own heart. I'm praying God would move on the inner cities, but I need Him to move on me. Bartimaeus had more desire for the healing of his physical blindness than I have for the healing of my spiritual blindness.*

At that realization, I cried out loud in the car, "Jesus, Son of David, have mercy on me!" Who was I to pray for change in others when I myself remained unchanged? That experience began a revival in me that still today influences my life and ministry.

We need to see our own hearts so God can change us—personal revival—and then use us to improve our homes, our workplaces, our churches, and all of society.

Before I suggest some steps in the process of life-changing prayer, let me warn that one of the greatest hindrances to developing a personal relationship with God is packaged programming that tells you how to pray. A man must be drawn to God alone, there to find his own "how-tos."

Moses found God in the burning bush.

David wrote many of his prayers in the form of poetry and music.

Elijah hid in a cave and heard God's still, small voice.

Jesus met with the Father in the wilderness.

You need to find for yourself the things that keep your prayer relationship with God fresh. However, most people can benefit from a few practical suggestions to help them understand where to begin.

The Holy Spirit leads us into a personal prayer relationship with God through four stages. I believe they are inevitable steps in the growing process in which we move from focusing on our own needs to focusing on the privilege of worshiping God. After all, worship, in its truest sense, means giving ourselves to God. It means forgetting about ourselves for the sheer joy of knowing Him.

These four words summarize the four stages of entering into a prayer relationship with God: love, intimacy, privilege, and responsibility. Let's look at each of them in turn.

LOVE

The initiative of love is always first with the Father. "For God so loved the world that he gave his one and only Son, that whoever believes in him shall not perish but have eternal life" (John 3:16). Even our salvation is a response to God's love. Scripture says it is the goodness of God that leads men to repentance.

The first time we yield to God is when we come to Him for salvation. We acknowledge our sinfulness. We thank Him for giving His Son to be our Savior. He embraces us. We are immersed in His love. And we find oneness with the Father.

INTIMACY

When we're alone with God, there are no more distractions to the development of intimacy. It is just us and Him. The rest of the world must wait.

True prayer is not a rhetorical stream of eloquent words; it is the expression of a deep longing for God that is born out of love. When we're in love with someone, we always look for ways to spend time with the person. We press through with the development of the relationship in every way.

Finding God is the beginning. Getting to know Him is the journey. Scores of people have found Him in saving grace but have not yet come to know Him in intimacy, the place where He begins to impart a sense of divine separation for His purposes.

PRIVILEGE

Out of the atmosphere of intimacy, trust is born. Where there is trust, there is the granting of privilege. What a privilege to understand and know God! What a privilege to comprehend Him through a living relationship! The greatest privilege any believer can have is access before Almighty God with the confidence that He will answer prayer.

RESPONSIBILITY

If we truly believe Christ is alive, we will do anything for Him because we can believe God for anything, and we know He is omnipresent. We know He identifies with us as His body. We recognize He is not only Lord over our lives, but He also takes responsibility for us and gives us responsibilities to carry out for Him.

When God grants you the privilege of knowing Him, He does not do it so you can get your needs met. He does it so He can accomplish His will. Unanswered prayer is a failure to approach God on the basis of His will, because "this is the confidence we have in approaching God: that if we ask anything *according to his will*, he hears us" (1 John 5:14, emphasis added).

PRAYING FOR REVIVAL

One thing we know God wants His people to pray for is revival. But if revival is to come, there must be a change in the prayer lives of the men of America. It is time for us to return to our knees and remain there until something happens.

The prophet Hosea said, "Sow for yourselves righteousness, reap the fruit of unfailing love, and break up your unplowed ground; for it is time to seek the LORD, until he comes and showers righteousness on you" (Hosea 10:12). God is looking for a company of men of courage who are willing to do whatever it takes to bring another great spiritual awakening.

In our ministry, we have an acronym for the type of prayer life that is necessary to bring about change. The word is PUSH, which stands for:

Pray Until Something Happens.

This acronym also stands for four steps you need to take in order to see personal, family, and national revival.

P: Purify yourself.

Search your heart. Repent from any known sin. The prophet Hosea said, "Sow for yourselves righteousness." Paul wrote, "Let us purify ourselves from everything that contaminates body and spirit, perfecting holiness out of reverence for God" (2 Cor. 7:1).

You need to sow the Word of God into yourself until you see that you are a sinner under the searchlight of God's righteousness. The psalmist wrote, "The unfolding of your words gives light" (Ps. 119:130).

When you sin, be quick to turn away from it and cry out for God's mercy.

U: Understand God's mercy.

We need to receive mercy from God, and we need to deliver mercy as ambassadors for Christ to a lost generation. "Be merciful to those who doubt" (Jude 22). Jesus said, "Blessed are the merciful, for they will be shown mercy" (Matt. 5:7).

Your personal revival awaits your willingness to forgive all who have wronged you and to seek forgiveness of others you have wronged (see Mark 11:25–26).

S: Sanctify yourself.

Learn to live a life of personal accountability to God. Regardless of what others consider to be righteous, keep yourself "from being polluted by the world" (James 1:27). Be separated for the purposes of God. "As God has said: 'I will live with them, and walk among them, and I will be their God, and they will be my people. Therefore come out from them and be separate,' says the Lord" (2 Cor. 6:16–17).

Separation for God does not mean we leave the world or neglect our families. Just the opposite. It means that our commitment to the living, righteous, holy God becomes evident to all those around us.

Hosea said, "Break up your unplowed ground." We must learn to obey immediately everything God tells us to do. We never want to have a wrong heart toward Him.

H: Hold fast in prayer.

Pray Until Something Happens. Prayer is work. It is blessed work, but it is work. As in any relationship, it takes effort to give up some of your own pleasures to bring pleasure to another. The chief sin of the church today is laziness. We are lazy about prayer. We're lazy about changing ourselves. We're lazy about good works. We're certainly lazy about praying through for a great spiritual awakening in America.

God has made available incredible power to change this nation, and yet we remain in our dulled state of sin, complaining about the condition of America, crime in the inner cities, and corruption among politicians.

Just think of all the power that could be unleashed if the fifty thousand men who attended the Promise Keepers rally in Colorado in 1993 would begin to PUSH for America. What would happen if each of those men made a commitment to Pray Until Something Happens? Can you see what a serious force that would be?

THE POWER FOR REVIVAL

Our problem is that we have no understanding of the great power within us. We're unwilling to give up our comforts, like morning sleep, for a few precious moments with God. "I love them that love me; and those that seek me early shall find me" (Prov. 8:17, KJV).

We call ourselves men of God, but we are too often men of our own needs. All needs are met on our knees. We must substitute "knees" for "needs."

America is sick and dying because the people have lost hope and vision (see Prov. 29:18). Even the church is aimless. Why? Primarily because of a lack of faith in God. But why do people lack faith? Because those who say they are men of God are so seemingly helpless to bring about change. They say they pray and study the Word, but their wives and children see little evidence in their lives. Our prayer and study lives should have an immediate, ongoing effect on our families. They should be so moved by our love and mercy that they want to emulate what they see in us of the character and qualities of Christ.

Do we really believe that Jesus has risen from the dead and that God answers prayer? If we do—if we continually develop that perspective through time with God on our knees—we will become the source of faith, hope, and vision that the world so desperately needs.

When the world sees men of God overcome with the lusts and pride of the self-life and trying to find a sense of purpose, however, its vision of God is distorted. A passage in Isaiah captures well the futility of American Christian men over the past thirty or so years: "As a woman with child and about to give birth. . . . We were with child, we writhed in pain, but we gave birth to wind. We have not brought salvation to the earth" (Isa. 26:17–18).

THE NEXT GREAT AWAKENING

But by God's grace, on our knees, that is all changing. Promise Keepers have become impregnated with personal revival. Our changed lives are obvious. Like a woman who is pregnant and nearing the end of her term, we Christian men are about to burst forth with the coming of the Lord in ways we have never experienced.

"In the last days, God says, I will pour out my Spirit on all people" (Acts 2:17). We have not had our last revival.

"'Before she goes into labor, she gives birth; before the pains come upon her, she delivers a son. Who has ever heard of such a thing? Who has ever seen such things? Can a country be born in a day or a nation be brought forth in a moment? Yet no sooner is Zion in labor than she gives birth to her children. Do I bring to the moment of birth and not give delivery?' says the LORD. 'Do I close up the womb when I bring to delivery?' says your God" (Isa. 66:7–9).

I believe that the church is in travail and that God is about to birth the next Great Awakening. And it will start with you.

 # Becoming a

Man of God's Word

by Joseph Stowell

Roy Regals was a walk-on player at the University of California. Only a year later, he was living every football player's dream as the starting center in the Rose Bowl. He never expected much fame as a center—centers rarely make the winning touchdowns in a bowl game. Then suddenly, the ball was spinning on the ground in front of him. He reached down, recovered the fumble, tucked the football under his arm, and, bouncing off a couple of players, saw himself in the clear! Roy Regal strained with every fiber of his being toward that goal line for his moment of glory.

Out of the corner of one eye, Regals saw his teammate Benny Lam running after him and shouting at him. It sounded like Benny was saying, "You're going the wrong way!"

Roy Regals later said he thought to himself, *What's wrong with him?* And he continued to go the wrong way. California lost the game to Georgia Tech 8 to 7. Roy was branded indelibly, "Wrong-Way" Regals. This incident occurred in 1929. Yet, even now they replay the clips on nationwide TV of Roy Regals picking up the fumble, running the wrong way, and losing the game.

To Regals the play seemed right. It seemed good. It was his moment to shine. His instincts empowered him, but they drove him blindly the wrong way. If we are not careful, we could be men of his legacy—men whose whole lives are driven by instincts.

PROMISE KEEPERS ARE WORD KEEPERS

Think for a moment. What drives your life? Why do you run the way you run and go to the places you go? Is it for pleasure? Prosperity? Possibly, fear drives you. Or testosterone. Some look for significance. Others strive to be culturally correct.

Rather than men driven by instincts; God calls us to be men formed by the inspired Word of God. Promise keepers are Word keepers. We are to raise up the standard of the Word of God as the sole authority for all of life. Probably the clearest statement about what God's Word is to the man of God is found in the Book of 2 Timothy: "All Scripture is inspired by God and profitable for teaching, for reproof, for correction, for training in righteousness; that the man of God may be adequate, equipped for every good work" (3:16–17, NASB).

All Scripture is inspired by God and it is *profitable*. Unfortunately, many of us look at God's Word and laws as some kind of divine rip-off. "Yeah, right. I'll submit to the laws of God. I'll submit to His Word, but I won't be happy or prosperous. He will send me to Africa. It will just be a bummer all the way home to glory."

The truth is that God's Word profits you. Specifically, it is profitable for teaching, reproof, correction, and training in righteousness—so that you and I, as men of God, may be equipped for every good work.

GOD IN YOUR HAND

God's Word is inspired. Literally, the word *inspired* means "God-breathed"—the expression of the very essence of His being. As I encounter the Word of God, I encounter God. The Bible is really like God in my hand—holding Him, hearing Him, reading Him. It is power, wisdom, correctness, justice, fairness, and love.

God's Word is the supreme authority of the universe. When God speaks, worlds come out of nothing. When God speaks, terrible storms become quiet and waves cease to roll. When God speaks, blind eyes see and lame legs walk. When God speaks, dead men come forth from the grave. There is not one element in this universe that is not submissive to the authority of the Word of God—except, sometimes, we men of God.

UNCHANGING, IMMOVABLE

I'm reminded of the story of a ship captain who was guiding his ship through a night sea enshrouded in fog. A bright light in the distance was headed directly toward his ship when he got a radio message: "Adjust your course three degrees."

He thought, *Who is this to tell me what to do?* So he got back on the radio and said, "You adjust *your* course three degrees."

Undaunted, the voice on the radio insisted, "No. Adjust your course three degrees."

The ship's captain finally laid it on the line. "I'm the captain of this ship, a retired navy admiral. I will not adjust three degrees. Who do you think you are?"

The radio voice responded, "I am the keeper of the lighthouse. Adjust three degrees."

God's Word is clearly, finally, always true. It is the absolute standard and authority. God does not adjust to us; we adjust to Him. God in my hand—the wonderful, loving, fair, just, wise, powerful authority in my life. It is our guide in the darkness.

LEARNING TO THINK STRAIGHT

When we are redeemed, we are born into the family of God ignorant. We just don't know much about the kingdom. I don't think ignorance is bliss when this tough life demands so much of us. That's when God's Word comes alongside and teaches us. For example, we live in a world that says, "Real men ought to grab for power and position and credentials." God's Word says in Matthew 20:26, "He who would be great let him be your servant." And suddenly, I'm taught. I say to myself, *I never knew that before—that the highest end of a man of God is not his power or his position or his profile or his prosperity, but it is that he be a servant of God and a servant of others for God's sake.*

We think that our careers are platforms for our own significance. We think that we are at the job to please our boss, to get a bigger pay-check and maybe a promotion. That's what we think. God's Word comes along in Colossians 3:23–24 and says, "No, no, no. You do your careers to please God. He is watching how you work. Work to make Him happy."

Or we think that money exists so we can accumulate things for our own benefit and significance. But God's Word in 1 Timothy 6:17–18 says, "Tell those who are rich among you not to be conceited or to trust in their riches, but to be rich in good works. To be generous and to share." I'm thinking, *Really? I didn't know that. I am supposed to use my money to be a blessing to others, to use my things to be generous and share for the glory of God.*

When I married my wife, I thought, *Great! She will clean my bedroom, pick up my socks, wash my clothes, and kiss me good-bye when I go to work. She'll make my coffee, rear my kids. And when I come home at night, she'll welcome me at the door and hand me the paper, along with the remote control. She'll feed the kids early, make me my favorite gourmet meal, and be a tiger at 11:00 P.M.* But then God's Word teaches me: She's not for you; you are for her. "Husbands love your wives, just as Christ loved the church and gave himself up for her" (Eph. 5:25).

Some of us are loaded with guilt. We feel like abject failures . . . until we read God's Word: "Come to me, all you who are weary and bur-dened, and I will give you rest" (Matt. 11:28). And, "If we confess our sins, he is faithful and just and will forgive us our sins and purify us from all unrighteousness" (1 John 1:9). We live in a world that will never forgive you when you blow it. But Christ always forgives us, and His cleansing blood flows over us and makes us clean. How do I know that? God's Word taught me.

DO YOU REMEMBER IN THE WORD . . .

One Sunday morning, I was walking through the church lobby in my navy blue suit, my sermon in my briefcase. The Sunday school super-intendent and his wife stopped me and asked, "Pastor did you order the Sunday school material we requested?"

I didn't premeditate it. It was instinct all the way. But I said, "Yes," walked into my office and shut the door. Nobody knew that I had lied, nobody. I opened my briefcase and God walked into my office. Well, not really, but you know how He works you over? *Joe, do you remember in the Word where I talk about lying and truth?*

Then things got worse. *Joe, do you remember that passage about confessing your faults to one another? Where it says in Matthew that if you are bringing your gift to the altar for God. . . .* (That's what I was going to do that Sunday morning—give my gift to God by preaching His sermon.) I remembered: "Therefore, if you are offering your gift at the altar and there remember that your brother has something against you, leave your gift there in front of the altar. First go and be reconciled to your brother; then come and offer your gift" (Matt. 5:23–24).

I thought, *Oh, I can't do that. If I tell those people that I lied, the elders will kick me out of the church.* God's Spirit said, *Obey the Word.* His reproof was heavy. Then my flesh said, *Don't do that. Nobody will ever know. Ask the Lord to forgive you. It will be cool. They'll never know.*

The Spirit put me in a full Nelson, pinned me to my bookshelves and said, *Stowell, be a man of the Word!* I knew what I had to do. After I asked the Lord to forgive me, I went to find the Sunday school superintendent and his wife to tell them that I had lied and to ask them to forgive me. There was a silent pause when I told them. But then, my friend put out his hand and said, "Of course, Pastor, we forgive you." Tears welled up in his wife's eyes. It may have been the first time in her life that a man admitted to her that he was wrong. It was a lot for her to take in. Finally, she said, "Pastor, we forgive you."

God cleansed me, and He healed our relationship. Know this: If you become a man of God, He will chase you down with His Word. If you start running the wrong way, His Word is going to start screaming at you. It will not only teach you, it will reprove you. Thank God it does! I do not want at the end of my life to be known as "Wrong-Way" Stowell.

God's Word will not only make you smart and reprove you; it will also correct you. I fly on planes all the time, and it's kind of unsettling to think that the pilot, after he gets us off the ground, leans back, and puts the plane on automatic pilot. As the plane starts to veer off course a little bit, the instruments immediately nudge it back. I love that about the Word of God. I start to wander a little bit, and it comes alongside and corrects me, nudging me back to righteousness.

GROWING UP IN RIGHTEOUSNESS

The Word will train you. Like a loving parent, it will groom you in what is right. You will be tested—given opportunities to learn. First to walk, then to run, then to do marathons for God.

I am an incurable people person. But even people people can get peopled out. Sometimes after a busy day at work, I get in my car thinking that I hope I never have to see another person again. *Furthermore, when I get home I am going right to the closet. I'll tell my wife to slide supper and the newspaper under the door. And don't anyone talk to me for three hours!*

Then God reminds me: *Stowell, I thought you were a man of the Word! Well, of course I am. But I deserve a little alone time.*

He says, *Let's talk about this. I called you to love your wife. Does she have any needs? She is waiting at home for you, you know.*

Here's a test. Can I grow up and do this right? I know what I need to do. I have to walk through the door, lean on the counter, and say to my wife, "Marty, tell me about your day. Tell me every detail. And I can't wait to tell you what happened to me today."

Then there are the kids. All they want is to wrestle with me on the floor. That's all that counts. You know, I used to be impressed with myself when I was asked to speak at a Promise Keepers event. My kids are not impressed. They are only impressed with my time and attention. That's it. Period.

God says that fathers come up alongside their kids like God Himself would (see Eph. 6:4). I know what I need to do when I get done talking to Marty. I need to go out and wrestle with my kids on the floor because if God walked through that door, He would go wrestle with my kids. You can take that to the bank. That's the kind of Father He is.

READY FOR THE PRIVILEGE OF GOOD WORKS

Our lives cannot be driven by our instincts. We must surrender to the authority of the Word to guide us, teach us, reprove us, correct us when necessary, and groom us up to be men of righteousness. The bottom line is to be thoroughly equipped for every good work God sends us.

I was flying to minister for a week in Toronto a couple of years ago, the last flight out on a Saturday night. I was the first guy to arrive in my coach section on one of those huge planes—three-hundred-plus seats. A lady had been preboarded and was sitting by the window, face buried in her hands, bawling her eyes out. I glanced at my boarding pass and—out of three hundred seats—I was sitting next to her.

So now I had a problem. I had procrastinated all day, and I had a briefcase full of things I needed to go through to be ready for ministry the next day. My instinctive reaction was that I didn't want to ride next to this woman. Everybody else would be on reading their *Wall Street Journals* with their laptop computers looking so significant, and I would be taking care of some teary-eyed woman. I already had another seat picked out. . . .

God's Word pounced on me again, like the hound of heaven. *Stowell, I thought you were a man of the Word! Doesn't the Word of God say you should imitate Christ? Well, what do you think Jesus would do if He got on this plane?*

It was over. Jesus would sit in that seat. He would *want* to sit there. That was a sobering thought. So I sat down. As soon as I sat down, the young woman lifted her face, tears running down her cheeks, and said, "Oh, I miss my daddy so much!"

In her late twenties, I knew right away that she was mentally challenged. I thought, *My goodness, this is going to be a long trip.* She was so disruptive that the man behind me asked to be moved before we even took off.

As we talked, I asked where she was from. She said, "Wisconsin— Union Grove." Now, I happened to know that one of the finest Christian Homes for mentally challenged people is in Union Grove, Wisconsin. So I asked, "Are you from Shepherds?" Yes, she was.

Suddenly I got the picture. This precious lamb was from a Christian Home, and God had asked me to help grant her safe passage. I thought, *God, thank You for giving me this opportunity to be adequately equipped for a good work like this. This is what angels do.* It's as if God said, *We have to get Christa from Chicago to Toronto,* but when He brings all the angelic hosts together they are all busy. So He goes, *Stowell, sit in that seat!*

I have to tell you that I'm no angel. My wife knows that, and all my friends know that, but it was a wonderful privilege to be taught, corrected, and groomed in the privilege of righteousness. That would have been enough in itself. But God took it even further.

As I waited for my luggage at the baggage claim, I stood next to the guy who asked to be moved to another seat. Seeing me, he said, "Excuse me, sir, can I ask you a question? Did you know that lady that you were riding with?"

I responded that I'd never met her before. Then he asked, "Are you a therapist?"

"No."

"Are you a psychologist?"

"No."

"Well, what do you do?"

I said, "I'm a minister."

I'll never forget what this attorney from Chicago said next. He kind of got quiet and said, "I knew you had to have something different in your life to do what you did on that plane." Then the bags came, and he was gone.

I pray for that man. I pray he gets around a lot of Promise Keepers and that every time he gets around us he sees that our lives are equipped for good works. I pray that he sees the shortfall in his life and says, "God, I need what these Promise Keepers have." I hope I see him in heaven.

In the Life

of One Man

"God was turning me, and I didn't want to turn. Being a dentist was everything to me." Dick felt sorry for friends who didn't like their jobs, because he loved his so much. For Dick, dentistry was artistic, challenging, and rewarding. He enjoyed the independence of working for himself and making all the decisions in a practice only three minutes from his home. But all this was coming to an end.

Inexplicably, Dick began to feel very tired all the time. Although normally he was extremely active, he found it difficult to make it through his day. The doctors could not tell him what was wrong. He was frightened, confused, and frustrated. During this time, Dick was introduced to Promise Keepers and joined a small group that met faithfully every week. The group met a deep need in the lives of the men and proved an invaluable support for Dick as he awaited further direction from the Lord.

Months later, his illness finally diagnosed as chronic fatigue syndrome, Dick realized he had to give up his dental practice. "At the age of forty-nine—after twenty years in private practice—I was not feeling up to a career change. I had to redefine totally who I was. It never occurred to me that I would ever be anything but a dentist!"

It was one of the toughest times Dick ever experienced. Finding someone to take over his practice not only meant giving up what he did. He also was cut off abruptly from the community he had served for many years—people who were like family to him.

Finances quickly became another problem. His wife, previously a full-time mom, was forced to find work outside the home and began to dip into his retirement fund to make ends meet. They found themselves having to rely on God as never before.

"Why is God putting us through this radical life change?" Dick wondered. His question was answered one evening while he put his daughter to bed, his attention seized by a plaque on her wall. "Trust in the LORD with all your heart and lean not on your own understanding." He trembled as he read on: "In all your ways acknowledge him, and he will make your paths straight" (Prov. 3:5–6). *Acknowledge him*. The words leapt out of the frame and pierced his heart.

"Do with me as You will, Lord," he prayed. It was so cleansing to let go. It was the first time he had really *yielded* to God's plan. Now, six years later, God's perspective has become even more clear.

In one year alone, Dick spoke at more than one hundred churches, telling his story. "Ministering to others has healed me, but not in the way I expected. I now can relate to men who are hurting. I'm much less self-reliant and feel so much more a part of His plan." Before this trial, Dick admits that he wasn't serious about his walk. Now his relationship with God is the most important thing in his life. "I'm not always where I need to be, but I'm growing. I think I like the new 'me' better!"

PROMISE

A MAN AND
HIS FRIENDS

A Promise Keeper is committed to
pursuing vital relationships with a few
other men, understanding that he needs
brothers to help him keep his promises.

A Mandate

for Mentoring

by Howard Hendricks

The most compelling question every Christian man must ask is this: What am I doing today that will guarantee my impact for Jesus Christ in the next generation?

If I understand my New Testament correctly, there are only two things God is going to take off our planet: One is His Word, and the other is His people. If you are building His Word into people, you can be confident that will last forever.

That's why I am so passionate about mentoring. Mentoring is a ministry of multiplication. Every time you build into the life of another man, you launch a process that ideally will never end.

My life and ministry are the result of mentoring. I am a product of a core of individuals who built into my life ever since I came to Jesus Christ sixty years ago. One in particular, Walt, literally changed the course of my life.

I was born into a broken home in the city of Philadelphia. My parents were separated before I was born. I never saw them together except once—when I was called to testify in a divorce court. I'm sure I could have been reared, died, and gone to hell, and nobody would particularly have cared, except that a small group of believers got together in my neighborhood to start an evangelical church. That small group of individuals developed a passion for their community.

Walt belonged to that church, and he went to the Sunday school superintendent and said, "I want to teach a Sunday school class."

The superintendent said, "Wonderful, Walt, but we don't have any boys. Go out into the community. Anybody you pick up—that's your class."

I'll never forget the day I met him. Walt was six feet, four inches tall. He said to me as a little kid, "Hey, son, how would you like to go to Sunday school?"

Well, anything that had "school" in it had to be bad news.

Then he said, "How would you like to play marbles?"

That was different! Would you believe we got down and played marbles, and he beat me in every single game? I lost my marbles early in life! By the time Walt got through, I didn't care where he was going—that's where I wanted to go.

For your information, he picked up thirteen of us boys, nine from broken homes. Today, eleven are in full-time vocational Christian work. And Walt never went to school beyond the sixth grade.

That's the power of a mentor. You don't need a Ph.D. to be used by God in the ministry of mentoring.

Have you ever asked, "Who has most affected my life?" Think about the people who made a difference. What did they do? How did they do it? Why did they do it? Answer those questions and you will be hooked on mentoring the rest of your life.

WHY MENTORING?

I want to ask and answer two central questions, then apply those answers to your life. The first question is, *Why be concerned about mentoring?* Is this just another gimmick? Is this simply some secular idea imported from the corporate world that we've introduced into the Christian community and baptized with a few verses of Scripture? Or is it a biblically legitimate strategy for our generation?

I am convinced there are three compelling reasons you must become involved in a ministry of mentoring. First, *you need to be involved in mentoring because of the severe shortage of leaders.* Leaders are fast becoming an endangered species. Wherever I go, across America or around the world, the screaming need is for leaders. I meet few churches or Christian organizations that can afford to hang a sign outside their front door saying, "No Help Wanted."

We need leaders in our churches. The average church in America is operated by 15 to 20 percent of its membership. But God gives to every believer a spiritual gift with which to function in the body, not to spectate in the stands.

I tell my students there are only two groups of people in church: the pillars who support it and the caterpillars who crawl in and out week after week. The latter occupy eighteen inches, more or less, on a pew, shake the hand of the pastor, and say with something of a pious whine, "Pastor, that was a wonderful message. We'll see you next week." They seldom come closer to the truth, for the fact is that 80 percent of the churches in America have plateaued or are in serious decline.

We need leaders in our homes, too. The American family is unraveling like a cheap sweater. May I remind you of one historical fact: No nation has ever survived the disintegration of its home life. Once the home goes, it's just a question of time before it all goes.

Pierre Mornell, distinguished West Coast psychiatrist, wrote a book titled *Passive Men, Wild Women,* and in that book he says,

> Over the last few years I've seen in my office an increasing number of couples who share a common denominator. The man is active, articulate, energetic, and usually successful in his work. But he is inactive, inarticulate, lethargic, and withdrawn at home. In his relationship with his wife he is passive. And his passivity drives her crazy. In the face of his retreat, she goes wild. [1]

Where are the men willing to step up to the plate and assume the leadership role God has given them in their homes?

We need leaders in our society as well—in politics, in business, in industry, in education, in agriculture, in the professions, in the military. I don't need to remind you that the landscape is littered with the bodies of men who have forfeited their right to be leaders because they were not men of integrity. They were not men we could trust.

Second, *we need mentoring because of the perceived need for mentors.* There's a severe deficiency in our culture, and it's seen in a number of areas. The first is the absence of fathers. I'm not talking only about physically absent; I'm talking about fathers who are emotionally and spiritually absent. The result is that the average boy in our society grows up and doesn't have a clue what a good father looks like.

The pedestals are empty! There's a shortage of older male models. It was well expressed by a little kid in a barbershop some time ago when I asked, "Hey, son, whom do you want to be like?"

He looked me straight in the eye and said, "Mister, I ain't found nobody I want to be like."

Do you think he's an exception? No, there is a terrifying void of affirming maleness in our society.

Recently my wife and I were in Jerusalem, visiting the Wailing Wall. We counted five bar mitzvahs going on. It was an exciting thing to watch those boys hoisted on the shoulders of their fathers, uncles, and friends, paraded around that sacred area with people clapping and singing and women throwing candy. Those boys will never forget that day. But what do we have in American society that even partially replicates that?

Someone asked me in a television interview, "What would you say has been your greatest contribution as a seminary professor?"

I answered, "To affirm the maleness of many of my students."

That's what we must do as men. Everywhere I go—to university campuses, evangelical churches, or the business and professional community—I find many young men asking, "Where can I find a mature friend?" And I find most older men asking, "Where can I find a ministry?" The result is the younger men are frustrated and the older men are unfulfilled. Intellectual honesty compels me to tell you: I find more younger men looking for older men to mentor them than I find older men willing to become involved in the lives of younger men. I say that to our shame.

Third, *we need mentoring because of the rape of existing leadership.* Two of the greatest curses ever perpetrated on a society have been crammed down our throats. One of them is the generation gap. There is no generation gap in the body of the Christ! You cannot drill any man out of the corps regardless of his age. Young people desperately need older people, and older people seriously need younger people who are going to carry on in the next generation.

The second curse is that of retirement. Retirement is a cultural, not a biblical, concept. You may retire from your company—you may not have an option—but you never retire from the Christian life and ministry. The only thing society knows to do with older men is to put them out to pasture and encourage them to play with the toys they have accumulated.

Have you noticed how many men there are over fifty who are reaching for the bench, who are sliding for home? At the very time when they ought to be tearing the place apart for Jesus Christ, they're caving in. May I remind you, the statistics are alarming of how many men die shortly after retirement. The reason is simple—they have no purpose for living. I'm finding an increasing number of guys blowing out their aorta on the way to Sarasota. The result? We're losing a great leadership pool in the body of Christ.

WHAT IS MENTORING?

You say, "I'm convinced, but *what is mentoring?*" That's our second key question.

Let me answer with a simple definition. Mentoring is a process involving people.

Sometimes it's a whole series of individuals whom God brings into your life at various stages and for various purposes. In every case, those people are committed to helping you grow and perpetuate the learning process.

The apostle Peter, in 2 Peter 3:18, said: "Grow in the grace and knowledge of our Lord and Savior Jesus Christ." He was saying, "As long as you live, you learn. And as long as you learn, you live."

Unfortunately, the epitaph of many a man is well expressed in the words, "Died, age twenty-six; buried, age sixty-four."

If you stop learning and growing today, you stop ministering tomorrow.

Bear in mind that mentoring is not a new concept. The trades, the arts, and the guilds have engaged in mentoring for centuries. Craftsmen not only know what to do and how to do it, but they also know why they do what they're doing. They're suffused with basic attitudes, particularly a pride in their work. And they know what to get excited about!

All of us know about the great artist Michelangelo. But few know about Bertoldo, his teacher. There's a debate in art circles about who was the greater—Michelangelo, the pupil, or Bertoldo, the teacher who produced him.

Christian mentors are people who have a spiritual commitment. They're not playing games; they're committed to life change. And they have specific values. High on their priority list is the development in another individual of excellence so that the individual grows in his Christian life to hate the mania of mediocrity, the attitude that anything is good enough for God.

Mentoring, whether through one person or a group of people, can help a person reach his maximum potential for Jesus Christ. In Colossians 1:28–29 we read, "We proclaim him, admonishing and teaching everyone with all wisdom." Why? "So that we may present everyone [mature] in Christ." And Paul added, "To this end I labor, struggling with all his energy, which so powerfully works in me."

Why was the apostle Paul committed to mentoring? Because he had clear-cut objectives. Your objectives determine your outcome. You achieve that for which you aim. Paul knew that the most important contribution he could make in terms of the next generation was to build into the life of the present one.

I'm finding an increasing number of men who are ending their lives at the top of the pile in terms of their field and at the bottom in terms of fulfillment. I believe the primary reason is that they have fuzzy objectives.

Paul not only had clear-cut objectives, but he also had clear-cut priorities. He not only answered the question, "What do I want at the end of life?" but also, "What price am I willing to pay for it?"

I happen to be a Van Cliburn fan, and, some time ago, a friend who plays in the Dallas Symphony Orchestra said to me, "Howie, are you going to the Van Cliburn concert?"

"I wouldn't miss it!" I said.

"How would you like to meet Mr. Cliburn?" she asked.

"You've got to be kidding!"

"No! You meet me behind the stage at the end of the concert, and I'll introduce you to him."

You can be sure I was there. And I had a question I wanted to ask him. "Mr. Cliburn," I said, "how many hours a day do you spend practicing the piano?"

Very casually he said, "Oh, eight or nine hours a day. Two hours doing nothing but finger exercises."

And to think my grandmother wanted me to play the piano!

Would I like to play the piano like Van Cliburn? You'd better believe it! But not that badly.

Often a guy will come to me and say, "Hendricks, I'd give my right arm if I had a marriage like yours."

To which I say, "That's precisely what it may cost you."

I sometimes ask men, "If you had an option—I mean, just one choice—either a great job or a great marriage, which would you choose?" Your priorities enable you to answer that searching question.

In 1 Corinthians 9, Paul said the Christian life is a race—not a hundred-yard dash but a marathon. Its success is determined at the end. Paul said it's a unique race because all can win. Not all will, but all can.

But Paul had a fear: He wanted to be sure that "after I have preached to others, I myself will not be disqualified" (1 Cor. 9:27).

If that was a live option to the apostle Paul, what about us?

WHERE TO FIND MENTORS

Every man reading this book should seek to have three individuals in his life:

You need a Paul.

You need a Barnabas.

And you need a Timothy.

You need a Paul. That is, you need an older man who is willing to build into your life. Please note: not someone who's smarter than you are, not necessarily someone who's more gifted than you are, and certainly not someone who has life all together. That person does not exist. You need somebody who's been down the road. Somebody who's willing to share with you not only his strengths, but also his weaknesses. Somebody who's willing to share his successes and his failures—in other words, what he's learning in the laboratory of life.

Hebrews 13:7 reads: "Remember your leaders, who spoke the word of God to you. Consider the outcome of their way of life and imitate their faith." Please note what you're not to imitate: not their method; not their giftedness; not their personality. Comparison is carnality. The Israelite women sang, "Saul has slain his thousands, but David his ten thousands." The comparison to David so embittered Saul that he spent the rest of his life pursuing David rather than the Philistines.

You also need a Barnabas. That is, you need a soul brother, somebody who loves you but is not impressed by you. Somebody who is not taken in by your charm and popularity and to whom you can be accountable.

By the way, don't miss your wife's role in this regard. I've never been able to impress my wife and kids. I tried! I used to think my kids would be impressed that I'm a seminary professor. That's impressive, don't you think? You don't think so? Neither did they.

My younger son once asked, "Hey, Dad, when are you going to get a new job?"

"What's the matter with my job?" I asked.

"I can't explain where you work," he said. "Everyone thinks you work in a cemetery!"

Sometimes I think I do, too!

My kids are not impressed that I studied Greek and Hebrew. They're probably not even impressed that I wrote this chapter for the Promise Keepers! My kids, like yours, are only impressed by the reality of Jesus Christ in our lives.

Have you got anybody in your life who's willing to keep you honest? Anybody who is willing to say to you, "Hey, man, you're neglecting your wife, and don't give me any guff! I know it, everybody else knows it; it's about time you knew it!"

Who's the person in your life who can say, "Hey, man, you talk too much!" without you saying defensively, "Well, I don't see any wings sprouting out on you."

Paul said in Galatians 2:11, "When Peter came to Antioch, I opposed him to his face, because he was clearly in the wrong." That's the kind of Barnabas you need.

Third, you need a Timothy. You need a younger man into whose life you are building. If you want a model, look at 1 and 2 Timothy. Here was Paul, the quintessential mentor, building into the life of his protégé. Notice the issues he addressed. He spoke of the need for somebody who can affirm and encourage you, for somebody who will teach you and pray for you, for somebody who will correct and direct you. That's the kind of person young people are looking for.

Now, how do you get these three men in your life? Let me give you two suggestions. First, *pray that God will bring into your life a Paul, a Barnabas, and a Timothy.* I happen to believe that where prayer focuses, power falls. You may not take God seriously, but He takes prayer very seriously. I am seeing an increasing number of men, younger and older, who are praying for Pauls, for Barnabases, and for Timothys to be brought into their lives. And God is wonderfully answering!

Second, *you need to begin to look for these men.* Put up your antennae. We have a lot of single students at the seminary who come and say, "Hey, Prof, I'm thinking about getting married."

"Oh," I say, "that's wonderful! You got any gal on the line?"

"No."

"Are you dating any?"

"No."

"Well, how do you expect to find a wife? You think God's going to let her down on a sheet out of heaven?"

Obviously, you've got to become involved in the process. And by the way, don't be surprised if it takes more than one or two experiences before you find that person, because there has to be a personal resonance. There's a chemistry that grows in a good mentoring relationship.

Now, I hear somebody out there saying, "Why are you so excited? You're fairly frothing at the mouth! This mentoring thing really has you." You're right. And it's not because I read some books on mentoring. It's not because somebody came along and said, "Hendricks, here's something else you need to get involved in." No, it's because it's the story of my life.

Remember Walt? Here's what's interesting—I can't tell you a thing Walt ever said. But I can tell you everything about him, because he loved me more than my parents did. He loved me for Christ's sake.

And I'm ministering today not only because of a man who led me to Christ and discipled me, but also because he started that mentoring process.

I want to leave you with a passage from Ecclesiastes 4. The wise man says, "Two are better than one." Why?

> Because they have a good return for their work: If one falls down, his friend can help him up. But pity the man who falls and has no one to help him up! Also, if two lie down together, they will keep warm. But how can one keep warm alone? Though one may be overpowered, two can defend themselves. A cord of three strands is not quickly broken. (vv. 9–12)

I want to recommend a cord of three strands—a Paul, a Barnabas, and a Timothy. An older man building into your life, a soul brother to keep you accountable, and a younger man into whose life you can build.

I can assure you after much experience that you haven't lived as a Christian until you have been mentored. And you haven't known fulfillment until you have been involved in the process of mentoring.

Gentlemen of God, go for it!

 **Strong Brotherly**

Relationships

by E. Glenn Wagner

Accepting the mandate for mentoring brings us to the tough part—overcoming the fear and barriers that hinder significant brother-to-brother relationships. I am convinced the benefits of such mentoring far exceed the risks of having to face those fears and barriers.

THE FRIENDLESS AMERICAN MALE

Men have difficulty being emotionally intimate with other men, which hinders the development of friendships. Why is that? The socialization of men and the lack of realistic role models are two significant factors. Here's what we've been taught:

"Men are self-reliant." Men have taken this to an extreme. Typically, we never ask for help, not even when we're lost. We're notorious for going it alone. The Lone Ranger of TV fame kept his mask on and kept mostly to himself—like many men in the church.

"Men don't feel." Actually, men do feel, but we have an innate or learned aversion to showing and sharing our emotions. This began when we were young and were told, "Suck it up! Big boys don't cry. Be a man!"

"Men don't touch." Touching, so common to friendships among women, is largely absent among men in our culture, except in contact sports.

"Men don't need fellowship." We tend to be so task-oriented, especially in our business relationships, that we cannot accept an invitation ("Let's do lunch") without asking, "What's up?" or "Why?"

"Men use people, love things." Acquiring things is important to many men. They tend to have relationships of convenience in which they use people to gain wealth and power.

"Men are too competitive." Men are so competitive with each other that enmity, not camaraderie, characterizes most recreational friendships. For many men, the only thing they get emotional about is losing. They buy Vince Lombardi's motto: "Winning isn't everything, it's the only thing."

"Men are too macho." On the silver screen and in the news, men who show bravado and violence are defined as "real men." Rarely do the media define manhood in terms of male friendships.

Yet these traditional stereotypes are changing.

THE SO-CALLED NEW MAN

Many men do desire to share their deepest feelings—but mostly with a *woman* they admire rather than another man in a mentoring relationship. We are told that women like this sort of sensitive and vulnerable friendship, whereas men resist it.

The New Man is described as being sensitive, caring, in touch with his own emotions. He has been disparaged by people on both sides of the gender gap who prefer men to be more macho—in the mold of John Wayne or Sylvester Stallone.

Clint Eastwood used to be on everyone's top ten list of macho men, but now he typifies the new manly man. Eastwood is breaking the mold by taking on male roles that call for more feelings, friendship, even forgiveness. According to reviewers, his movies "Unforgiven" (1992) and "In the Line of Fire" (1993) show us the face of the New Man:

• the steely blue eyes have a softer glint

- the taut jaw muscle is more relaxed
- he reveals some of his softer side—his emotional vulnerability

Nonetheless, the macho male is still the traditional one we were raised with. This causes confusion in the minds of men, and so we wonder: Can a "real man" enjoy a deep and meaningful, nonsexual relationship with another man?

The answer is *yes*. We can and should develop strong mentoring relationships. It won't be easy, however. To break the cultural stereotype and fulfill the biblical mandate to develop man-to-man friendships requires time spent in those relationships. According to George Barna's 1992-93 report, Americans consider friends (relationships) to be most important, yet we spend an ever *decreasing* amount of time with them. Barna wrote:

> Most churches claim they are "friendly." But that may not be enough these days. In a culture where time is always lacking and communication skills are minimal, people may not even know how to go about establishing meaningful relationships with friendly people. The Church has the chance to establish community by offering outlets that create and nurture real relationships.
>
> Small group systems, social events, relational teaching, and modeling relational development are effective methods of providing adults with both the emotional and tangible security they are searching for. (*The Barna Report* [1992-93], pp. 39-40)

The Scriptures give us the mandate for mentoring. Due to the pressures of our culture, many men recognize their need for mentoring relationships. This presents us with a tremendous opportunity. But we must overcome the barriers to friendship. Progress toward that end can be realized in seven steps.

Step 1: Follow the Golden Rule and Be a Friend

The Golden Rule applies directly to building strong man-to-man relationships. To find and keep a friend, you must first be a friend. As Jesus said, "Do to others as you would have them do to you" (Luke 6:31). We begin a mentoring relationship by asking ourselves how we like to be treated. The qualities men look for in a mentoring relation-ship embody one or more of these ideals:

Acceptance—to be fully known, accepted for who I am, without becom-ing someone's "project."
Understanding—to be listened to without interruption and without unsolicited advice.
Loyalty—to keep confidences without ever wanting to hurt me.
Self-disclosure—to risk revealing innermost feelings without fear of rejection or manipulation.
Availability—to be there for me, night or day, even at 2:30 A.M. in time of need.
Genuineness—for him to be who and what he says he is.

Develop these qualities in yourself and, as like attracts like, you will soon find them in someone else.

Step 2: Obey the "One Another" Commands of God

In strong mentoring relationships, we obey what God commands us to do within the Body of Christ. All issues of spiritual growth and maturi-ty are framed in the context of relationships. This is obvious from the many "one another" passages in the New Testament. Here's a sampling:

- *Love one another:*
  "A new command I give you: Love one another. As I have loved you, so you must love one another" (John 13:34).
- *Accept one another:*
  "Accept one another, then, just as Christ accepted you, in order to bring praise to God" (Rom. 15:7).
- *Encourage one another:*
  "And let us consider how we may spur one another on toward love and good deeds. Let us not give up meeting together, as some are in the habit of doing, but let us encourage one another—and all the more as you see the Day approaching" (Heb. 10:24-25).
- *Forgive one another:*
  "Be kind and compassionate to one another, forgiving each other, just as in Christ God forgave you" (Eph. 4:32).

- *Honor one another:*
  "Be devoted to one another in brotherly love. Honor one another above yourselves" (Rom. 12:10).
- *Instruct one another:*
  "I myself am convinced, my brothers, that you yourselves are full of goodness, complete in knowledge and competent to instruct one another" (Rom. 15:14).
- *Serve one another:*
  "You, my brothers, were called to be free. But do not use your freedom to indulge the sinful nature; rather, serve one another in love" (Gal. 5:13).
- *Submit to one another:*
  "Submit to one another out of reverence for Christ" (Eph. 5:21).

The list of "one another" passages goes on, but you get the point. It is impossible for men to fulfill the commands of Scripture without being in significant relationships with one another.

Step 3: Seize the "Teachable Moments" in Your Life

Being open to change is another component in building strong relationships with men. As Paul said, "Do not conform any longer to the pattern of this world, but be transformed by the renewing of your mind" (Rom. 12:2).

We cannot build lasting, significant relationships if we are unwilling to change sinful and hurtful attitudes or actions. But take heart; there are many ways to hurdle this barrier. Frequently a "teachable moment" will make us open to such change.

We are most teachable when: (1) struggling in a time of crisis; (2) overwhelmed by inadequacy; (3) confronted with an unresolved need or problem; (4) challenged or measured by a goal; or (5) searching for a more meaningful relationship.

One such teachable moment contributed significantly to the formation of a mentoring relationship for a Wisconsin Promise Keeper. As he tells the story:

I was due to be married in June but got cold feet and called it off one month before the wedding. My career in life insurance sales was also at a dead end. I had asked Dick, a seminary professor and sometime mentor over the years, to officiate at the wedding. Wanting to comfort me in my disappointment and guide me in my ongoing search for meaning-ful work, Dick came out from Boston to Wisconsin on the weekend the wedding would have happened.

As we shared heart to heart, Dick ended up inviting me to write for him. I changed careers to apprentice myself as a "Timothy" to this veteran communicator of the faith. That mentoring relationship has continued to this day, but it would not have begun had it not been for a crisis of confidence 15 years ago.

Teachable moments do not have to be life-changing experiences like that one to catapult you into a mentoring relationship, however. You just have to be open to change and acknowledge your need.

Step 4: Acknowledge Your Need of Others

Until you acknowledge your need for the gifts, talents, and perspec-tives of other men in your life, you will never pursue positive, nur-turing relationships.

Some years ago, while pastoring in New Jersey, I reconnected with a former college professor who had been a real encouragement to me. In the course of our phone call, I invited Stan to come and preach at my church. To hear him preach and watch the congregation respond so positively was great. Even greater were our times of "catching up."

That's when I began realizing my need for this mentor in my life and ministry. When I suggested the possibility of regular talks, prayer, and accountability with Stan, he was humble and honest enough to voice his need for me. Even though we have been called to minister in different states and must content ourselves with only a rare get-together, I have yet to come away from one of our monthly phone calls without feeling affirmed.

By acknowledging their need for each other, two men can make a positive impact on their respective lives, ministries, and families.

Step 5: Accept and Appreciate Differences in Others

We acknowledge our need for others by placing a high value on their opinions and ideas, even (and especially) when they differ with us.

Differences of culture, gifts, talents, temperaments, and physical abilities should all be valued with the special, unconditional love that Christ bestows on us.

After my move to Denver, Colorado, I continued to acknowledge my need to connect with other men of like heart. However, I had not been able to get beyond the acquaintance stage in any relationship. Then I followed the advice of an out-of-town friend and met Rod, who was teaching at a local seminary. Within minutes, I knew Rod was someone I could relate to, enjoy, learn from, grow with, and be held accountable to on important matters. But I also wondered if such a relationship was possible. How could two men so unlike each other grow together?

Our differences are obvious. I'm white; he's black. I was raised in suburbia; he was raised on a farm. My path took me through the rebellion of the late '60s and early '70s; he went through college and on to seminary, then graduate school—all with a positive focus and unswerving direction. We both love golf, but he often hooks his ball, and I often slice mine. We both love to preach, but our styles are so different. We both love to laugh, yet my humor is mostly in side comments, while his involves storytelling accented by hearty laughter.

Those very differences, however, are what make our relationship special and powerful. I have learned from Rod's personal pain; as he has grown through it, so have I. Thanks to our differences, I have a deeper appreciation for what is important in life.

Step 6: Devote Yourself to People

The very thing we're trying to develop and maintain—a mentoring relationship—could be jeopardized by shifting our focus and devoting ourselves to goals, programs, or tasks. When that happens, men are viewed as a means to an end rather than as an end in themselves. To remedy that, involve yourself in the lives of men quite apart from how they fit into your business agenda.

Devotion to people begins with a focus on your own family. You are the only husband or father they have. You may find it somewhat natural to develop mentoring relationships at work, with a built-in expectation for training and developing younger associates. When you intentionally invest in someone younger and bring him along with you, you multiply or generate your talents through others.

All the above-stated principles of developing and maintaining man-to-man friendships apply to a men's small group. This last step in building mentoring relationships may also be the first.

Step 7: Band Together in Small Groups for "PPP"
When pairs of men in strong mentoring relationships band together for mutual edification, support, and accountability, you have a small group of Promise Keepers. Conversely, existing small groups are an excellent source of brother-to-brother friendships that could develop into mentoring relationships.

Assuming you are committed to keeping your promises and will take the risk of being a friend—even if that means caring enough to confront—you are ready to band together with other men and make mentoring relationships happen on a small-group scale.

Coach Bill McCartney, founder of Promise Keepers, has a handy way of remembering the basic agenda of men's small groups. He calls men together for "PPP," which stands for prayer, pages (of Scripture), and pain.

- *Prayer* is conversing with God—acknowledging His supreme place in our lives, giving thanks for all things, and bringing the needs of others and ourselves before the One who can do something about them.
- *Pages* of Scripture are what we use to find out more about God and His provision for us. The divine-human encounter is life-changing. Referring to Scripture as the final arbiter in all matters of faith and practice keeps us from merely pooling our ignorance or giving unsubstantiated advice.
- *Pain* is our reason for going to prayer and Scripture in the first place. Men are most genuine with one another when they are vulnerable and share their pain—in their marriages, with their children, or at work—with each other.

HANDLE CONFLICTS WITH CARE

Despite the best of intentions, conflicts will arise in most friendships and small groups. In such times, you find out who your real friends are.

Conflicts are neutral; it's how you react that makes—or breaks—the friendship. Here are some pointers for handling conflicts constructively.

- *Give others the benefit of the doubt.* Rather than always looking for a hidden agenda, trust people to keep their word and live up to their agreements.
- *Double check your own attitude.* Assert your opinion and don't be defensive, but do defend the other person's right to speak his mind and hold an opinion different from yours.
- *Separate people from the problem.* Go soft on people, hard on issues—that is, love people more than opinions.
- *Focus on interests, not on positions.* Do not bargain over the substance of a position, but do build on common interests, which are vested in maintaining the relationship.
- *Invent creative options* for mutual gain. Go for a win-win solution to the conflict by broadening the range of options and agreeing on objective criteria or principles by which you will decide what's best.
- *Compromise on matters of taste or personal convenience.* Stand firm with integrity, however, on matters of principle or personal values.

Confrontation and Care

A balance between confrontation on issues and care for people will strengthen and lengthen any mentor relationship. Many men in Scripture model this tough love. It was used, for example:

- by the prophet Nathan with the adulterous David (see 2 Sam. 11–12);
- by Jesus with Peter, who had denied his Lord three times (see John 21:15-19);
- by Paul with Peter, who had compromised on the issue of justification by faith for Jews and Gentiles alike (see Gal. 2:11-16).

This need for honest confronting of issues with genuine caring for people is made practical for mentors in the following chart (adapted from David Augsburger, Caring Enough to Confront [Ventura, Calif.: Regal, 1980]).

Remember that the Bible commands both the one who has been offended and the one who did the offending to seek reconciliation. Acknowledge whatever actions and attitudes on your part led to the break in the relationship. Admit the hurt and consequences to the people involved, as well as remorse over the offense itself. Yet the repentant person cannot restore himself; someone else must take the initiative.

Barnabas (see Acts 4:36) was noted for his ministry of restoring broken people. He took the government agent Saul under his wing, defending him when Saul was newly converted and the early church did not yet trust him. On another occasion, years later, Barnabas sided with the young John Mark, who had suddenly dropped out of the missionary team and was rejected by Paul (see Acts 15:36-41). Thanks to a mentoring relationship with Barnabas, John Mark later proved useful to Paul (see 2 Tim. 4:11).

You get the point. Mentoring relationships are not for the faint-hearted. But those who go the extra mile and show biblical love will reap the rewards. Restoring a brother may be the toughest job a mentor has to do. However, only a mentor—one who has proved his faithfulness as a friend—will be trusted at those critical, teachable moments that make or break a man's ministry.

CONCLUSION

You can be a Barnabas to a Saul and a John Mark. Or you can be a Paul to a Peter and a Timothy. In either case, follow the mentor's creed (2 Tim. 2:2): "The things you have heard . . . in the presence of many witnesses [your Barnabases] entrust to reliable men [your Pauls] who will also be qualified to teach others [your Timothys]."

The mentor's creed, coupled with the mandate for mentoring, is essential to being a Promise Keeper. We need a few trusted brothers to help us keep our promises. That's all there is to it. It's that simple. And it's that hard.

 **In the Life**

of One Man

By his own admission, Kurt Stansell is a sex addict. Kurt is also one of those men most acquaintances regard as someone who "has it all." Married to a wonderful wife and the father of two children, Kurt is one of the founding elders of his church. In short, Kurt is one of the last people anyone might suspect of having a problem with sexual addiction. But he did. And he does.

Kurt grew up in a strong Christian home, his dad a military chaplain. His downfall came with his initial exposure to pornography as a youth living in the Far East. "It was a casual, almost accidental thing at first," he recalled. "I was walking along the streets of Manila when I passed a newsstand overflowing with pornographic magazines. Everything was out in the open—plastered all over. I didn't stop to look that day. But after that, every time I walked past a newsstand, I'd slow my pace ever so slightly and cast a few furtive glances at those magazines. Just that small exposure proved enough to fuel my adolescent fantasies."

When Kurt graduated from college, he and Martha were engaged and planned to be married the following year. Kurt thought, *Marriage will be terrific. That'll be the end of this kind of temptation. I'll have a legitimate sexual release. That'll be the solution.* Unfortunately, it wasn't.

A pattern developed and continued for years. There were periodic stops at convenience-store magazine racks, an occasional X-rated video rental when Martha wasn't at home, and excuses made during shopping trips together so he could slip into a bookstore by himself. Visits to live entertainment clubs were reserved for out-of-town business trips.

Following a work-related move to a new city, Kurt and Martha got involved in an exciting new church. Kurt was quickly drawn into a leadership role. Desperate for fellowship, he joined a weekly men's prayer breakfast and even made a commitment to a one-on-one accountability relationship with Stan, a new church friend.

"I really liked Stan," Kurt said. "He was a terrific Christian guy—someone I thought I could relate to and be honest with. Not that I was very honest with him in the beginning. I'd tell myself, *As soon as I get my act together with this pornography business, I'm going to have 100 percent accountability with Stan. There's no way I can share where I've been; it's just too shameful. He'd never be able to accept me.*"

The two men started meeting for breakfast every week, and Kurt used a lot of euphemisms to avoid getting too specific. Despite the limited openness, Kurt's relationship with Stan was positive and encouraging. They challenged each other to be better Christian men, better husbands, and better fathers. Yet the sexual sins continued. All the patterns of temptation, all the trigger points were still there.

On his next business trip, after a week alone, Kurt began to feel the urge. He went to a topless entertainment club and paid one of the women to dance for him. Back in his hotel room later, he thought, *Now I've really hit bottom.* He had never interacted with a person before.

The incident scared him enough that he determined to make his accountability work by being honest with Stan. Then Kurt learned that a man who had played a major role in his spiritual life had been accused of sexual misconduct and his ministry had come to an end. Kurt confessed, "That was what said to me, 'Kurt, you are going down in flames unless you can be 100 percent honest.'"

One night when their families had gotten together, Kurt and Stan went for a walk. Out on the street, Kurt asked, "Stan, what's the worst thing you've ever done in your whole life?"

Stan described a sexual experience he had years before. "I could see it was hard for him to tell me; it was something that still haunted him," Kurt observed. Hearing Stan's story made Kurt want to tell his. "I nearly choked on the words," Kurt recalled, "but I got them out. Stan listened. He didn't condemn me. We prayed for each other."

Kurt noticed an immediate difference after sharing and praying with Stan. If he felt temptation building, he'd tell Stan. Many times, just knowing that he would have to tell Stan if he gave in helped Kurt overcome an urge to sin. He began to understand what shame does when Christians try to hide something in the darkness, giving Satan license to work in their lives. He learned that the more open he could be, the less hold Satan seemed to have.

Kurt is quick to admit that the struggle isn't over—the war goes on. But he now has weapons to use in the battle. The first is honesty and communication with Martha. He eventually told her about his addiction, and, by God's grace, they were able to work through their issues and feelings and make their marriage even stronger.

Still, Kurt believes strongly in the need for a guy like Stan, to whom he can go without burdening Martha with the emotional load of his day-to-day temptations.

Last but certainly not least, Kurt is developing a level of trust in God that is deeper than ever. "He really does want what's best for me; He's not making up the rules arbitrarily. And when we follow His plan and work for His ideal, He amazes us with His blessing."

A MAN AND HIS INTEGRITY

A Promise Keeper is committed to
practicing spiritual, moral, ethical,
and sexual purity.

Godly Men:

Hope for Our Times

by Crawford Loritts

There is something in the wind today in Christian circles that concerns me deeply. Regrettably, we have mistaken our processes for the power of God. That is, we embrace events, magazine articles, books, radio programs, and information *about* God, rather than surrender ourselves to the presence and movement of the Spirit of God. So, despite all that we know, all that we've been exposed to, and all that we have received, the body of Christ has a tragic case of "spiritual constipation." We are informed, fed, manualed, and notebooked. We have stacks of tapes, stacks of books, and stacks of information. We even have prominence, popularity, and name recognition. And yet there seem to be limits on our growth and development to impact the world for the cause of Jesus Christ.

Tragically, many men all across the country will come to Promise Keepers events and miss the point. They will think that somehow by association and osmosis—having a PK T-shirt, a PK hat, and a PK notebook—they are godly men. Let me be clear: Information is not transformation, and exposure is not experience.

The body of Christ is arrogant, not broken. We are riddled with classism, separatism, and a fraternity mind-set. An insidious, biblical pride imprisons and isolates us from one another—from being vulnerable and real. We are fighting one another. We are criticizing one another. We are writing articles about one another. And we've forgotten who the real enemy is! Brothers, racism and the many other kinds of problems in our culture will not be solved by seminars. They will not be solved by a sociological exposition of "the problem." They will not be solved by relationship alone. It's going to take the power of the Holy Ghost washing over our hearts, over our minds, and over our lives. To shed all of this "stuff" we are carrying and to lay it at the foot of the cross, we need a real gully-washer of the Spirit—*and a genuine brokenness.*

DOING THE RIGHT THING FOR THE RIGHT REASON

Some months ago, I had a car accident. It was a brand-new car. I had just dropped off my two younger children at school when a man ran a stop sign at about sixty miles per hour. He caved in the whole side of my car. Six inches more, the rescue crew said, and I would have either been dead or the left side of my body mangled. As it was, I only had a slight friction burn on my right thumb from the airbag and a little bruise on my right knee.

As I got out of the car, the man who hit me was yelling. I couldn't figure this out. He hit my car, and *he* was yelling at *me*. He yelled, "I hope you die! I hope you die! I hope you die!"

I looked at him and said, "Mister, this is nothing but a car—a piece of metal. What is important is that you're standing here and I'm standing here."

And then he said these words to me, with anger and hatred in his eyes: "This is white folks' country, *nigger.*"

Now, he had hit my car so hard that the impact had knocked the cell phone off its cradle onto the front seat. And I want to tell you when he said that, I had that cell phone in my hand and he was only about fifteen feet away from me. I don't want to pretend to be more spiritual than I am. I began walking toward him, and I was going to bury that cell phone right upside his head. I was going to put the send button right in his ear!

And then a woman appeared out of nowhere. I've never had an experience like that before. I'm not saying that she was an angel, but this woman grabbed my arm and said to me, "Mister, you are not to go over there. You are *not* to go over there!" And it took just that much for me to get a little bit of spiritual sense in my head, and I backed off.

After the emergency vehicles came and towed our cars away, my wife came to pick me up. This man was standing on the side of the road, and I still wanted to hurt him. But as I was getting into my wife's car, something said to me, *Crawford, go shake his hand.*

And I answered out loud, "Not in this life." Now, I have never heard the voice of God speak audibly to me, but I tell you, this was the closest I've ever gotten in my life. As I was getting into my wife's car and pulling the door closed, it was as if the Spirit of God grabbed my shirt and said, *You'd better go shake that man's hand!*

I got out of the car and walked over to him. As I put one hand on his shoulder, I looked him straight in the eye, stuck out my hand, and said, "Mister, are you all right?" And he melted.

A few days later in court, I put my arm around him again, and I told him about the love of Jesus. I told him about the death of Christ on the cross for his soul and about the empty tomb. You see, what God was teaching me through this experience was, *Crawford, are you willing to go through embarrassment and the perceived rape of your dignity to do what is right?*

What God is teaching us in Promise Keepers is all about doing what is right in the context of human history. It's not about how you're treated. It's not about what people do for you. But the real test of transformation is a decision in your soul—that no matter what circumstance you find yourself in, you will represent the King's business in this world. You've got to do what's right.

ISAIAH SAW THE LORD

In the Book of Isaiah, chapter 6, God gives us a picture of what happens to a man when he has a deep encounter with his Maker. I want to use this passage to draw out some principles for you to grasp and understand about God's action in your own life.

Most scholars believe that the event described in this chapter actually occurred in the latter part of Isaiah's prophetic ministry. Isaiah was a contemporary of King Uzziah, who reigned in Jerusalem for approximately twenty-six years. Isaiah had been Uzziah's number-one prophetic confidant. But Uzziah went into the temple and trespassed God's sovereignty by taking on the mantle of a priest when God had clearly called him to be king. Because of Uzziah's spiritual arrogance and pride, he was stricken with leprosy and died a hideous death. This sets the stage for the vision that changed Isaiah's life forever.

Isaiah begins his chronicle by writing, "In the year that King Uzziah died, I saw the Lord" (v. 1). He saw the Lord. And the very essence of everything that followed in his life springs from the fact that Isaiah embraced this call to intimacy with God. Intimacy with God is the center of what is needed today in the body of Christ.

Many of us have been laboring in the church for years. Our efforts may be basically sound, but they have degenerated to the status of "professional ministry." Others of us are laymen who have known Christ for a long time but have gotten rather ho-hum in our relationship with Him. There is very little power, very little freshness in life, and very little zeal for the things of the kingdom. In this state, there is little evidence of the supernatural in our daily experience, and our hearts become cold and callous. Our problem is that we lack an intimate relationship with God.

THE ULTIMATE PARADIGM SHIFT

There are four principles leading to intimacy with God revealed in this passage from Isaiah: bask in His worthiness, confront your own unworthiness, experience His work, and submit and surrender your will to pay the price for revival and renewal in your life. Let's look at each of these more closely.

1. Bask in His Worthiness.

Isaiah tries to put in human terms the awesomeness of what he had seen and experienced. He says, "I saw the Lord!" The spiritual glaucoma had been taken away. The distraction Uzziah and all his greatness and grandeur represented had been put to death. And Isaiah saw God as never before.

Once you have been into the inner sanctuary, you begin to plumb its depth and cultivate the power of your walking relationship with

God. Once you begin to initiate the process of godly disciplines in your life, God will indelibly etch in your soul an experience that you'll never forget.

2. Confront Your Own Worthlessness.

I believe in self-esteem to a point, but you cannot get around this truth: You have no worth of your own. This is not just some Christian hobby-horse horse or ancillary concept to the deeper spiritual life; it is solid, biblical territory. The path to intimacy with God requires great brokenness.

Notice Isaiah's reaction following his vision: "'Woe to me!' I cried. 'I am ruined! For I am a man of unclean lips, and I live among a people of unclean lips, and my eyes have seen the King, the LORD Almighty'" (v. 5). There is a double entendre here. He says not only are my lips not clean, literally, but in a figure of speech, my whole life is unclean. He says, "I am ruined." I like the old King James Version, which says, "I am undone."

Now, in all intellectual honesty, what kind of categorical fool would stand in the presence of God holding up his résumé and biographical sketch? What do we have to bring to the table when we enter into the holy presence of a great God? Isaiah didn't talk about his great initiatives, proposals, and spiritual perspective. He said, "Woe is me, for I am undone." I'm unraveled!

3. Experience His Work.

I think the process is very interesting here because God responds to Isaiah in verse 6. He says, "Then one of the seraphs flew to me with a live coal in his hand." I don't want to milk that image too much for its intention, but I do want you to grasp the immediate reaction and response of God to us when we fall down in brokenness. If you want the touch of God, you have to be transparent with God. You will never get His touch until you express truth. In fact, cleansing always precedes clarity, according to Scripture. And fire—especially in the Old Testament—is a picture of deep, scouring cleansing.

Some of you may still be wrestling with strongholds in your life that are displeasing to God. And you've been hiding out. People may think that you're godly. They may think that you're wonderful! You can dazzle them with your evangelical, theological articulation and smoke and mirrors. You can say the right words. You can look holy. But you know in your heart of hearts that there is a compartment in your life that is tearing you up. And you have not heard the voice of God in so long that there is a drought in your soul.

For some of you, that stronghold is legalism, and you are trying to shout away the disease, rather than repent of the sickness. You think that by having rules, regulations, and standards that are higher than what God intended, somehow or other people will not see the real crud you have stored in your heart. So you pick on other Christians and criticize other movements. You say how this or that one is not godly, but it is because you have not experienced the touch and the cleansing of God for your own soul. Once you experience God's forgiveness, when you must confront somebody because of sin or heresy, there will always be a tear trickling down your cheek.

Isaiah continues in verse 8, "Then I heard the voice of the Lord saying. . . ." The point here is not that God just began to speak. The problem was not in God's ability to communicate. The problem was that Isaiah couldn't hear Him. But only after he had received cleansing. Oh, hallelujah! His ears were unstopped and he could hear the voice of the Lord clearly. Do your ears need to be unplugged? Are you missing the messages, the divine assignments from God because you're satisfied to dwell with spiritual paupers? It is possible to think that by coddling your sinful habits, you can control your life. But you really are impeding the process of God.

4. Submit and Surrender Your Will.

Consider carefully the word order of Isaiah's response to God's call in verse 8. He did not say, "Here I am." He said, "Here am I." There is a very important distinction between the two. "Here I am" is a statement of being: "Yeah, I can do that. I've got something to bring to the table. Here I am. I've got expertise. I've got skill. Here's my education, here's my background. . . ."

Instead, Isaiah says, "Here am I"—a statement of location. In other words, "If You can use me, You know my frailties. I've seen You, Lord. There is none like You. Nobody can compare to You. I have nothing to bring to the table. You don't use me because I'm all that great."

True greatness is not recognition or popularity. Greatness is godliness. Greatness is obedience. Greatness is faithfulness. I am willing to go anywhere, to do anything, to be anything that God wants me to do or to be. I take my hands off my life, and I say to Him, "No more telling You how to use me." I want to lay it on the line. I want to make a difference. I'll pay the price. Life is too short, and, at any moment, God may say, "Give Me back My breath!"

I want to be a vehicle of revival. But I want to be real, Lord. Help me to make it home before dark, spiritually.

Black-and-White
Living in a Gray World

by Gary Oliver

The judge looked down from his bench and, in a somber voice, declared, "Mr. Wilson, this is your day of reckoning!" Then he sentenced him to seven and one-half years in federal prison.

In response, Wilson's lawyer requested that he be allowed a few minutes with his family and friends before surrendering to the authorities.

The judge replied, "Mr. Wilson is going to be taken by the marshals right now. You should have thought of that before."

Wilson was one of four California men convicted of financial fraud and sentenced to prison in that particular case. Five men were originally investigated, but the fifth, Mark Jacobs, was not arrested and charged.

Jacobs had been invited to join the financial scheme by four friends (the men sent to jail) in a weekly Bible study. They had assured him their plan was totally legal. Yet something inside him said it wasn't right. While it was hard to say no to good friends, he chose to go with his conscience and tell them he wouldn't participate.

The lawyers for the four convicted men pleaded with the judge that their clients had simply made mistakes of poor judgment. They were good men who loved their wives and kids, gave to charities, and were active in their churches. Their crime involved a "gray" area, crossing a line that wasn't clear.

The judge disagreed. "It is not hard to determine where the line is," he said. "The guy who drew the line is Mark Jacobs. He knew what was right and what was wrong, and he didn't hesitate. Hopefully, now we will have fewer people who are willing to walk up to the line and dabble with going over the line. We will have people like Mr. Jacobs, who wouldn't touch this thing with a ten-foot pole."

That case is just one example of the moral and ethical crises sweeping our nation. While the cast may change and involve stockbrokers, bankers, lawyers, or television evangelists, the script is the same. We are a generation that isn't sure where the line is between right and wrong. Many don't believe there is a line, or, if there is, they don't care.

In 1966, an American professor named Joseph Fletcher published an influential book called *Situation Ethics*. His basic premise was that nothing is universally good or bad, right or wrong. There are no absolutes. Morals are determined by the situation. An act that is right in one situation may be wrong in another.

What was only a philosophical discussion in 1966 has become today the basis for morals in our society. Thirty-five years ago, our country followed the Judeo-Christian ethic. Few people questioned that chastity was a good thing, that hard work was the duty of every responsible man, that homosexual conduct was wrong, and that it was never right to lie, cheat, steal, or commit adultery. But today our ethics and morals are no longer based on Jerusalem; they're based on Sodom and Gomorrah.

If you take situation ethics to its logical conclusion, you end up with Auschwitz, Dachau, and Buchenwald. In fact, at the entrance to the Auschwitz concentration camp is a sign with Adolf Hitler's words: "I want to raise a generation devoid of conscience." He almost succeeded.

Every day, we're influenced by the philosophy and values of those around us. In a famous experiment, some students put a frog in a container of water and began to heat the water slowly. The water finally reached the boiling point, yet the frog never attempted to jump out. Why? Because the changes in the environment were so subtle that the frog didn't notice them until it was too late.

As Christian men, it's easier than we think to end up like the frog. Many godly men—pastors, seminary professors, respected and beloved Christian leaders—have yielded to the world's values because they failed to discern the subtle changes occurring around them. Before they knew it, they were in hot water. They didn't want that. They didn't intend to get there. They didn't think it could happen to them. But it did.

If the desire of your heart is to be a Promise Keeper, you need to think seriously about the connection Jesus made between Christianity and morality. Who we are should determine what we do. The Bible commands us to become "holy and blameless" (Eph. 1:4), to "live a life worthy of the calling you have received" (Eph. 4:1), to be "mature" (Eph. 4:13) and "imitators of God" (Eph. 5:1).

What do you think of when you hear the word *holy*? Most of us think of someone else, not ourselves. In both the original Hebrew and Greek of the Bible, the word *holy* refers to "something or someone separated and set apart for God." A major characteristic of a holy man is purity. Something that is pure is spotless, stainless, containing nothing that does not properly belong, free from moral fault or guilt.

Purity isn't an accident, and it doesn't just happen overnight. Peter compared it to the process of purifying gold (see 1 Pet. 1:6–7). Gold has to be heated and reheated several times for the alloys and impurities to be brought to the surface, where the goldsmith can remove them. If you forget that becoming pure is a process, you risk becoming overwhelmed by discouragement when you experience those inevitable setbacks.

Still, it's not enough that you desire to be pure, nor will sincerity or hard work necessarily get you there. You also need a plan to "be conformed to the likeness of his Son" (Rom. 8:29). As the ancient saying goes, a journey of a thousand miles begins with the first step. What will be your first step? Where can you begin? The rest of this chapter presents seven simple steps that God can use to help you move beyond good intentions and down the path to purity.

Step 1: Make a decision.

When Babylon's King Nebuchadnezzar conquered Judah, he ordered thousands of the best and brightest young men to be taken as captives to Babylon. His goal was to immerse them in the seductive culture of Babylon and thus remake their character. He would turn their hearts from the God of their fathers to the idolatry of the Chaldeans.

Daniel was one of those men. The king changed his name to Belteshazzar, which means "a servant of the god Bel." Then the king ordered the captives to go through three years of special training, which included a certain diet. That's where Daniel drew the line. He couldn't avoid the king's education, but he could refuse food that had been offered to idols. In Daniel 1:8, we read that "Daniel resolved not to defile himself with the royal food and wine."

Daniel made a decision not to compromise and defile himself. Webster defines *defile* as "to make unclean or impure, to corrupt the purity or perfection of, debase, sully, taint, dishonor, contaminate, pollute, dirty, soil, poison, smear, blot, blur, smudge, stain, tarnish, profane, infect, dishonor, or disgrace." That's not a pleasant list of words. Daniel chose to stand tall for what he knew to be right. The influence of social morality was nothing. Being God's man was everything.

Almost every day, you come to some kind of fork in the road. Like Daniel, you face tough choices. What you decide at that fork is greatly influenced by the choices you made the day before about the kind of man you are.

Step 2: Choose to put first things first.

It's not easy to be pure in an impure world. Even if you become a cultural ostrich and avoid all movies, listen only to Christian radio, and read only Christian books and magazines, you are still going to struggle. You will never become a godly man by negation. A pure, pollution-free environment doesn't make pure people. In Mark 7:15, 20–23, Jesus made it clear that what's inside a man defiles him. That's where we need to start.

If a farmer doesn't plant seed in the ground, he will never harvest a crop. It doesn't matter how weed-free his ground is; he must also plant and cultivate good seed. In the same way, we can only reap a harvest of purity and integrity by planting the good seed of God's Word into our lives. I'm not talking about merely reading the Bible. I'm talking about allowing the Holy Spirit to plant the truths of

Scripture deep into our hearts and minds through consistent Bible reading and memorization, meditation, and prayer.

To be effective, truth must be planted in our hearts daily. After thirty-five years of being a Christian, I'm convinced that the best time to do this is in the morning. Keep in mind that this is being written by someone who is not a morning person. However, a statement by Dietrich Bonhoeffer greatly challenged this reluctant morning person:

> The entire day receives order and discipline when it acquires unity. This unity must be sought and found in morning prayer. . . . The morning prayer determines the day. Squandered time of which we are ashamed, temptations to which we succumb, weaknesses and lack of courage in work, disorganization and lack of discipline in our thoughts and in our conversations with other men, all have their origin most often in the neglect of morning prayer. . . . Temptations which accompany the working day will be conquered on the basis of the morning breakthrough to God.[1]

Step 3: Determine where the line is, and then stay a safe distance behind it.

Most Christian men want to be strong and victorious. We want to hear God say, "Well done, good and faithful servant." We want our lives to be characterized by integrity. The problem is that each of us has blind spots, weaknesses, and deeply entrenched habits that can sabotage our best intentions.

We need to move beyond the biblical absolutes and determine what kinds of things are healthy for us and what kinds are unhealthy. What one man can watch or listen to with no problem may open the door to unnecessary temptation for another man and increase his vulnerability to sin. Satan's first step in the battle for our minds is to distract us (see James 1:14–15). The distraction itself may not be sin. It may seem small and insignificant. However, whatever distracts us or weakens our resolve puts us at risk.

To help determine your line, honestly answer these questions:
- In what areas of your life do you consistently struggle?
- Are there any particular sins to which you are consistently vulnerable?

- Do any activities consume too much of your time?
- Over the past years, what has been Satan's most effective "bait" to attract you?

Moral failure is rarely the result of a blowout; almost always, it's the result of a slow leak. For some men, it starts with the healthy desire to provide for their families, and they end up becoming workaholics, driven by an insatiable appetite for more. For other men, it starts with something as seemingly innocent as lingering too long over the swimsuit issue of *Sports Illustrated* or the latest *Victoria's Secret* catalog.

Look at Samson. He was physically strong and attractive, born of godly parents, and appointed to be a judge in Israel. He had everything going for him. Yet he never drew a line and dealt with his tendency toward lust. For that he paid a heavy price.

Determine where the line is. If it's not something that is clearly spelled out in Scripture, pray about it and seek the counsel of several wise friends. Once you've decided where the line is, walk ten yards back and make that your line! Always leave yourself a margin. Don't see how close you can get to the line without going over. That's like a scuba diver seeing how little air he can leave in his tank and still get to the surface. Only a fool would do something like that.

Step 4: Guard your heart.

Jesus made it clear that we can't serve two masters. Where our treasure is, there our hearts will be also (see Matt. 6:21). As Chuck Swindoll wrote,

> The quest for character requires that certain things be kept in the heart as well as kept from the heart. An unguarded heart spells disaster. A well-guarded heart means survival. If you hope to survive the jungle, overcoming each treacherous attack, you'll have to guard your heart.[2]

Only the passionate love of purity can save a man from impurity. When Jesus met Peter on the seashore after His resurrection, He didn't bawl him out for his lack of faith in denying Him. Three times He asked Peter the simple question, "Do you love Me?" A growing affection for our Lord Jesus Christ is the only antidote for the kind of apathy that leads us down the primrose path to compromise.

Step 5: Guard your mind.

There's a large railroad switchyard in St. Louis. One switch that begins with just the thinnest piece of steel directs a train away from one main track and onto another. If you follow those two tracks, you'll find that one ends in San Francisco, the other in New York.

Our thought life is a lot like that switch. The seemingly simple choice of what we set our minds on can determine the outcome of our spiritual warfare. Just a small deviation from God's standard can put us at risk and lead us far afield from our desired destination. Someone once said:

> We have never said or done an ungracious or un-Christlike word or action that was not first an ungracious and un-Christlike thought. We have never felt dislike or hate for a person without first of all thinking thoughts of dislike that have grown into hate. We have never committed a visible act of sin that has shamed us before others that was not first a shameful thought. We have never wronged another person without first wronging that person in our thoughts. What we habitually think will, sooner or later, manifest itself clearly in some visible expression of that thought.

The mind is the place where decisions are made for or against the truth. What we choose to read, watch, and think about will determine, to a great degree, whether we will be victims or victors, conquered or conquerors.

Step 6: Guard your eyes.

In Genesis 39, we see that Joseph was smart enough to know you can't play with fire and not get burned. Job also knew the importance of guarding his eyes. He wrote, "I made a covenant with my eyes" (Job 31:1). David, however, lingered too long, stared a bit too much, and unwisely entertained an unhealthy fantasy. He didn't guard his eyes and ended up committing adultery with Bathsheba and murdering her husband.

The little Sunday school song has some powerful wisdom for us:

Oh, be careful little eyes what you see.
Oh, be careful little ears what you hear.

Oh, be careful little lips what you speak.

There's a Father up above, looking down in tender love,

Oh, be careful little eyes what you see.

Step 7: Guard the little things.

Jesus said that "whoever can be trusted with very little can also be trusted with much" (Luke 16:10). As a young man, I didn't understand why that was so important. Now I know that in the process of becoming a godly man, there are no "little" things. In fact, how we handle the seemingly little things determines, over time, our response to the big things.

If you allow one thought or activity in your life that you know is not best for you, even though it may not be sinful in itself, you will find that your spiritual eyes will become darkened, your spiritual ears hard of hearing, and your soul numb to the "soft promptings" of the Spirit. Beware of the temptation to justify or rationalize. Many of my own failures started by moving in a direction my head rationalized by saying, "It isn't sin," but my heart said, "Don't do it." Be on guard for statements such as, "It's not that bad," "I've seen worse," or "The Bible doesn't have anything to say about that." Don't ask what's wrong with a certain behavior or choice; ask what's right with it. Ask, "Is what I'm considering more likely to move me closer to or farther away from my goal of being a Promise Keeper?"

If there is any hope for our marriages, our families, our cities, our nation, and our civilization, we men must passionately embrace the biblical standard for who God would have us to be and to become. It's not enough to give mental assent to truth. We must make a commitment to be men who aren't afraid to count the cost and then stand tall—at times seemingly alone, but in truth with thousands of other men who want to make their lives count.

Remember: "Blessed—happy, enviably fortunate, and spiritually prosperous—are the pure in heart, for they shall see God" (Matt. 5:8, AMP).

God Owns It All

by Ron Blue

I'm not a singer, and I'm not a preacher. In the Old Testament, the penalty for missing a prophecy was death. So I choose not to be a prophet. And I'm not a tax expert. April 15 has occurred every year for the last fifty-five years that I have been on this planet. But if you want to reduce your taxes, I have a guaranteed, sure-fire, 100 percent no-risk-of-audit way: *reduce your income.* It works every time.

I'm not an economist either, but I do know that the world has never seen an economy like we see in the United States of America. The British didn't experience it, the Romans didn't experience it, and the Japanese haven't experienced it. The citizens of the United States of America comprise about 2.5 percent of the world population, and we own one-third of the world's assets.

And yet, according to some recent statistics, fifty million families—about one-half of all the families in the United States—consider themselves to be in trouble financially. There is $370 billion in credit card debt in America today. The average debt is $6,000 per card, and we pay an average of $1,000 per year in credit card interest. There were one million bankruptcies in 1996. There were two billion credit card solicitations mailed (I think I got half of them).

Every citizen in America—man, woman, and child—receives about seventeen credit card solicitations per year. Credit cards are the most profitable area for banks. In fact, if you pay your credit cards off early, or on time, there are two terms for you: "deadbeat" or "freeloader." The reason for these names is because you're cheating that bank out of the interest that it expected to earn. So, you're a deadbeat!

The reason given for 50 percent of the divorce cases in the country today is money problems. Think for just a moment. Did you spend money today? Yesterday? Did you think about money today? Have you discussed money with a family member in the last week? With your spouse? Have you ever worried about money?

Would you like the answer to financial security, financial success, financial significance, and financial survival? If you would, I have good news for you. The Bible has more to say about money and money management than any other topic. There are two thousand verses in the Bible dealing with money. Two-thirds of the parables deal with money; there is more written about money than faith, more written about money than prayer, more written about money than heaven and hell combined. The Bible has the answer to financial security, financial survival, financial success, and financial significance. And it transcends economic systems, political systems, and incomes.

THE KEY TO FINANCIAL SECURITY

In the Book of 1 Chronicles, David says: "Praise be to you, O LORD, God of our father Israel, from everlasting to everlasting. Yours, O LORD, is the greatness and the power and the glory and the majesty and the splendor, for everything in heaven and earth is yours" (29:10–11). Do you believe that God owns it all? Do you really, really, really believe that God owns it all? Because if you believe that God owns it all, that means that everything that you have you hold with an open hand, and God can put into your hands whatever He wants, and take out whatever He wants—whenever He wants.

I don't know how much is enough to live in America today, but I know the answer to how much is too much. It's when you take what God has entrusted to you and close your hands on it. Yeah, that hurts, doesn't it? But the key to financial security is to hold everything with an open hand. It's not an income issue. God owns it all. If God owns it all, you can't lose something you don't own. So, there's no fear of loss. How about guilt?

If God owns it all, does He give us principles to deal with His resources? You bet. Can you have conflicts with your spouse if you're dealing with God's resources? No, because you're both dealing with *His* resources, not her resources or your resources. So there's freedom from failure.

SIGNIFICANCE, SURVIVAL, AND SUCCESS

The key to financial significance, survival, and success: Spend less than you earn. And keep doing it long term. Now think about that. Financial success is no more difficult than living within your income. I don't care whether you make $10,000 or $10 million. You still have limited resources. This principle works at any income level. It is not new truth. You need to accept your income as God-given and live within it.

I know that it's un-American to live within your income. Americans spend on the average 110 percent of their incomes. How do we do that? We do that by debt. Credit card companies have allowed us to fund a lifestyle for which God has not given us an income. The average credit card and consumer debt in America today is $12,500.

If you borrow $2,000 on your credit cards and repay them with the minimum monthly payment, it will take you thirty-two years to repay $2,000. And you will pay a total of $10,000 for the privilege of borrowing $2,000. If Christian men were committed to getting out of credit card and consumer debt by the year 2000, we would free up literally billions of dollars just within the Christian community—money that would then be available for kingdom work in families, churches, and communities.

GETTING OUT OF DEBT

There are four simple things that you need to do in order to get out of debt.

1. Be brutally honest about how much you owe.

Figure out and write down how much you owe and to whom you owe it. Eighty percent of American families in America today have more debt than they have assets. That's the bad news. The good news is they don't know it.

2. Stop going into debt.

If you have a problem with credit cards, I have a solution. Preheat your oven to 450 degrees, spread them all out on a cookie sheet, stick them into the oven, and you will no longer have a problem with credit cards. I'll also guarantee you this: You'll get seventeen more solicitations within the next twelve months. (So you can always get them back if you want them back.) But ultimately, credit cards are never the problem. The person who holds the credit card is the problem. Credit cards never get anybody into debt; people get people into debt. You can't blame the credit cards, and you can't blame the lending institutions.

3. Develop a repayment plan.

Note: repayment *plan*, not repayment *hope*. Be realistic. I think a lot of American Christians are counting on the Rapture to get them out of debt. Jesus may not come back before the year 2000, and I'd like to see you out of debt by the year 2000. Simply start with the smallest credit card, and pay that one off. Then take the next smallest, and next smallest, and so forth until you're out of debt.

4. Make yourself accountable to someone.

It is very, very difficult to get out of debt, and I don't think that you can do it unless you're accountable to someone. And that someone cannot be your spouse. You can be accountable to another group of men, or to a small group, or to your pastor. You need support. Getting out of debt is a lot more difficult than getting into debt, believe me.

A friend of mine once told me he got saved in 1960 and his pocketbook got saved in 1962. You know, along with other spiritual disciplines, I believe that we write a prayer journal in our checkbook. Our checkbook reveals more about our spirituality than probably any other thing that we have. Pray for the work of the Holy Spirit in your life and the life of your spouse in the area of your finances.

Remember: God owns it all. And abandon yourself to be available to the Lord to do whatever He wants, whenever He wants, and in whatever way He wants.

The Call to Sexual Purity

by John Maxwell

Many church historians cite 1987 as the most tragic year of the twentieth century for the body of Christ. In 1987, many well-known and influential Christian leaders were exposed for moral failure. And it seemed to open up a floodgate across America. Every time you turned around, you heard of yet another leader who had fallen morally. There seems to be a philosophy within the church that says, "I love to sin, and God loves to forgive." It must be stopped.

Now, it is important to remember that God invented sex. It was His idea. And I say, "Yea, God!" There is no problem with sex as long as it's within its proper bounds. But every one of us knows what it's like when lust or sex goes out of bounds. Water is also a wonderful thing, but too much water and you drown. And every one of us knows of our own bent toward sin.

E. Stanley Jones, a great Christian missionary, once interviewed a Hindu ascetic who had removed himself from temptation by living in the wilderness. The ascetic's first words—after forty years of being alone, forty years without talking to anyone—were, "I haven't thought of a woman in forty years!"

Every one of us knows what it's like to be consumed with lust, and every one of us knows what it's like to have our heart turned from God to things that are wrong. And it is true that when lust begins to fill our mind and to fill our body, God begins to be very unreal to us. He begins to grow small, and He begins to vanish.

PRACTICAL WAYS TO DEAL WITH TEMPTATION

1. Run!

The Bible tells us that we are to flee the evil desires of our youth, to flee from sexual immorality—to run as fast as we can! Don't put yourself into a position to see how good your resistance is. We're not to act brave; we're not to act like we have all answers; we're not to act bold. In fact, the Bible doesn't even say to pray. As fast as you can, get out of there.

In Genesis 39, we have the well-known story of Joseph facing temptation. Potiphar's wife began making eyes at him. Every day that Joseph came to work, there she was, waiting for him. And every day he got out of her way as much as possible. One day she grabbed him by the sleeve. It says that he ran and tore off his jacket. Five times in the rest of this story, the Bible talks about the fact that Joseph left his jacket. Joseph didn't go back. He didn't call the next day to say, "Hey can I drop by? I'd like to get my jacket if I could." He left the jacket, didn't go back to get the jacket, and did without a jacket. Run! Leave your jacket!

2. Accept responsibility.

Addictive lust feeds on the darkness of denial. People will often say, "I can't believe I'm in this affair. I can't believe what happened, but it's become bigger than both of us." But God's Word teaches us that what we sow is what we reap and that we need to accept responsibility for where we are.

3. Be accountable.

Satan's best weapon is to keep Christians isolated. God's Word says, "Therefore confess your sins to each other and pray for each other so that you may be healed" (James 5:16). I have a friend who has been my prayer partner for thirteen years. We get together every month to pray.

Bill has a list of questions that I asked him to ask me: (1) Are you spending time alone with God? (2) Is your thought life pure? (3) Are you misusing your power? (4) Are you walking in total obedience to God? (5) Have you lied about any of the previous questions?

4. Listen to your wife.
If your wife is like my wife, she has a sixth sense. She's amazing. God created her with an antenna that I don't have. She'll say, "John, you better watch out for that gal over there." And I go, "What gal?" She's my best friend. Many, many times she'll keep me from falling into a hole if I just listen to her words.

5. Be on guard.
Most men who have fallen morally never thought it could happen to them. We have to plan ways to protect ourselves when we are vulnerable. Travel is prime time for temptation. It's very rare that I'm by myself anymore when I travel, and I call my wife, Margaret, every night so we can just enjoy each other. I am seldom alone with a woman—I don't eat alone in a restaurant with a woman, and I don't counsel alone with a woman. I always talk positively about my wife to other people.

6. Choose close friends carefully.
Bad company will corrupt good character, so I'm very careful of those I have as close friends. I want them also to have a good, solid, Christlike marriage.

7. Determine to live a pure life today.
Jesus told His disciples, "Come, follow me, . . . and I will make you fishers of men" (Matt. 4:19). He asked them to turn from what they were doing, to take an action before they had the feeling. If you are flirting with an affair, whether mentally or physically, you cannot wait for your feelings to change to make it right. You must make the right decision, and God will honor your action. The Holy Spirit will change the feeling as time passes.

8. Realize that sexual sin assaults the lordship of Jesus in your body.

Sexual sin prostitutes the pure body of Jesus. Paul said, "Do you not know that your body is a temple of the Holy Spirit, who is in you, whom you have received from God? You are not your own" (1 Cor. 6:19).

9. Recognize the consequences of sexual sin.

And how many times I've heard the words, "If I could just turn the clock back. If I could just go back." Recognize the consequences of sexual sin. Proverbs 6:32 says, "The man who commits adultery is an utter fool, for he destroys his own soul" (TLB). Proverbs 6:26 says, "An adulteress may cost him his very life" (TLB).

10. Think about your children.

I was in my senior year of college, right before Margaret and I were to be married and I was to enter the ministry. Dad wanted to talk to me about his moral life. He said, "I want you to know that I have been faithful to your mother, and I want to tell you why. It's not because I haven't been tempted; it's not because I haven't had opportunities," he said. "I've been faithful to your mom because as I look in the Bible I find that when the father is unfaithful, so many times there's a tendency for the son to come behind and also be unfaithful. I have been faithful to give you a strong foundation to stand upon." And he said, "If you go out and mess your life up, I'm gonna love you, but I never want you to be able to look back at me and say, 'Dad I just did what you did.'"

We want our kids to be pure. We want our kids to be holy. We want our kids to love Jesus. And if it's gonna happen for our kids, it's got to start with us. It's got to start with *me*. I've got to take responsibility—I'm the dad, I'm to be the spiritual leader, the model for holiness.

Some of you know you have already blown it. You've been unfaithful and failed your family. But this is where the grace of Jesus Christ comes in. Go to your knees and tell God, "Although I've blown it in the past, from this moment on, I am going to live a godly, holy, pure life and become the father and the husband that You want me to be." Today.

 **In the Life**

of One Man

Suppose you're in charge of the biggest project in your company's history, and, due to factors beyond your control, things aren't going as well as everyone would like. To obscure that fact, you're asked to play accounting games. Failure to do so might cost your company the contract and could cost you your job. What course would you choose?

That's the kind of dilemma Jeff Vaughn faced some years ago in applying his faith to his responsibilities at a leading aerospace company.

Every program handled by Jeff's company is assigned a management team responsible for overseeing the fulfillment of the contract. Jeff, as one of those executives, was responsible for cost and schedule management. "In other words," he explains, "it was my job to make sure my company delivered a piece of hardware or software to our client on schedule and for the price specified in our contract."

Part of the challenge of managing such long-term, multimillion-dollar contracts is keeping up with the constant changes in specifications and plans being made by the client's engineers or at the whim of politicians who ultimately control the purse strings of any government project.

Jeff began work on a space-station program that was the most challenging and troublesome project he and his company had ever tackled.
The sheer size of the overall program and the multitude of subcontractors involved made logistics difficult enough. To complicate
things even further, constant engineering changes by NASA and higher-
level contractors resulted in literally hundreds of contract changes.
And Jeff, whose job it was to monitor every change so costs and
schedule could be adjusted accordingly, was sometimes months and
hundreds of contract changes behind because their client wasn't communicating those changes in a timely manner.

It was a logistical and managerial nightmare. Routinely, in such
programs contractors seldom acknowledge cost overruns during the
early years. Instead, for example, a contractor given an annual budget
of $100 million will issue reports indicating it did, indeed, spend no
more than the budgeted amount—with the overruns then scheduled
to come out of next year's budget. But ultimately—unless costs can be
cut somewhere else (an unlikely scenario)—a snowball effect kicks in,
with ever-increasing amounts pushed into the following year. When
the truth finally gets out, everyone usually has too much invested to
abandon the project, so all that can be done is to appropriate addi-
tional funds for the remaining years of the program or extend the project a few years.

This is just what happened with Jeff's project. "Every year I was on
the program, we fought a constant battle, because of the continuous
changes, to live within the funding for the year and to deliver what
we'd promised on schedule," Jeff reported. "The pressure came right
down the line from NASA to our client and all the other contractors. If
everyone failed to deliver everything we were supposed to deliver at
the cost we had contracted for, not only would we look bad, but our
client and its client would look bad, all the way up to NASA. And then,
when Congress scrutinized NASA's budget, if the program looked as
though it had serious overrun problems, the politicians might well ter-
minate the entire project. This would mean not only the loss of billions
of dollars a year to corporate America, but also thousands of jobs both
in our company and throughout the entire aerospace industry."

Jeff said he lost a lot of sleep trying to figure out how his company
was going to meet the terms of the contract. He eventually concluded

it simply couldn't be done—that there would indeed be cost overruns. He wrestled with just what to tell his superiors, because he knew they wouldn't like the unvarnished truth. Ultimately, however, as a Christian man of integrity, Jeff decided that the full truth was the only way to go. But when he delivered his conclusions, he received intense pressure to manipulate his figures.

One of his bosses called Jeff into his office and said, "You can't tell me that you can know for a fact that we can't make up enough ground in the remaining years of this program to meet our delivery schedule. Surely you have to admit there's a *chance* we can deliver on time."

Jeff admitted he couldn't say with certainty what would happen five years down the road. "But the possibility is very, very slim," he maintained. "And based on my evaluation, I feel there is no way we can fulfill the contract."

Despite that kind of pressure from within his own company, Jeff felt he had no choice but to be just as honest with his company's client—who was no more eager than his bosses to face the truth. After Jeff and the rest of his team presented the numbers and got a cold reception, they retreated to a conference room to rehash their projections. In time, they all agreed there was no way to do the contracted work for less money. So when the team leader argued for the usual postpone-some-of-the-work-to-a-later-date trick, the team finally agreed—but only after Jeff and others who backed him insisted on being completely open with the client. They would agree to the original amount of funding budgeted as long as they spelled out in careful, written detail what parts of the contract could not be fulfilled or would have to be delayed until the following fiscal year.

As a man of integrity, Jeff says, "I had an obligation to my company and our client to make sure they clearly understood my position—that we could no longer expect to do what we'd promised on the schedule or at the cost we'd agreed to when we signed the original contract. I had to do what I thought was right. And it was up to my superiors, our client, and ultimately their clients to decide what to do with the information I provided."

Someone somewhere made the decision to continue hiding the truth about cost overruns. But the whole thing blew wide open the following year. Congress held hearings, calling in NASA officials and executives from numerous contractors and subcontractors. As a result, the entire space-station program was scaled back and restructured to include a new partnership with the Russians. In the process, several companies, including Jeff's, lost huge contracts. Many jobs were lost, including those of some of Jeff's superiors. But Jeff was transferred to another team overseeing the cost and scheduling management of one of his company's contracts with the Pentagon.

Jeff will never know for sure, but his carefully documented insistence on honestly reporting his company's part of the space-station program may be one reason he's closing in on a twenty-five-year project while so many in his industry are out of work. "God has been good," he says. "And I now sleep better than ever."

PROMISE

A MAN AND
HIS FAMILY

A Promise Keeper is committed
to building strong marriages
and families through love,
protection, and biblical values.

Five Secrets of
a Happy Marriage

by Gary Smalley

If I could convey only one message to men, the contents of this chapter would be it.

As I've traveled the world ministering to families, I've noticed five things consistently displayed among couples with healthy, vibrant marriages and families. As I tell you about my friends the Brawners, see if you can identify the five elements in their home.

The Brawners are a normal family—not perfect by any means. They've got their shortcomings, and they've got their strengths. But if I knew you were living with your wife and kids the way Jim is with his, I would be very encouraged about the direction of our world.

Jim and Suzette Brawner live in a small town in Missouri and have three children: Jason, who's nineteen at the time of this writing, a national swimming champion and a freshman in college; Travis, their seventeen-year-old son, who's an outstanding three-sport athlete in high school; and Jill, their beautiful and talented thirteen-year-old. Jim and Suzette are in their early forties. Jim came from a home that had dysfunctional elements. But he realized that while his background could lead to unhealthy behavior in his own marriage, he could do something about it. He has worked hard to build a strong marriage and to rear, with Suzette, three emotionally healthy children.

Recently Jason came home for the first time from college. He was unusually nervous because, as part of his initiation into the swim team, he had been coerced into wearing an earring. None of the men in his family had ever worn an earring, and it just wasn't done among their circle of friends. Jason felt the roof might come off when Mom and Dad saw him.

Jason pulled into the driveway and found his mom. She was so excited to see him that she gave him a big hug before she noticed his earring and gasped. Then she laughed. "What a great joke!" she said. "I assume it's one of those stick-on kinds?"

"No, Mom, this is the real thing," Jason answered. "I had my ear pierced. Everybody on the swim team has an earring, and I was the only one who didn't, so I gave in."

Suzette became nervous, not because she was upset with her son, but because she wondered how her husband would react when he got home. After taking Jason's laundry and getting him something to drink, she called two friends. Then, while Jim was still at work, she made a trip to the home of one of those friends and discussed how she should handle the situation.

Both Jason and his mother were anxious as Jim arrived home.

When he walked in the door, Jason said, "Hi, Dad, I'm home for the weekend."

Jim immediately hugged his son—on the side opposite the earring—then said, "Well, how's college going?" He hadn't noticed, and Jason just kept waiting for the explosion. Finally, Dad saw it. "Hey-y-y, what's this?" he said.

Jason thought, *Oh, no! He's going to rip it off my ear.*

Suzette gently suggested, "Now, don't overreact."

But Jim didn't react at all. Calmly and sensitively, he asked, "What's going on?"

Jason answered, "Dad, everybody on the swim team has an earring. I knew you'd be upset, but, Dad, I was the only guy who didn't have one. The seniors said either I do it or, you know, I'm in trouble."

"If you want to wear the earring, that's your business," Jim answered. "It's not up to me. Only God knows how much I love you.

Personally, I wouldn't wear an earring, but, hey, I understand the pressure you were getting."

Suzette calmed down immediately. "I thought you were going to be mad," she told Jim.

"No, we need to support our son," he said. "Actually, I'd like to do something about it, but I don't think anything would help."

While they were in the middle of that discussion, my wife, Norma, and I showed up. We're a part of the Brawners' support team. Along with three other couples, we meet weekly in a small group, plus we meet socially and pray for each other. The Brawners know about our family and everything that goes on, and we know the same about their family.

My wife gave Jason a big hug and said, "That's a good-looking earring."

Then I gave him a hug and asked, "How's the temperature in the house today?"

He had an embarrassed smile on his face as he said, "So far, so good."

So what's the big deal about this ordinary family conflict? What the Brawners did is what I wish millions of families would do. Even though they may seem small, this brief encounter contained all five qualities that are extremely important.

FIVE QUALITIES OF HEALTHY COUPLES

In many respects, that was a typical family conflict. What's not so typical is the way the Brawners handled it. Did you catch the five things Jim and Suzette did in their relationship and family? They aren't all immediately obvious, but all were definitely there and operational.

They had a clearly defined menu of expectations.

They understood and used meaningful communication.

They were involved in a small support group.

They recognized their personal emotional wounds and had learned how to compensate for them.

They were dependent on the Lord Jesus Christ for their quality of life.

In any family, one thing you can count on is crisis. It may be a child having poor grades or breaking up with a friend. It may be the disappointment of not making an athletic team. It could be a major event, such as a long-term family illness or a job change that forces the family to move across the country. Whatever the issue or crisis, those five things the Brawners have will hold the family together and greatly increase the likelihood that their marriage will thrive.

Let's look more closely at each of the five elements and see how we can use them in our own marriages and families.

1. Healthy couples have a clearly defined menu of expectations. When you go to a restaurant, you look at a menu, and you expect to be able to order anything you want from it. The owners know that if they provide good food and service, you'll come back.

The same is true in a successful home. When a family agrees, preferably in writing, on a menu of options for quality life and relationships, they will enjoy a healthy, successful family life. Here is just a sample of things you might consider putting on your menu:

Honor for your loved ones. Honor means "to place a high value on." It's the decision we make that someone has great worth. From that decision and God's power comes our ability to love others genuinely and consistently.

You can determine that each member of your family is highly valuable and to be honored. You can do that by first honoring God, then building security into your wife and your children by verbally praising them and protecting them.

A plan for dealing with unresolved anger. Scripture admonishes us not to let the sun go down on our anger (see Eph. 4:26). Every family needs a healthy process for resolving anger and keeping it low. Jim and Suzette could have let anger erupt when they saw Jason wearing an earring. Instead, they dealt constructively with their emotions and honored their son.

Activities that foster emotional bonding. You can't just sit at home and talk every day. You need to do things together outside your home that will draw you together.

Many other areas can be covered in your family's menu. They should be agreed upon together during periods of calm. Some resources in the back of this book will help you develop your menu.

2. *Healthy couples understand and practice meaningful communication.*

Picture yourself driving through a fast-food restaurant. You pull up to that little speaker box and announce, "I'd like two hamburgers, two fries, an onion ring, and two Diet Cokes."

After a moment, you hear from the speaker, "Did you say a hamburger and a cheeseburger, two fries, an onion ring, and two Cokes?"

You clarify, "No, I didn't say that. I said *two* hamburgers, two fries, an onion ring, and two *Diet* Cokes."

In a similar way, I recommend that couples practice "drive-through talking." Take the time to repeat back to one another what you think you heard your partner or your children say. It's very honoring and meaningful.

Within marital and family communication it's important to remember that you're always trying to move toward the deepest level of intimacy. Healthy families are connected emotionally, spiritually, psychologically, and physically. They feel two big things: They feel connected, and they feel safe in that connection—they can say things and feel they're not going to get rejected or belittled.

Experts have identified five levels of communication, and healthy families operate on all five levels.

The shallowest level is when you just use clichés like "Hi." "How are you?" "Did you have a good day?" "Is everything going okay?" "Give me five." Clichés are little phrases that have little meaning. They're pretty safe. You can say them and know you're not going to get in trouble.

The second level of communication is when you relate facts. "Did you see that in the paper today?" "It looks like it's going to rain tomorrow." "Do you think the Dodgers [or your home team] are going to win?" "The football team doesn't seem that good this year."

The third level of communication is riskier, and a lot of couples, especially when they're starting out, are hesitant to go to it because of potential conflicts. It is the stating of opinions: "I think this is going to happen," "I believe this is the way things ought to be," or "We ought to have a date one night a week."

Whenever you state opinions, you increase the possibility of conflict. That's a good time to use drive-through talking and repeat back what you think you hear your mate saying until you achieve clarity and understanding. Keep in mind that conflict with your mate or your children is healthy and normal. What's not healthy is walking off and not talking about it, or else reacting, getting angry, and dishonoring each other. But handled properly, conflicts are doorways to intimacy. They open up the last two areas of communication.

The fourth level is expressing and understanding each other's feelings. This can best occur when you feel safe.

Not long ago, Norma and I went on a short trip with the Brawners. In the driveway before we left, Suzette said to Jim, "I feel so nervous about leaving Travis [their seventeen-year-old] home alone the first week of two-a-day football practices. Who's going to cut the watermelon for him at six in the morning? Who's going to make his breakfast? Who's going to have his sandwiches ready? I just feel so uncomfortable. Isn't Travis going to feel he's been abandoned?"

Suzette felt safe expressing those feelings. But that openness can be shattered when we're insensitive. Without thinking, Jim said, "Come on, Suzette, will you relax? We've got to take vacations once in a while. Let the kids grow up."

Then he realized what he was doing, and he stopped attacking his wife's feelings. He hugged her and said, "I see you're really hurting, and that's okay. Should we cancel the trip?"

"No, I want to go. It's just hard," she said.

We men need to understand that in healthy homes, everyone feels free to express feelings without fear of hearing, "That's stupid!" "Only an idiot would feel like that," or "Why don't you grow up?" Maybe the feelings are immature, but they're real nonetheless. It's not our job to analyze; it is our duty to love, value, and understand our mates and our children.

The fifth and deepest level of communication is when we feel safe in revealing our needs. I can say I need a hug. I can say I need to hold and kiss my wife and be involved sexually. Or she can say she needs to go shopping and ask if I'll go with her.

Norma and I were talking recently as we prepared to fly to Colorado to speak at a physicians' conference. She had learned there was going to be a western dinner on Friday night, so she had bought a western outfit. She brought it home and said, "I need to have you look at this outfit I bought. What do you think?"

In the past, I might have said, "Hey, I'm busy. Can I do it later?" Or I would have looked at the outfit and said, "What difference does it make? Just buy it if you want it."

But I have learned that such words are dishonoring. So I looked at my wife and said something like, "I love the outfit! It makes you look younger." (Most men know from experience that that's something women like to hear.)

Then she said, "I don't have a coat to go with it. But I found one at this outlet mall, and I really like it. I need you to go look at it with me and tell me what you think."

Norma hasn't always felt free to reveal her needs to me. I used to be very controlling, rigid, critical, and prone to giving lectures. The damage I did in the first few years of our marriage still lingers. But I want her to feel increasingly safe, because then I know we're going to go increasingly deep in our intimacy.

3. Healthy couples are associated with a small, healthy support group.

I suggest you meet regularly with three—at the most four—other couples who have the same commitment to God and their marriages that you have. In a healthy group, each person feels the freedom, safety, love, and commitment to think out loud. In fact, group members want you to think, reason, and grapple with important issues.

An effective support group is built on deep friendship. Members give each other hugs and affection when needed. They do things together like camping or dining. But they also have a definite purpose for meeting every week. It may be to study a marriage book or to discuss ways to improve their parenting skills. Whatever the purpose, it must be specific if the group is to stay on course. The weekly meeting is not a gossip session. It's not a time to criticize your pastor or other church members. And it's definitely not a time to put down your mate. Sure, every once in a while, someone's going to slip, but you can't have a steady diet of that. There must be freedom to feel, think, and discuss your feelings and needs with each other.

Why are support groups so important? First, they give you power to make the changes we all need to make to stay healthy. There's a dynamic that takes place where you actually experience energy from someone else hugging you and saying things like, "We can do this together," "I know you're in conflict, but it will get better," and the all-important words, "We love you."

Second, you get the tremendous power of accountability, knowing that once a week you're going to ask each other, "How's it going?" in the area of your purpose for meeting together. You know you're going to have honesty, so when you say it's not going well, someone will ask, "What are you doing about it? What steps are you going to take to make this better?"

Third, if you come from an unhealthy home, a good small group gives you a chance to be re-parented. You get to see how couples can interact in a healthy way. That leads to the next area of strong family life.

4. Healthy couples are aware of unhealthy or offensive behavior stemming from their heritage.

The Bible says that the sins of a father are visited on the children up to four generations. So some of the things I'm doing to my wife and children today could be directly related to my great-grandfather, his behavior and offensive ways toward my grandfather, then my father, and so on down the line. Now, that doesn't mean I'm to blame my great-grandfather or my father. But it helps to understand who I am so I can take 100 percent responsibility for my life today and do whatever is necessary to raise a new generation that God will bless.

What you need to do is to look at your life and ask, "Did I come from an unhealthy environment?" You might rate your parents on a scale from zero (not at all) to ten (all the time) in such areas as the following:

____ were like dictators, demanding obedience

____ were rigid, forceful, with strict rules, values, beliefs, and expectations

____ were critical, judgmental, with harsh punishment

_____ were closed to talking about certain subjects like sex, religion, politics, feelings

_____ were poor listeners to my thoughts and feelings

_____ used degrading names like "stupid," "lazy," or "no good"

The higher the score, the more potential there is for an unhealthy relationship in your home. Based on your score, you may need some specific help from a counselor to analyze where you came from and develop a plan for healing.

Unlike a lot of couples, Jim and Suzette Brawner understand the families they came from and the strengths and weaknesses they inherited. They struggled in their marriage until Jim got some help. Now he's in charge of a small-group ministry called Homes of Honor, and through it he trains couples to overcome past mistakes and to gain support for the changes they want to make.

5. Healthy couples have a vibrant relationship with Jesus Christ.

Norma and I, Jim and Suzette, and many other couples have entered into a relationship with Jesus Christ in which we are dependent on Him as our primary source of abundant life. That life includes love, peace, joy, patience, kindness, and self-control. The Holy Spirit gives us the spirit of completeness, or contentment, so we don't have to struggle and look for anybody else to get our needs met.

The apostle Paul wrote, "My God will meet all your needs according to his glorious riches in Christ Jesus" (Phil. 4:19). He also wrote that we can know the love of God "that surpasses knowledge—that you may be filled to the measure of all the fullness of God" (Eph. 3:19).

Over and over, the Bible talks of how Jesus is our life and that we're not to have any other gods, nor are we to look to anything else as our source of life. Everything else—wives, kids, cars, homes, jobs—is overflow to the relationship we have with Him. When that permeates our relationship as husband and wife, we experience what Scripture calls a calm or quiet spirit. We're relaxed because we know that Jesus filters everything that comes into our lives. Plus, He can take any trial we experience and, as He said in Isaiah 61:3, turn that sorrow into gladness. Our kids will tend to pick up that spirit and follow in our footsteps as long as they're not angry with us.

Do you have a home like Jim and Suzette's, where there is a clear menu of expectations and communication is open and goes deep in the five levels toward intimacy? Do you recognize problems from your childhood, and do you have a support group to help you grow as a couple? And finally, do you recognize Jesus Christ—not your wife, family, job, or anything else—as the source of life?

I suggest that, with your wife, you rate your marriage in each of those five areas on a scale from zero to ten. Then choose one of the five and talk about how you can move it closer to a ten. That will put you on the road to a healthier and more rewarding marriage.

The Servant
Who Leads

by Ken Davis

The topic of this chapter is "The Servant Who Leads." You can turn it around, and it's "The Leader Who Serves." But no matter how you look at it, it comes out this way: to lead is to serve. Jesus sat with His disciples just before He was going to be crucified. The Bible says in John 13, just before the Passover feast, Jesus knew that the time had come for Him to leave this world and go to the Father. And it says that He showed them the *full extent* of His love, not just an expensive gift or a flowery note. Jesus got up from this last meal with His disciples— with all of His authority, with all of His power—wrapped a towel around His waist, and began to wash their feet.

To be a leader for Almighty God means to serve. How do we serve? Men don't like to serve. In our culture, we believe it is only the weak who serve. We want to *be* served, and the more power we have, the more we want to be served. But the Bible tells a different story. Servanthood is not a sign of weakness; it is a sign of great inner strength. Only those who are secure in their true source of power, their true source of identity, are capable of serving. They serve because they're free to do so. They serve because they want to. They serve because they know that taking on the attitude of a servant does not diminish their authority.

The challenge to be a leader in our home is not a ticket to abuse our authority as head of the household, but instead we must understand that our wives and our children are not our possessions. They are not extensions of our egos. They are beloved children of God who will be blessed and influenced beyond our imagination, who will have their minds and hearts blown away by our willingness to serve them. Leadership and authority are not weapons to be wielded; they are trusts to be administered. But how do we serve?

SERVE YOUR FAMILY WITH YOUR TIME

They desperately need your time! We get so busy creating careers and building what we think are foundations of authority that we forget the very people whom we love the most. The time spent with your child isn't a distraction from the main events. The time spent with your child *is* the main event. That's what life is about! And the window of opportunity for doing that is very short.

I remember when my first child was born, I didn't even want to have children. I had a bad attitude! When my wife told me she was going to have a baby, I said, "Why did you do that?" I got kicked out of Lamaze class. They showed a movie and I said, "Run it backward!" The lady teaching the course didn't have a sense of humor.

I took a camera to the delivery room. (I confess to you that I am a recovering jerk.) So I sat in that room with two cameras to take pictures, but I don't have any pictures because God did a miracle in my life. When that child was born, I fell in love with her. I would have died for her. The doctor brought her over to me and asked, "Would you like to hold her?"

I said, "No! She'll break!" I had never seen anything so fragile! Anyway, he brought that baby over and placed her in my arms. Tears streamed down my face; I had never seen anything so beautiful in all of my life. Her little hand reached up and grabbed my little finger— her whole hand wasn't any bigger than my thumb. And I made a fatal mistake: I blinked! And when I opened my eyes again, she was still in my arms, I was still weeping, but I was leaving her in a college dorm room eight hundred miles from our house.

And it went just like a snap of my fingers! And last December, I walked down an aisle with that child, and her little hand was wrapped around my arm. I walked to the front of that church, and I kissed that tiny little hand one last time. Then I placed it in the hand of her husband-to-be.

The opportunity to spend time with your children is so short. One man took his son fishing. They didn't catch anything all day. In his journal he wrote these words: "Went fishing with my son, didn't even get a bite. Whole day wasted." Years later, he was going through a big trunk and found his son's journal lying on the bottom. He opened that journal and read what his son had written about that very same day: "Went fishing, didn't get a bite all day. Spent the whole day with my dad—the best day of my life!"

Giving our time is how we show what Christ has done in our heart! Many of us stopped dating our wives the day we got married. They are desperate for a romantic moment, for a dinner alone with you—a dinner where no telephone rings, no beeper goes off, and they are the focus of your attention.

Many years ago, my wife got cancer. I remember as she lay in bed one night, I looked at her lying there and God brought to my heart how dearly precious this woman was to me. I no longer treated her with the same attention, with the same intensity, with the same gentleness that I treated her when we were dating. I reached over as she slept and touched her lips. And I ran my fingers across her eyebrows, I was so grateful for what God had given me. And as I did that, I saw a huge tear pooling in the side of her eye. I said, "Sweetheart, what's the matter?" as I held her in my arms.

And she answered, "Don't stop. Don't stop."

Do you want your wife to know, do you want your children to know, do you want your family to know that you love them? Spend time with them. That's what Christ did with us. Aren't you glad God didn't send us a fax declaring His love? Aren't you glad He didn't leave a message on your e-mail or send you a telegram? He came down here to spend time among us and die on the cross so we would know He loves us! There's no doubt He loves us! Aren't you glad?

SERVE THEM WITH YOUR WORDS

We live in a culture that is desperate to hear the words, "I love you." When's the last time you looked your son in the eye and said, "I love you"? When's the last time you looked your dad in the eye and said, "I love you"?

I was on a plane at thirty thousand feet one day. I had just received a national award and had thousands of people applaud as I went to the platform to receive that award. I only wished that my dad had been there. So I took out a sheet of paper and wrote a letter to my dad. Basically I said, "Dad, all my life I have achieved a lot of things." And I added, "Dad, you know, all I wanted is for you to be proud." You see, my dad grew up in an era when you didn't say "I love you." It wasn't the manly thing to do. That era was wrong, men! It was wrong! Now, I'm not putting my dad down. He grew up to believe that's the way it was. But I wrote him this letter, and at the bottom of the letter, I said, "You know the award I'm most proud of, Dad? I'm most proud that you're my dad." As I concluded the letter, I wrote the words I couldn't remember saying to my father for years: "I love you."

And then I folded up the letter. I dared not mail it because I was afraid he wouldn't respond. What if he didn't acknowledge my love? I wasn't sure that was a pain I could handle. I held that letter for two weeks until I sent it. Then I waited by the phone to get that call. I finally came to believe the letter didn't make any difference, because the call never came. I had struggled through this emotional crisis to tell my dad I loved him, and he couldn't even call me and acknowledge he got the letter!

Several months later, I was visiting my parents. I remember pulling into the driveway, a ball of fire burning in my stomach! I resented the fact that I desperately needed to hear this man say to me, "I love you, too!" When I walked into the house, my mother greeted me in that way that moms do when something's up. My dad went into the garage. Then my mom ushered me into the guest room. Hanging there, framed in a homemade frame that my dad had made, was the letter I had written him months before. My mother said, "No one comes into this house but that he ushers them into this room and shows them that letter and makes them read it."

My dad loves me! My dad loves me! I grabbed ahold of his body when he came out of that garage. I said, "I love you, Dad!"

He said, "I love you, too." *Agape* love, God's love. Do you know what it meant for my dad to see that his son had written on a piece of paper, "I love you"? We call each other all the time now, we say it all the time. It has transformed our relationship. A lot of bitterness drains away when you say the words, "I love you." We're desperate to hear them.

SERVE THEM WITH YOUR ACTIONS

I grew up in an era that believed all the housework belonged to the woman. I thought that God put women on the earth to make sure that everything went well for men. I didn't help my wife at all. For years, I was in ministry and I made $8,000 a year working for God. My wife made $22,000 a year working for a bank. You figure it. But I liked it that way. I didn't want it to change.

She was gone day after day after day, and I never lifted a hand to help her around the house. And I wondered why she didn't respond to me! Oh, our courtship had been full of passion and fire. She wanted me and I knew that I deserved to be wanted . . . then we got married. And she began to sense in our relationship that perhaps I was not demonstrating to her the love that I had proclaimed with my mouth. Our marriage grew cold. The passion and fire were gone. The little moves that I had made that I thought were so sexy and so alluring repulsed her. Soon I began to repulse myself.

I sat in the house one day, and—I'll never forget this—the door to the closet was open and the vacuum cleaner was in there. I had never touched that vacuum cleaner. The amazing thing is, I paid good money for that vacuum. Some salesman came and showed me a bunch of demonstrations—amazing things! That vacuum could float a Ping-Pong ball in a stream of air! Then he took out a golf ball and the golf ball floated in the air! He told me that other vacuum cleaners couldn't do a golf ball. So I bought it. To this day, that vacuum won't suck dirt!

But I saw it sitting there, so I thought, *I'm going to try it*. Oh, did I learn some things. We need to do these things just to learn what our wives put up with! Vacuum cleaners don't work—at least, not on the important stuff. They pick up little pieces of lint, hang on to them for an indeterminate amount of time, then drop them when you least expect! They will take a toothpick or anything that's got grab to it and not mess with it, even if you go over it a hundred times. The carpet is worn out, and the toothpick's still there!

I finally tired of the whole mess, so I just put the vacuum in the middle of the room, took off all the hoses and brought stuff to it! Then I put the hose back on and started to vacuum the rug. Here's a fascinating thing. When you go this way, it makes a color of one stripe; if you come back the opposite way, a different colored stripe! I got so fascinated I striped the whole house! Then I figured, *While I'm at it, I might as well dust!* So I dusted! And then I went the other way with the vacuum and made a little checkerboard pattern all over the house.

I sat back down in the chair that I was usually in when she came home. She got home, opened the door, and came in. She had two big bags of groceries, so she kicked the door shut. I'm sitting on the recliner, reading the paper, working a crossword puzzle, being lazy like I had been all my life. Then she looked up and saw the checkerboard and that everything was picked up and neat! And I still can remember being surprised when one sack of groceries fell, then the other sack of groceries fell, and she said, "Who did this?"

I looked up stupidly and said, "I did!" She came running over and jumped on the chair with me. We broke that chair. It was wonderful!

One of the reasons that the passion is gone from our marriages is because we have for too long stopped saying, "I love you." We have stopped demonstrating, "I love you."

Suppose you are single. What can you do? You treat the lady that you're dating with the dignity that God gave her. You serve her as the Bible says that Christ served us. Gentlemen, you won't be single long. There is an entire society of women out there who have never been treated like that—not ever.

Kids need our tangible expressions of love, too. One little girl wanted her daddy to tell her the three little pigs story over and over again. Well, if you're like me, I used to do that, and then I would start to skip pages. (The three little pigs story lasts a long time.) Her dad tried that, but she wouldn't let him skip pages. Finally, he tape-recorded the story, gave it to his daughter, and showed her how to play it. He came home one night, busy working on the stuff that men do, and the little girl came in with the tape recorder. She said, "Daddy, tell me the three little pigs story."

He said, "It's on the tape recorder, sweetheart!"

And she said, "Daddy, I can't sit in the tape recorder's lap!"

How desperate our children are to be able to touch us, to know that we care. Those are actions of love. Serving God has to be practical.

PLUGGED INTO THE SOURCE OF POWER

I guarantee you that unless you're tied into the tree of life, with a personal relationship with Jesus Christ, your bouquet is going to wilt the first time you run into a challenge. And people will point and say, "See? It doesn't mean anything." Some of you have that little bouquet clutched in your hand, but you have rejected the Person who is the source of the power to serve. Jesus said, "Love each other like I have loved you." But you can't love out of emptiness. Unless you know the love and forgiveness of Jesus Christ, you have nothing to love from. But your family is waiting. And they're waiting to be served by you and loved by you. Jesus wants to help you do that. So, in your own heart, right now, do whatever you need to do to make that commitment.

The Priority

of Fathering

by James Dobson

I was walking toward my car outside a shopping center a few weeks ago, when I heard a loud and impassioned howl.

"Auggghh!" groaned the masculine voice.

I spotted a man about fifty feet away who was in great distress (and for a very good reason). His fingers were caught in the jamb of a car door which had obviously been slammed unexpectedly. Then the rest of the story unfolded. Crouching in the front seat was an impish little three-year-old boy who had apparently decided to "close the door on Dad."

The father was pointing frantically at his fingers with his free hand, and saying, "Oh! Oh! Open the door, Chuckie! They're caught . . . hurry . . . Chuckie . . . please . . . open . . . OPEN!"

Chuckie finally got the message and unlocked the door, releasing Dad's blue fingers. The father then hopped and jumped around the aisles of the parking lot, alternately kissing and caressing his battered hand. Chuckie sat unmoved in the front seat of their car, waiting for Pop to settle down.

I know this incident was painful to the man who experienced it, but I must admit that it struck me as funny. I suppose his plight symbolized the enormous cost of parenthood. And yes, Virginia, it is expensive to raise boys and girls today. Parents give the best they have to their children, who often respond by slamming the door on their "fingers"—especially during the unappreciative adolescent years. Perhaps that is why someone quipped, "Insanity is an inherited disease. You get it from your kids."

Without wanting to heap guilt on the heads of my masculine readers, I must say that too many fathers only sleep at their homes. And as a result, they have totally abdicated their responsibilities for leadership and influence in the lives of their children. I cited a study in my previous book *What Wives Wish Their Husbands Knew About Women* that documented the problem of inaccessible fathers. Let me quote from that source:

An article in *Scientific American* entitled "The Origins of Alienation," by Urie Bronfenbrenner best describes the problems facing today's families. Dr. Bronfenbrenner is, in my opinion, the foremost authority on child development in America today, and his views should be considered carefully. In this article, Dr. Bronfenbrenner discussed the deteriorating status of the American family and the forces which are weakening its cohesiveness. More specifically, he is concerned about the circumstances which are seriously undermining parental love and depriving children of the leadership and love they must have for survival.

One of those circumstances is widely known as the "rat-race." Dr. Bronfenbrenner described the problem this way, "The demands of a job that claim mealtimes, evenings and weekends as well as days; the trips and moves necessary to get ahead or simply to hold one's own; the increasing time spent commuting, entertaining, going out, meeting social and community obligations . . . all of these produce a situation in which a child often spends more time with a passive babysitter than with a participating parent."

According to Dr. Bronfenbrenner, this rat race is particularly incompatible with fatherly responsibilities, as illustrated by an investigation in the 1970s which yielded startling results. A team of researchers wanted to learn how much time middle-class fathers spend playing and interacting with their small children. First, they asked a group of fathers to estimate the time spent with their one-year-old youngsters each day, and received an average reply of fifteen to twenty minutes. To verify these claims, the investigators attached microphones to the shirts of small children for the purpose of recording actual parental verbalization. The results of this study are shocking. The average amount of time spent by these middle-class fathers with their small children was thirty-seven seconds per day! Their direct interaction was limited to 2.7 encounters daily, lasting ten to fifteen seconds each! That represented the contribution of fatherhood for millions of America's children in the 1970s, and I believe the findings would be even more depressing today.[1]

Let's compare the thirty-seven-second interchanges between fathers and small children with another statistic. The average preschool child watches between thirty and fifty hours of television per week (the figures vary from one study to another). What an incredible picture is painted by those two statistics. During the formative years of life, when children are so vulnerable to their experiences, they're receiving thirty-seven seconds a day from their fathers and thirty or more hours a week from commercial television! Need we ask where our kids are getting their values?

Someone observed, "Values are not taught to our children; they are caught by them." It is true. Seldom can we get little Johnny or Mary to sit patiently on a chair while we lecture to them about God and the other important issues of life. Instead, they are equipped with internal "motors" that are incapable of idling. Their transmissions consist of only six gears: run, jump, climb, crawl, slide, and dive. Boys and girls are simply not wired for quiet conversations about heavy topics.

How, then, do conscientious parents convey their attitudes and values and faith to their children? It is done subtly, through the routine interactions of everyday living (see Deut. 6:4–9). We saw this fact illustrated in our own home when Danae was ten years old and Ryan was five. We were riding in the car when we passed a porno theater. I believe the name of the particular movie was *Flesh Gordon*, or something equally sensuous. Danae, who was sitting in the front seat, pointed to the theater and said, "That's a dirty movie, isn't it, Dad?"

I nodded affirmatively.

"Is that what they call an X-rated movie?" she asked.

Again, I indicated that she was correct.

Danae thought for a moment or two, then said, "Dirty movies are really bad, aren't they?"

I said, "Yes, Danae. Dirty movies are very evil."

This entire conversation lasted less than a minute, consisting of three brief questions and three replies. Ryan, who was in the back-seat, did not enter into our discussion. In fact, I wondered what he thought about the interchange and concluded that he probably wasn't listening.

I was wrong. Ryan heard the conversation and apparently contin-ued thinking about it for several days. But amusingly, Ryan did not know what a "dirty movie" was. How would a five-year-old boy learn what goes on in such places, since no one had ever discussed pornography with him? Nevertheless, he had his own idea about the subject. That concept was revealed to me four nights later at the close of the day.

Ryan and I got down on our knees to say his bedtime prayer, and the preschooler spontaneously returned to that conversation earlier in the week.

"Dear Lord," he began in great seriousness, "help me not to go see any dirty movies . . . where everyone is spitting on each other."

For Ryan, the dirtiest thing he could imagine would be a salivary free-for-all. That would be dirty, I had to admit.

But I also had to acknowledge how casually children assimilate our values and attitudes. You see, I had no way of anticipating that brief conversation in the car. It was not my deliberate intention to convey my views about pornography to my children. How was it that they learned one more dimension of my value system on that morning? It occurred because we happened to be together . . . to be talking to one another. Those kinds of subtle, unplanned interactions account for much of the instruction that passes from one generation to the next. It is a powerful force in shaping young lives, if! If parents are occasion-ally at home with their kids; if they have the energy to converse with them; if they have anything worthwhile to transmit; if they care.

My point is that the breathless American lifestyle is particularly costly to children. Yet 1.8 million youngsters come home to an empty house after school each day. They are called "latchkey" kids because they wear the keys to their front doors around their necks. Not only are their fathers overcommitted and preoccupied, but now their mothers are energetically seeking fulfillment in the working world, too. So who is at home with the kids? More commonly, the answer is nobody.

Have you felt the years slipping by with far too many unfulfilled promises to your children? Have you heard yourself saying,

Son, we've been talking about the wagon we were going to build one of these Saturdays, and I just want you to know that I haven't forgotten it. But we can't do it this weekend 'cause I have to make an unexpected trip to Indianapolis. However, we will get to it one of these days. I'm not sure if it can be next weekend, but you keep reminding me and we'll eventually work together. And I'm going to take you fishing, too. I love to fish and I know a little stream that is jumping with trout in the spring. But this just happens to be a very busy month for your mom and me, so let's keep planning and before you know it, the time will be here.

Then the days soon become weeks, and the weeks flow into months and years and decades . . . and our kids grow up and leave home. Then we sit in the silence of our family rooms, trying to recall the precious experiences that escaped us there. Ringing in our ears is that haunting phrase, "We'll have a good time . . . then. . . ."

Oh, I know I'm stirring a measure of guilt into the pot with these words. But perhaps we need to be confronted with the important issues of life, even if they make us uncomfortable. Furthermore, I feel obligated to speak on behalf of the millions of children across this country who are reaching for fathers who aren't there. The names of specific boys and girls come to my mind as I write these words, symbolizing the masses of lonely kids who experience the agony of unmet needs. Let me acquaint you with two or three of those children whose paths I have crossed.

I think first of the mother who approached me after I had spoken some years ago. She had supported her husband through college and medical school, only to have him divorce her in favor of a younger plaything. She stood with tears in her eyes as she described the impact of his departure on her two sons.

"They miss their daddy every day," she said. "They don't understand why he doesn't come to see them. The older boy, especially, wants a father so badly that he reaches for every man who comes into our lives. What can I tell him? How can I meet the boy's needs for a father who will hunt and fish and play football and bowl with him and his brother? It's breaking my heart to see them suffer so much."

I gave this mother a few suggestions and offered my understanding and support. The next morning I spoke for the final time at her church. Following the service, I stood on the platform as a line of people waited to tell me good-bye and extend their greetings. Standing in the line was the mother with her two sons.

They greeted me with smiles and I shook the older child's hand. Then something happened that I did not recall until I was on my way back to Los Angeles. The boy did not let go of my hand! He gripped it tightly, preventing me from welcoming others who pressed around. To my regret, I realized later that I had unconsciously grasped his arm with my other hand, pulling myself free from his grip. I sat on the plane, realizing the full implications of that incident. You see, this lad needed me. He needed a man who could take the place of his renegade father. And I had failed him, just like all the rest. Now I'm left with the memory of a child who said with his eyes, "Could you be a daddy to me?"

Another child has found a permanent place in my memory, although I don't even know her name. I was waiting to catch a plane at Los Angeles International Airport, enjoying my favorite activity of "people watching." But I was unprepared for the drama about to unfold. Standing near me was an old man who was obviously waiting for someone who should have been on the plane that arrived minutes before. He examined each face intently as the passengers filed past. I thought he seemed unusually distressed as he waited.

Then I saw the little girl who stood by his side. She must have been seven years old, and she, too, was desperately looking for a certain face in the crowd. I have rarely seen a child more anxious than this cute little girl. She clung to the old man's arm, whom I assumed to be her grandfather. Then as the last passengers came by, one by one, the girl began to cry silently. She was not merely disappointed in that moment; her little heart was broken. The grandfather also appeared to be fighting back the tears. In fact, he was too upset to comfort the child, who then buried her face in the sleeve of his worn coat.

"Oh, God!" I prayed silently. "What special agony are they experiencing in this hour? Was it the child's mother who abandoned her on that painful day? Did her daddy promise to come and then change his mind?"

My great impulse was to throw my arms around the little girl and shield her from the awfulness of that hour. I wanted her to pour out her grief in the protection of my embrace, but I feared that my intrusion would be misunderstood. So I watched helplessly. Then the old man and the child stood silently as the passengers departed from two other planes, but the anxiety on their faces had turned to despair. Finally, they walked slowly through the terminal and toward the door. Their only sound was the snuffling of the little girl who fought to control her tears.

Where is this child now? God only knows.

If the reader will bear with me, I must introduce you to one other child whose family experience has become so common in the Western world. I was waiting at Shawnee Mission Hospital for word on my dad's heart condition, after he was stricken in September. There in the waiting room was an *American Girl* magazine that caught my attention. (I must have been desperate for something to read to have been attracted to the *American Girl*.)

I opened the cover page and immediately saw a composition written by a fourteen-year-old girl named Vicki Kraushaar. She had submitted her story for publication in the section of the magazine entitled "By You." I'll let Vicki introduce herself and describe her experience.

That's the Way Life Goes Sometimes

When I was ten, my parents got a divorce. Naturally, my father told me about it, because he was my favorite. [Notice that Vicki did not say, "I was his favorite."]

"Honey, I know it's been kind of bad for you these past few days, and I don't want to make it worse. But there's something I have to tell you. Honey, your mother and I got a divorce."

"But, Daddy—"

"I know you don't want this, but it has to be done. Your mother and

I just don't get along like we used to. I'm already packed and my plane is leaving in half an hour."

"But, Daddy, why do you have to leave?"

"Well, honey, your mother and I can't live together anymore."

"I know that, but I mean why do you have to leave town?"

"Oh. Well, I got someone waiting for me in New Jersey."

"But, Daddy, will I ever see you again?"

"Sure you will, honey. We'll work something out."

"But what? I mean, you'll be living in New Jersey, and I'll be living here in Washington."

"Maybe your mother will agree to you spending two weeks in the summer and two in the winter with me."

"Why not more often?"

"I don't think she'll agree to two weeks in the summer and two in the winter, much less more."

"Well, it can't hurt to try."

"I know, honey, but we'll have to work it out later. My plane leaves in 20 minutes and I've got to get to the airport. Now I'm going to get my luggage, and I want you to go to your room so you don't have to watch me. And no long good-byes either."

"Okay, Daddy. Good-bye. Don't forget to write."

"I won't. Good-bye. Now go to your room."

"Okay. Daddy, I don't want you to go!"

"I know, honey. But I have to."

"Why?"

"You wouldn't understand, honey."

"Yes, I would."

"No, you wouldn't."

"Oh well. Good-bye."

"Good-bye. Now go to your room. Hurry up."

"Okay. Well, I guess that's the way life goes sometimes."

"Yes honey. That's the way life goes sometimes."

After my father walked out that door, I never heard from him again.[2]

Vicki speaks eloquently on behalf of a million American children who have heard those shattering words, "Honey, your mother and I are getting a divorce." Throughout the world, husbands and wives are responding to the media blitz that urges and goads them to do their own thing, to chase impulsive desires without regard for the welfare of their families.

"The kids will get over it," goes the rationalization.

Every form of mass communication seemed mobilized to spread the "me first" philosophy during the seventies and early eighties. Frank Sinatra said it musically in his song, "I Did It My Way." Sammy Davis Jr. echoed the sentiment in "I've Gotta Be Me." Robert J. Ringer provided the literary version in *Looking Out for Number One*, which became the best-selling book in America for forty-six weeks. It was flanked by *Open Marriage*, *Creative Divorce*, and *Pulling Your Own Strings*, among hundreds of other dangerous bestsellers. The est program then sold the same sickness under the guise of psychological health.

It all sounded so noble at the time. It was called "the discovery of personhood," and it offered an intoxicating appeal to our selfish lusts. But when this insidious philosophy had wormed its way into our system of values, it began to rot us from within. First, it encouraged an insignificant flirtation with sin (perhaps with a man or woman from New Jersey) followed by passion and illicit sexual encounters, followed by camouflaging lies and deceit, followed by angry words and sleepless nights, followed by tears and anguish, followed by crumbling self-esteem, followed by attorneys and divorce courts and property settlements, followed by devastating custody hearings. And from deep within the maelstrom, we can hear the cry of three wounded children—two girls and a boy—who will never fully recover. "Then when lust hath conceived, it bringeth forth sin; and sin, when it is finished, bringeth forth death" (James 1:15, KJV).

For those younger fathers whose children are still at an impressionable age, please believe the words of my dad, "The greatest delusion is to suppose that our children will be devout Christians simply because their parents have been, or that any of them will enter into the Christian faith in any other way than through their parents' deep travail of prayer and faith."

If you doubt the validity of this assertion, may I suggest that you read the story of Eli in 1 Samuel 2–4. Here is the account of a priest and servant of God who failed to discipline his children. He was apparently too busy with the "work of the church" to be a leader in his own home. The two boys grew up to be evil young men on whom God's judgment fell.

It concerned me to realize that Eli's service to the Lord was insufficient to compensate for his failure at home. Then I read further in the narrative and received confirmation of the principle. Samuel, the saintly man of God, who stood like a tower of spiritual strength throughout his life, grew up in Eli's home. He watched Eli systematically losing his children, yet Samuel proceeded to fail with his family, too! That was a deeply disturbing truth. If God would not honor Samuel's dedication by guaranteeing the salvation of his children, will He do more for me if I'm too busy to do my "homework"?

Having been confronted with these spiritual obligations and responsibilities, the Lord then gave me an enormous burden for my two children. I carry it to this day. There are times when it becomes so heavy that I ask God to remove it from my shoulders, although the concern is not motivated by the usual problems or anxieties. Our kids are apparently healthy and seem to be holding their own emotionally and academically. (Update: Danae finished college in 1990 and Ryan was completing his junior year at the time this was written.) The source of my burden derives from the awareness that a tug-of-war is being waged for the hearts and minds of every person on earth, including these two precious human beings. Satan would deceive and destroy them if given the opportunity, and they will soon have to choose the path they will take.

This mission of introducing one's children to the Christian faith can be likened to a three-man relay race. First, your father runs his lap around the track, carrying the baton, which represents the gospel of Jesus Christ. At the appropriate moment, he hands the baton to you, and you begin your journey around the track. Then finally the time will come when you must get the baton safely into the hands of your child. But as any track coach will testify, relay races are won or lost in the transfer of the baton. There is a critical moment when all can be lost by a fumble or miscalculation. The baton is rarely dropped on the back side of the track when the runner has it firmly in his grasp. If failure is to occur, it will likely happen in the exchange between generations!

According to the Christian values that govern my life, my most important reason for living is to get the baton—the gospel—safely into the hands of my children. Of course, I want to place it in as many other hands as possible, and I'm deeply devoted to the ministry to families that God has given me. Nevertheless, my number-one responsibility is to evangelize my own children. In the words of my dad, everything else appears "pale and washed out" when compared with that fervent desire. There is no higher calling on the face of the earth.

(Taken from *Straight Talk: What Men Need to Know, What Women Should Understand,* by Dr. James C. Dobson [Dallas: Word, 1991], 59–60, 63–66, 68–73, 77–79, 82. Used by permission.)

 **In the Life**

of One Man

As his son began growing up, Mel Franklin wondered, *Will I be a better dad to him than my own father was to me? Or will I end up hurting my son in all the ways my father hurt me? What can I do to break the chain of our bad relationship?*

It's not that his dad was evil; in fact, Mel looked up to his dad. He wanted to grow up to be just like him—brave, strong, never letting his emotions show. But Mel was the antithesis of his father. He had fears—lots of them—and he couldn't keep his emotions in check. He felt weak compared to his father and was sure that his father knew it.

Mel couldn't remember his dad telling him that he loved him, but he could remember him lighting up when quoting Mel's accomplishments. It was great to hear his dad—his hero—brag about him.

So Mel began a pattern of performing for acceptance. He thought, *Maybe if I am "the best" at everything, Dad will play catch with me in the backyard, or show up for my basketball games, or take time off work for a school event.* But his dad never did—not even once.

So Mel tried harder. And it worked, sort of. Hearing his dad's praise wasn't the same as hearing the words, "I love you," but it felt good, and it was better than nothing. Performing also impressed others like coaches, scoutmasters, and teachers. All he had to do, he thought, was continue to perform, and all would be well.

But then he learned about the downside of the performance equation: *failure*. If performance gained acceptance, then failure must mean rejection. Since failure is an unavoidable part of life, he had to find ways to deal with it. Deceit became a major part of Mel's life—maintaining the perfect image at all costs. He also avoided any activity that had a high risk of failure. Consequently, he came to live a very controlled and structured life—at eleven years old!

One day, when he was twelve, Mel's dad came to him and said, "Your mom and I are getting a divorce, and we want to know whom you want to stay with."

This came as a shock! Mel had no idea their marriage was in trouble, but he remembers having absolutely no desire to live with his father. "I'll stay with Mom," he answered. "She'll need a man around the house." Showing no outward emotion and asking no questions, Mel just turned away and went upstairs to bed.

His dad moved out a few days later. The pressure to perform was greater than ever. Despite Mel's attempts to manage everything around him, his life was falling apart. And his entire being yearned for his dad's love and affection.

Then he discovered something to fill the void, something that he believed gave him physical and emotional comfort: pornography. When he was in pain, looking at pornography made him feel good—at least for a few minutes.

At nineteen, Mel left home for college. Although his high-level performance was paying dividends, he soon realized how ill equipped he was for this new stage of life. The risk of academic and social failure was so great that his fear caused him to drop out of school, even though he was on the dean's list!

Guilt and shame drove him into deeper levels of hiding and deceit. He did not have any close friends for fear that they might find out who he really was. He was losing control. He needed to do *something* about the increasing emptiness inside him. So he added drugs to his pornography obsession and rapidly became addicted to both.

But he still knew how to perform. Landing a job in a large aerospace company, he immediately moved into management. On the outside, he appeared to have it all; on the inside, he was dying.

Then he met Maria. She was beautiful, charming, and most importantly, she loved Jesus. And through this relationship, Mel came to know Jesus, too. With his newfound faith, Mel knew he would have to give up his addictions. He kicked the drug habit but could not shake the pornography problem.

Mel and Maria began to date and soon became engaged. Mel thought that once he got married, he wouldn't need the pornography anymore. But it had a death grip on him. He could not understand it, for he loved Maria deeply and for the first time in his life began to feel complete.

Then came the scariest thought of his life: What if Maria found out who he really was? For years, he hid the pornography addiction from her and fought the battle alone. He thought that if he could just do enough for God, He would take this sin away. But performing for God did not work.

At a men's retreat, Mel finally surrendered his own control. He remembers, "God was telling me I had to confess to my wife. It was one of the hardest things I've ever done. Only by the grace of God did our marriage survive."

Throughout months of Christ-centered counseling, he began to see the root causes of his destructive behavior. While taking full responsibility for what he had done, Mel also came to understand the severe impact of not receiving unconditional love from his father and vowed not to make the same mistake with his own children.

Mel has discovered that as he learns to exchange his performance-based mentality for God's unconditional love, he also is beginning to give unconditional love to those around him—especially his family. This love is fleshed out in practical ways. He never misses his son's sports events and even coaches the baseball team. Recently, he took a day off work to go to an event at his daughter's school. He and Maria are communicating on a deeper level than he ever thought possible.

And God had one more wonderful surprise. When diagnosed with cancer, Mel's dad suddenly discovered what was most important in his life: He reconfirmed his commitment to the Lord and began to spend more time with his children. His relationship with Mel blossomed. At the end, as he sat at his dad's bedside, Mel put his arm around his father and told him he loved him. His father turned to him, looked into his eyes and softly said, "I love you, too, son."

The chain was broken.

A MAN AND
HIS CHURCH

A Promise Keeper is committed to
supporting the mission of his
church by honoring and praying for
his pastor, and by actively giving
his time and resources.

Honoring and

Praying for Your Pastor

by Dale Schlafer

I was in Cincinnati for a conference in which I was playing a significant role, and I was afraid. I had been given a large responsibility, and I questioned my ability to handle it. I had told my church these feelings on the Sunday prior to my two-week absence. I had pleaded with them for prayer. Now, nine days later, I returned to my hotel and stopped off at the front desk to see if I had received any mail. I had a telegram, the clerk said; it contained only three words: "We Love You!"

That message was followed by twelve pages of single-spaced, typed names of people from my church. During the announcements at church the day before, the congregation had been reminded that the upcoming Tuesday was my big day. Anyone who wanted to encourage me was invited to stop in the back and sign up for the telegram. As I read those names, all twelve pages, I felt ten feet tall. I knew they were praying and thinking about me. At that moment, I felt I could have done anything because I was so affirmed and supported.

That evening, one of my best friends (also a pastor) and I went to see the Cincinnati Reds play a baseball game. While we were sitting in the stands, I told him about the telegram. Even years later, as I sit writing this, I can still see his face. He looked me straight in the eyes and, with tears running down his cheeks, said, "Once, just once, I wish somebody in my church would tell me they loved me."

What I have discovered since that night, and what surveys of pastors show, is that an overwhelming number of ministers share my friend's sentiment. They feel unloved, unappreciated, and unprayed for.

Promise Keepers is committed to changing this situation by calling men to "honor and pray for their pastors."

HONOR

All Christians are called to practice honor. Romans 12:10 says, "Honor one another above yourselves." God calls us to esteem, respect, and show deference to each other in the body of Christ. When it comes to pastors, however, the Word of God says something unique. We read in 1 Thessalonians 5:12–13, "Now we ask you, brothers, to respect those who work hard among you, who are over you in the Lord and who admonish you. Hold them in the highest regard in love because of their work."

The phrase "Hold them in the highest regard" is unusual in the original Greek of the New Testament in that it takes the adverb and triples its intensity. This verse could read, "Hold them beyond the highest regard in love." Or it might be rendered, "Honor, honor, honor in love those who work hard among you." In today's wording, we might paraphrase it, "Esteem to the max in love those who work hard among you." What we sense here is the apostle Paul's struggle— almost being at a loss for words—to express adequately what the Holy Spirit wants to communicate to the church, just how much the people in a congregation are to hold their pastor in super-highest regard. Pastors are not to be esteemed for their office, degrees, age, or spiritual gifts, but "because of their work."

The biblical pattern, then, is for all Christians to show honor to one another, and triple honor to their pastors.

Now, if that's the case, why are pastors not honored in our day? First, our culture encourages us to not show honor to anyone. We live in a day of egalitarianism that doesn't allow for differences and appears to treat all people the same. Political and sports cartoonists ridicule those in authority. Comedians poke fun at anyone in a place of prominence. And the average Christian carries that same attitude into the church.

I believe the major reason pastors are not honored, however, is that church members don't know it's one of their responsibilities in following Jesus Christ. Some church members simply enjoy tearing down their pastor, but the vast majority fail to honor their pastor just because they are ignorant of God's Word. One pastor, Steve, with whom I spoke in preparation for writing this chapter, brought some men from his church to the Promise Keepers '93 conference. He told me that since then, things had changed dramatically because his men heard Coach McCartney talk about a man's responsibility to his pastor. "The men of my church didn't have bad hearts," Steve said. "They just needed an external source to explain the truth of God's Word to them."

How is it that people in the church don't know this teaching to honor their pastors? The answer is that it hasn't been taught. I searched through the books of sermons in my library, some many years old and others quite contemporary, but I could not find one sermon on this topic. Given our society, it's obvious why this is the case. Can you imagine your pastor standing in the pulpit next Sunday and stating, no matter how smoothly, "You as a church body are to give me triple honor"? As soon as you entered your car, you would be saying, "What an egotist! I can't believe the turkey would say something like that. Wow, is he ever full of pride!" Because that's the way most people would react, pastors shy away from this teaching, and the American church continues in its ignorant disobedience to this clear command of God.

Promise Keepers is committed to seeing that this biblical truth is recaptured in the church. By the grace of God, we are determined to eliminate the neglect and dishonor of our pastors. With fierce determination, Christian men are being called to take the lead in bringing triple honor to our pastors.

What would it look like to honor our pastors? Let's take a closer look at Steve's story.

In his own words, Steve was "at a point of depression." Disheartened with the ministry at his church, he had already written a letter of resignation. In fact, the letter was signed and on his desk when he and some of his men left for the Promise Keepers conference. As the men listened to Coach Mac, they came under strong conviction for their failure to honor their pastor. And during a sharing time in the worship service the next Sunday, a number of them stood and repented of their sin of not honoring and encouraging their pastor. They also acknowledged their sin of expecting him to do all the ministry while they stood on the sidelines and griped.

"Overnight there was a change in my church," Steve said. "The entire dynamic of our church is changing. They have freed me to do what I was called to do. Beyond that, they have started a Monday morning prayer time where a part of the time is devoted to prayer for me." With great delight, Steve ripped up his letter of resignation, and he and his church are now working together as a team. Why? Part of the answer has to be that the men came to see the biblical necessity of honoring their pastor. As a result of their obedience, God is now free to pour out His blessing.

Perhaps you're thinking at this point, *Could this honoring thing go too far? Could this feed an ego problem? Might this cause jealousy?* Undoubtedly, those concerns are possibilities. If I were writing to pastors, I would digress at this point to deal with the sins of pride and arrogance with which pastors might be tempted. But right now, at this point in the history of the American church, those sins are not the problem. The hurt, the neglect, the dishonoring have gone on for so long and with such intensity that large numbers of pastors are turning in their resignations because they feel so alone and unsupported. One recent poll revealed that 80 percent of the pastors responding had thought about quitting in the last three months. Yes, in some immature men, triple honoring might cause a problem. But for the vast majority of godly pastors, honoring and lifting them up will cause them to be more motivated and even harder workers. They will be encouraged, and their churches will be blessed.

As a pastor, I, too, stood on the floor of the football stadium at Promise Keepers '93. I reveled in the prolonged standing ovation the more than fifty thousand gathered men gave to all the pastors who were there. In the providence of God, I stood next to a pastor I didn't know. He said, "This will be enough for me to be able to put up with all the abuse I'll take at my church for the next six months!" Honoring him in this manner had put a new resolve and a new desire in his heart to go back and pastor his church in what was obviously a tough situation. Now, if the men of that church honored and encouraged him regularly, what effect would it have?

What would happen if you regularly honored and encouraged your pastor? I believe your church would begin to receive blessing as never before. Why? Because the blessing of God comes when we obey His Word.

PRAYER

Promise Keepers are also committed to praying for their pastors. The concept of praying for all Christians is clearly spelled out in the Bible: "And pray in the Spirit on all occasions with all kinds of prayers and requests. With this in mind, be alert and always keep on praying for all the saints" (Eph. 6:18).

When it comes to praying for our pastors, we have a special responsibility. Paul, an apostle and pastor, said, "I urge you, brothers, by our Lord Jesus Christ and by the love of the Spirit, to join me in my struggle by praying to God for me" (Rom. 15:30). In another place, he reminded his readers that they could help him and his ministry team "by your prayers" (2 Cor. 1:11). In other words, pastors especially are in need of prayer.

Why is that the case? Satan's desire is to destroy the work of Christ in the world. One of his most effective ways of doing that is to destroy pastors. If Satan can bring them down, causing disgrace and ridicule to taint the work of Christ, the nonbelieving world will not be attracted to Jesus. We have all seen the carnage left around us as pastors have failed morally or have simply left the ministry because of disillusionment.

Several years ago, a pastor in Denver told his congregation the following true story. A lady from his church was flying back to Denver, and, as the meal was served, she noticed the woman sitting next to her did not take a meal. To make conversation, the Christian woman asked, "Are you on a diet?"

"No," came the reply, "I am a member of the church of Satan, and we are fasting for the destruction of the families of pastors and Christian leaders."

Pastors are at risk because they are the church's leaders. If Satan can get them, the church of Jesus Christ will be crippled.

In no way am I trying to excuse the pastors who have fallen or bailed out of the ministry in recent years, but I do have a question. How many of those pastors had men in their churches who daily brought them before the Lord in prayer? I wonder how many men's groups gathered to pray for them? I am not surprised by the number of pastors who have fallen. To be truthful, I'm surprised the number is not larger. The job of being a pastor is enormously difficult and is made even more so because the men of the church are not praying.

Pastors need prayer, especially for their preaching and teaching of the Word. Again I ask, why are pastors not preaching what they really believe is the Word of God to their congregations? The answer is, I believe, that they are afraid—afraid the people of their churches will not accept the kind of preaching that clearly and powerfully confronts sin and sinners. Afraid they will be fired and lose their financial security. As a result, in many cases, God's purposes are thwarted and our churches remain weak and sick.

The apostle Paul regularly asked for prayer so that "boldness might be given." Pastors need to know their men are with them and are praying for them so they can be emboldened to share the whole council of God and not cower in the face of opposition within or without the church.

E. M. Bounds said it this way:

> The men in the pew given to praying for the pastor are like poles which hold up the wires along which the electric current runs. They are not the power, neither are they the specific agents in making the Word of the Lord effective. But they hold up the wires upon which the divine power runs to the hearts of men. . . . They make conditions favorable for the preaching of the Gospel.[1]

I don't understand it all; I just know that when the men of the church start praying for the pastor, something happens.

Dr. Wilbur Chapman often told of going to Philadelphia to become the pastor of the Wanamaker Church. After his first sermon, an older gentleman met him in front of the pulpit and said, "You are pretty young to be the pastor of this great church. We have always had older pastors. I am afraid you won't succeed. But you preach the gospel, and I am going to help you all I can."

"I looked at him," said Dr. Chapman, "and said to myself: 'Here's a crank.' But the old gentleman continued: 'I am going to pray for you that you may have the Holy Spirit's power upon you, and two others have covenanted to join me.'" Then Dr. Chapman related the outcome:

> I did not feel so bad when I learned he was going to pray for me. The three became ten, the ten became twenty, the twenty became fifty, the fifty became two hundred who met before the service to pray that the Holy Spirit might come upon me. In another room, eighteen elders knelt so close around me to pray for me that I could put out my hands and touch them on all sides. I always went into the pulpit feeling that I would have the anointing in answer to the prayers of two hundred and nineteen men. It was easy to preach, a very joy. Anybody could preach with such conditions. And what was the result? We received eleven hundred into our church by conversion in three years, six hundred of which were men. I do not see how the average preacher under average conditions preaches at all. Church members have much more to do than go to church as curious, idle spectators, to be amused and entertained. It is their business to pray mightily that the Holy Ghost will clothe the preacher and make his words like dynamite.[2]

Imagine what would happen if you and the other men from your church determined to pray for your pastor. The whole dynamic and atmosphere of your church would be different.

What would it look like to start such a prayer ministry? In the church I serve, men are asked once a year to sign up to be prayer partners with me. At least one man is assigned to pray for me each day of the month. When that list is drawn up, I pray for the man who is praying for me on that day as well. To further assist my prayer partners, I regularly send them a letter to keep them current on answers to their prayers and new things for which they can be praying.

The entire group that signed up is also divided into four teams. Each team is assigned one Sunday a month to come to the church to pray for me. (Fifth Sundays are left unassigned, and any team member can come. Usually, the meetings are packed!) The men arrive at 8:15 A.M., as our first service is at 9:00. They disperse throughout the entire church facility. Some stay in the worship center, praying for the worship team and others participating in the service as well as for those who will attend the services. Others move through the classrooms, praying for teachers by name. Still others walk in the parking lot, asking God to keep things organized and friendly and that the sweet Spirit of Jesus will be sensed by folks as they pull into the lot. At 8:30, we all gather in my office, and they pray for me. I tell them what I think God wants me to do that day, plus how I am feeling both physically and spiritually. Then I kneel and the men gather around, lay hands on me, and begin to pray.

The results have been dramatic. I have sensed a new power and authority in my preaching. The men who pray have a sense of personal ownership of Sunday mornings. They know their prayers are essential if anything of eternal significance is to take place. Further, the Lord has built a wonderful sense of teamwork through this prayer partnership. Sometimes as I'm preaching, I catch the eye of one of them, and he'll wink or give me the thumbs-up sign. When that occurs, I know they are praying and are *for* me, and then I really "go to preachin'!"

Let me suggest that you go to your pastor and tell him you want to organize a team of men who will pray for him every day. Tell him you and this group of men wish to meet with him on Sundays before services to pray for the anointing of the Holy Spirit to come upon him. If you do this, it will be one of the greatest joys your pastor has ever had in his ministry.

Why do I know that's true? Because the overwhelming majority of pastors feel unprayed for and isolated in their ministries. One pastor said to me not long ago, "Nobody in my church cares about me or the ministry of this church." Suppose the men of his church came around him and asked to pray for him. What do you think would happen? That church would never be the same again.

CONCLUSION

Promise Keepers is seeking nothing less than a paradigm shift in the life of America's churches. Until now, in the vast majority of situations, pastors have not been honored, loved, esteemed, or prayed for. By God's grace, however, that is going to change as Promise Keepers in every church see it as their personal responsibility to support the pastor. That's why I say we want a paradigm shift. A paradigm is a model or pattern for understanding and interpreting reality.

When there's a paradigm shift, everything gets changed. As Promise Keepers begin to honor and pray for their pastors, a new life and vitality will start to grow in congregations. A new teamwork will blossom between pastor and people. A new sense of call will dominate the pastors of this land. A new holiness will spring forth because of changed preaching. And we will find ourselves in the middle of revival.

At Promise Keepers '93, Coach McCartney said the following:

I see us going home to our churches and asking our pastors for permission, praying fervently for the favor of God, to stand before the congregation and say: "Things are going to change around here. We're going to start to lift up our pastor. We are going to start to stand in the gap for our preacher. We're going to pray around the clock! We're going to build this man up. We're going to take him where he has never been before." I see us exploding in our churches.

Indeed! That is our goal—to see revival spread across our country. How will that occur? Revival will come as churches are revived. The churches will be revived as the pastors are revived. And part of what God will use to revive them will be Promise Keepers, men who keep their word to honor and pray for their pastors.

"Church"
Means "People"

by Jesse Miranda

I learned early in life that the church is supposed to be much more than a handsome building or a pastor preaching in the pulpit. Where I grew up, the churches were the most beautiful buildings in the community, but that was about it. In spite of their beauty, they never seemed able or willing to meet anyone's practical, day-to-day needs. My father attended his church once or twice a year, and my mother took us on special holidays. As a result, I was never connected spiritually or physically to those church buildings. But I was connected from an early age to the people of God.

This began in a special way with an incident that occurred when I was three years old. A Christian couple came knocking on our door, asking to talk to my parents. My father was at work, and my mother was sick in bed. In fact, Mother was so sick that my sister, who was then five, and I had been caring for her for five days. The couple were warm and caring. There was something different about them that, even as a toddler, I could detect. They offered to pray for my mother, explaining that Jesus Christ was Lord, that He cared for us, and that He could even heal us. They prayed, and my mother was healed. Our family had never heard or seen anything like that before. This was my introduction to the good news of Jesus Christ. It was to become my lifelong impression of the incredible blessing of God's people.

That episode taught me a valuable lesson. The ministry of God is done by the people of God, not just by ordained pastors. That means you and me—children, adults, new believers, laymen, and clergy alike. Scripture makes it clear that God intends for all those who call on the name of the Lord to be involved in His ministry. God easily could have called on His angels to fulfill His will on earth, but He chose you and me, as members of His church, to carry out His work. He designed it to be a highly personal calling according to the gifts He gave each one of us (see 1 Cor. 12:8–10). And the vehicle He provided for us to pour our gifts into is His church.

SPECTATOR CHRISTIANS TAKING A TOLL ON THE CHURCH

As the twentieth century draws to a close, however, we're seeing a disturbing trend among God's people. Too many are relinquishing their awesome responsibility for sharing in God's ministry. They've elected to stand on the sidelines while the pastor runs the whole show. In a sense, by abdicating this priceless birthright, they have accepted something far less for their lives than God intended. Rather than exercising their God-given gifts, creativity, and labor to build up the church, they've become passive "pew-sitters." These marginal Christians are functionally distanced from the daily activity of the church and emotionally detached from the needs, pain, and often hopelessness their chronic indifference has bred among God's shepherds.

Sadly, we live in a spectator society, where Christians and unbelievers alike grow up watching idly from the periphery, conditioned to hire something done rather than doing it themselves. Spectating, however, is not a luxury most pastors can afford. Without the daily support of dedicated servants, pastors today are running on empty. They're burning out at an unprecedented rate. God's chosen leaders are overworked, beaten up, stressed out, and ready, in many cases, simply to walk away from their life's calling.

To illustrate the point, I refer to a survey of pastors conducted by the Fuller Institute of Church Growth and reported by Dr. Arch Hart of Fuller Seminary in November 1991. It speaks to the loneliness, inadequacy, and stress many of our pastors privately experience every day.

90 percent work more than forty-six hours per week and often more than sixty.

80 percent believe pastoral ministry is affecting their families negatively.

33 percent say, "Being in ministry is clearly a hazard to my family."

75 percent have reported a significant crisis due to stress at least once every five years in their ministry.

50 percent feel unable to meet the needs of the job.

90 percent feel they were not adequately trained to cope with the ministry demands placed on them.

40 percent report having a serious conflict with a parishioner at least once a month.

70 percent do not have someone they would consider a close friend.

37 percent have been involved in inappropriate sexual behavior with someone in the church.

70 percent have a lower self-image after they've pastored than when they started.[1]

Can these possibly be the capable, courageous leaders we depend on to shepherd the church? Are these the people who committed their lives to serve God, minister in His Word, and pour themselves out as a drink offering to the glory of Jesus Christ? If so, what happened? And is it any wonder that God's purposes seem continually to be thwarted and many of our churches remain weak and sick?

Some might say, "Well, life's tough. We all have to work hard to survive, so quit complaining." But consider the pressures a typical pastor faces that are unique to the ministry. If the workloads of other professionals become heavy or unmanageable, they can simply refuse clients or refer them to another qualified expert. But most pastors don't feel the freedom to turn anyone away, regardless of how severely overworked they may be. Businessmen can postpone an appointment until they have a free slot in their schedules, but pastors (especially those without large staff) are often on call twenty-four hours a day, every day.

DEEDS SPEAK LOUDER THAN WORDS

I will say it again and again: The ministry of the church is our ministry—yours and mine—not solely the pastor's. The spiritual battles our clergy face every day are incredible. The battles are intensified by well-meaning congregations that give and praise with their lips, yet by their actions they make it clear they've lost respect for the pastoral position.

Our pastors need our loving support not just in word, but also in deed, or their chances of burning out—even failing—are enormous. Scripture urges us to honor and care for our pastors: "And now, friends, we ask you to honor those leaders who work so hard for you, who have been given the responsibility of urging and guiding you along in your obedience. Overwhelm them with appreciation and love!" (1 Thess. 5:12–13, THE MESSAGE). True honor requires us to pour our hearts, energies, and resources into the lives and families of these dedicated servants. Are we each doing our part?

"CHURCH" MEANS "PEOPLE," NOT BUILDINGS

As I've already mentioned, my earliest memories of church aren't of fine sanctuaries or cushioned pews. Once my mother got serious about church, "going to church" simply meant people meeting in one another's homes. It resembled Acts 2:46–47: "They broke bread in their homes and ate together with glad and sincere hearts, praising God and enjoying the favor of all the people." It was in this house church atmosphere that our family gathered with others to worship God and enjoy fellowship with our brothers and sisters in Jesus. I can remember hardly being able to wait to "have church."

Our family's house church eventually grew into a congregation that had its own building. It became organized and began to offer a variety of ministries. Our church was small, so everyone had to do his or her part.

In this supportive, nurturing atmosphere, I learned my earliest lessons in Christian servanthood. I learned, primarily, how important it is to honor and help one's pastor. My mother was my model in this. She was a housemaid and a cook, but she was also a faithful servant to the church. She served as the leader of the women's group and later became a "deaconess," one who would pray for and visit the sick. I also remember well how on Sunday mornings I would wake to the smell of delicious food. Mother was preparing our breakfast, but she was also cooking a large Sunday dinner. She would smile at me and say, "Today I'm inviting the pastor and his family over to eat."

As my family matured in the Lord, we learned to regard our pastors with the highest respect. We had several pastors serve in the church in which I grew up. They were all different and possessed a diversity of gifts and qualifications, but they were all loved. They were looked upon as special men of God. They were our father figures, our counselors, our teachers, and friends of the family.

They mentored me by showing an interest in me, and they kept me busy with church-related work. I was allowed to gain experience ministering in many ways. By the time I was fifteen, I was serving as Sunday school secretary. I also served in the youth department. At seventeen, I was assigned to a "preaching point," which today is known as church planting. While I was still a young man, I became a deacon of the church.

I came to hold the ministry in such high regard that I eventually spent fifteen years teaching in a Bible school developing future pastors. Then I became a pastor's pastor, that is, a district superintendent. I continue to serve the leadership of the church as the associate dean at the School of Theology of Azusa Pacific University and as a professor in the department of ministry, urging men and women to take up the mantle of leadership.

Because I learned to support and honor my pastor at an early age, I grew up loving the church. Because my childhood pastors taught me the importance of being actively involved in the life of the church, I have served it most of my life. This is the way God intended it. We worked alongside our pastors in the ministry, and they never felt isolated or inadequate. They knew we loved them by our actions.

HELPING OUR PASTORS FIND THEIR WAY

In one of the "Peanuts" cartoons, poor Linus is standing in the middle of a weedy, unkempt baseball field. He's talking to himself, saying, "I don't mind playing right field. I don't mind standing out here in weeds over my head if this is where I can do the team the most good. The only thing that bothers me," he concludes pitifully, "is that I don't know if I'm facing the right way."

That depicts the situation many pastors find themselves in today. Overworked, sometimes underpaid, under constant spiritual attack, many feel they're in over their heads. They're unable to discern if they're even facing the right way, much less ministering to the lost and hurting with power and authority. The challenges they face today are unlike any in history. Aside from the obvious pressures of trying to train and equip disciples in an age and culture in which "church" is largely regarded as irrelevant, legalistic, and often hypocritical, there are many unseen stress-inducers that conspire to disarm and demoralize our pastors.

Consider that pastors, more than any other profession, are expected to be all things to all people. They're often exposed to unfair comparisons with other, higher-profile clergymen. They're expected to be models of righteousness and holiness. Their families must be perfect. They're expected to meet the needs of everyone and have all the answers. They aren't allowed to have personal problems or marital conflicts. They can't get depressed. And they usually aren't given the leeway to simply be spiritually dry. Pastors are expected to be expert counselors, deft mediators, gifted financiers, and noble visionaries.

In the face of all these expectations, many have yet to find their vision for their ministry. I've spoken with many pastors who are frustrated because they don't feel their everyday work touches the actual structures of life; they wonder if the church has moved to the periphery of people's lives. Their best efforts—their prayers, their studied sermons, their devotion, and all their hard work—seem at best to address the symptom rather than the root of people's problems.

This state of affairs we're discussing isn't restricted to the United States, either. Pastors all over the world face similar stresses, challenges, and outright attacks. They are hurting and in need of genuine friendship, prayer support, and affirmation for what they do. As men of God, we must step off the sidelines and get in the game, involving ourselves in the life of our churches. We do this most effectively by coming alongside our pastors with our service and daily prayers for their families, their marriages, and most importantly, their continued growth in their relationship with Jesus.

FIVE WAYS TO HONOR YOUR PASTOR

Our family was poor, but we always gave honor and respect and the gifts we could afford to our pastors. Again, my mother set the example. I remember several times coming home from school and noticing that a rug was missing, some chairs were not in their usual place, or some other small items were gone. Instantly, I knew that the church had a new pastor who had moved into the parsonage. Mother had done some creative "housecleaning" on his behalf.

As a teenager, I came home from work one day to find that the first car I ever owned was gone. I asked Mother about my car, and she answered, "I noticed you've bought another car, so I gave your old one to the pastor. You're a single man and have two cars. The pastor has a wife and five children and only one car."

"But it was a good car," I argued.

"Yes," she responded, "I know. You should never give junk to the Lord."

Somewhat perplexed, I asked, "Why do you do so much for the pastors?"

"Son," she said, "I do for my pastors what I wish people will do for you someday, should the Lord call you into ministry."

That was a prophetic statement. I accepted a lifelong call to the ministry soon after. I also married into a pastor's family, the daughter of one of the pastors my mother blessed with her generous spirit. In turn, I reaped much of that same generosity. What my mother began turned into a wonderful legacy of blessing for God's appointed leaders.

Men, it's time for us—not just our wives or our mothers—to show the way in blessing and honoring our pastors. We're the men of the church, and God has given us the mantle of leadership. He has also given us the high calling of serving His shepherds.

In my travels and mission trips, I've asked dozens of pastors in churches large and small, denominational and independent, "What have the men in your church done to honor you?" Many scratch their heads at such a question. But they're full of stories that reveal subtle ways they've been ignored or dishonored. We must begin to honor these men as the Bible instructs. Below are five ways you can support your own pastor.

1. Initiate a relationship without an agenda.

One pastor recounted an experience that left him feeling used and confused. When he arrived at his first church, he was blessed by the invitations that poured in to treat him and his wife to dinner. He soon learned, however, that these gifts had strings attached. Person after person who called quickly betrayed that he wasn't interested in getting to know the pastor and his wife as friends but was pushing an agenda or making sure the new pastor heard his view on a personal or theological issue before someone else got to him.

If you're serious about honoring your pastor, spend time with him to build a relationship without an agenda. Make an appointment to see him and say, "I just wanted to come in and find out what I could pray for you about and to see if there's anything I could do to encourage you." Support the pastor and his wife as people, not some authority to lobby for your own ends.

2. Provide opportunities for your pastor to bless his family.

Another pastor I met was worried because he felt he was neglecting his family, especially his son. He arranged his schedule to spend all day with his boy one Saturday—and then the call came. A board member said he had tickets to a football game that same Saturday.

"Thank you," the pastor said, "I'd love to go, but I can't. I promised my son we'd spend the day together, and I need to keep my promise."

"You don't understand," the board member replied. "I'm not inviting you to go to the game with me. I've got two tickets so you and your son can go."

The board member had overheard the pastor expressing his need to spend time with his son, and he arranged for the tickets as well as a team ball cap and shirt for the father and son.

Helping your pastor bless his family is a tangible way of honoring him. For instance, I know a pastor who has two daughters. Each Christmas, a man in his church does something special. A few weeks before Christmas, he gives the pastor two crisp, new twenty-dollar bills—one for each daughter. But there's a stipulation: The girls must spend the money on a present for their mother. It has become a high point of the Christmas season, and all because someone takes the time and effort to help his pastor bless his family.

3. Be specific in praising his ministry in your life.
A common complaint from pastors is how often a well-meaning parishioner will say, "That was a wonderful sermon, Pastor." But if asked, "What was it that specifically touched you?" the person gives blank stares and finally the empty response, "I guess I liked everything about it!" That response doesn't carry much weight.

Your pastor spends a lot of time in prayer and study for his messages. Being specific in your praise is a way of letting him know you were actively listening.

4. Be a churchman, not a spectator.
Many people go to church today much as they go to the mall. They window-shop and browse, and their commitment to one "store" lasts only as long as they like what's being offered. If you want to honor your pastor, be a churchman, not a spectator. A churchman pitches in and helps in some capacity, attends services regularly, and supports the church financially.

5. Make your pastor and his family a key part of your prayer list.
Have you ever told your pastor, "I'll pray for you this week," and then forgotten your promise until you saw him again the next Sunday? I know one man who remembers to pray for his pastor by setting the alarm on his watch for 4:00 P.M. each day. When the alarm sounds, wherever he is, he lifts his pastor in prayer. That gentle reminder puts teeth in his commitment.

Like a family member, your pastor needs and deserves your best in prayer. Your prayers not only support and protect him, but they also empower him to live out his challenging, high calling.

It's Time for Men to Set the Godly Example
Obviously, there are many other ways to bless your pastor and his family. My hope is that this chapter serves as a wake-up call to the men of the church. I pray it convicts us of our responsibility to our

clergy and spurs our imaginations to new ways of expressing our appreciation. You and I have been placed in this world and given the gift of salvation to do ministry with our leaders.

We're not to bleed our pastors dry while we sit on the sidelines and cheer—or complain. We're not to engage them in relationships for our own benefit. Men of God must show the way; the time has come for us to set a godly example. If we acknowledge that the church is truly a body, it's clear that the pastor is but one appendage. Those of us who are the hands, feet, or legs can't forget to love, honor, and nourish those appointed as the head of the local church. We must each take personal responsibility for our commitment to our churches and pastors.

The church needs you. Your pastor needs you. And God calls you to meet those needs.

 # In the Life

# of One Man

"You may have lymphoma, Bud," the grim-faced doctor said. "I'd like to refer you to a cancer specialist at Cedars-Sinai Medical Center in Los Angeles."

Bud Schaedel was one of those people who had been blessed with lifelong good health. On rare occasions he caught a bug, but he never let it slow him down or even force him to miss a day of work.

Right after Christmas 1989, however, Bud came down with the flu, and a week or so later he noticed swelling in the glands along his neck. Then came the terrible diagnosis.

Bud had gone through a long period of spiritual drifting. But now, suddenly faced with cancer's undeniable reminder of his mortality, Bud evidenced a growing spiritual hunger.

Two years later, the lymphoma flared up and the doctors began the first round of chemotherapy. That was also when Bud and his wife, Connie, found a great church to attend. The more spiritual food he devoured, the hungrier Bud seemed. He even began listening to a Christian radio station as he drove to and from work. It was there, in the spring of 1993, that Bud first heard about something called a Promise Keepers conference.

Bud casually asked a member of the church staff what he knew about Promise Keepers and its upcoming conference. The man's face lit up, his eyes zeroed in on Bud's, and he said, "I've been looking for someone interested enough to attend the conference and then take the lead in finding ways to get the men of our church involved in Promise Keepers."

Bud literally backed away, held up a hand, and said, "Hey, I was just asking! I'm really too busy to consider going."

But eventually Bud did agree to attend the conference with his brother-in-law, Larry. He and Larry joined fifty thousand other men at the University of Colorado Folsom Stadium, under a blistering sun and scorching 104-degree heat, for the two-day conference.

Larry was concerned about how the brutal heat might affect Bud. But throughout the conference, Bud seemed oblivious to any physical discomfort. From the opening words of the conference, Bud was totally absorbed. On Friday night, when speaker Greg Laurie challenged the men to be sure they were trusting in Jesus as their Savior, Bud realized, *I've never done that. In all these years of going to church, reading the Bible, and everything else, I've never really given my life to Christ. I need to do that, and tonight's the night! Thank You, Lord!*

A few minutes later, when Laurie asked the men who wanted to commit their lives to Christ to come down in front of the stage, Bud turned to Larry and said with conviction, "I need to go down there!"

Laurie asked the throng of men to kneel as he led them in a prayer of confession, repentance, and commitment. Bud knelt with the others, quietly repeating Laurie's prayer even as he thought, *This is the best thing I've ever done. I've never been so sure of what I needed to do.*

That was only the beginning of Bud's transformation that weekend. He caught the first glimpse of what God just might be able to do through him.

More men from our church have got to come here next year, Bud thought. *If I tell them what God has done for me this weekend, they'll want to come, and He'll get ahold of them the way He's doing for me.* Bud's goal became recruiting as many men as possible to attend a Promise Keepers conference already scheduled for Anaheim the next spring.

Bud also immediately set about living up to the commitments he'd made to God and to himself in Boulder. He clearly intended to be a true man of God, and nothing was going to stop him.

At every possible opportunity in church, Bud wanted to talk about Promise Keepers and the upcoming conference. In one men's meeting, someone said, "Wouldn't it be great if we could get fifty men to go?"

Bud's response was, "Surely we can do better than that!"

"What about a hundred men?" another proposed.

"No, higher!" Bud urged.

The agreed-upon target eventually was one hundred fifty men. But everyone got the idea that Bud wouldn't be satisfied until every man in church had signed up. Sometimes it seemed he was out to recruit the entire world.

Then, during the fall of 1993, Bud's lymphoma worsened. This was much sooner than his doctors had expected. They proceeded with another round of chemotherapy in January.

Through the entire ordeal, Bud continued to recruit more people for the upcoming Promise Keepers conference in May. To enable some men to go who couldn't afford the registration fee, the Schaedels set up a scholarship fund.

As Bud intensified his efforts to sign up more men for the conference, the chemotherapy began to take its toll on his body, and he took a rapid turn for the worse. Bud was admitted to the hospital, and the seriousness of his condition was clear to anyone who walked into his room. Visitors who had last seen him at church or at work just the week before were shocked by his rapid deterioration. Yet his spirits remained high. When someone commented about how hard life can be, Bud responded, "Life isn't so hard. It's just a boot camp for heaven." And he continued to talk to visitors about Promise Keepers.

Bud's breathing became so labored that he was moved to intensive care and placed on a respirator. Once the tube was inserted down his throat, Bud could no longer talk. He had to resort to communicating by touch. But when the president of the church's men's group arrived that night, Bud excitedly held up ten fingers. Connie had to interpret: "Bud wants to tell you that he and I have decided to fund ten scholarships to the Promise Keepers conference. So on Sunday he wants you to announce that there's no reason for anyone to decide he can't afford to go."

That was Bud's last message to the world outside his family. He had done all he could to give as many men as possible the opportunity to experience Promise Keepers. By Friday morning, he was no longer conscious. And in the early hours of Saturday morning, Bud Schaedel died.

Just two weeks later, in the closing session of the conference in Anaheim Stadium, Bud's pastor, Lee Eliason, was called to the platform. He told the men filling the "Big A" about coming to know Bud Schaedel, a man whose life had been changed at the Boulder conference less than a year before. He spoke movingly about the impact Bud's love and support had had on him and his ministry.

Then Lee directed everyone's attention to a specific spot in the upper deck and asked the *two hundred fifty* men from Bud's church to stand in honor of the man who had worked so hard for them to attend.

One ordinary man, devoted to Jesus, simply served his church with all his heart and reaped an extraordinary harvest for the kingdom of God.

PROMISE

A MAN AND
HIS BROTHERS

A Promise Keeper is committed to
reaching beyond any racial and
denominational barriers to demonstrate
the power of biblical unity.

A Call to Unity

by Bill McCartney

It happened in the mid 1980s. I had been the football coach at Colorado University for a few years when a black Denver attorney by the name of Teddy Woods died at the age of 40. In his college days, Teddy had excelled as a student-athlete at C.U. Although he didn't play for me, I had met him and knew of his prowess and influence in the Denver area.

I arrived early for the funeral and found a seat in the front of the church. By the time the service began, the auditorium was full. Now, bear in mind that I didn't know the other people and had only met Teddy in passing. I was there to pay my respects because he had played football for C.U. and I was the current coach.

What happened to me that day changed my life. It may be hard for you to understand, but when I sat down and started listening to the music, I was deeply affected. The mournful singing of the mostly black congregation expressed a level of pain I hadn't seen or felt before. As I looked from side to side across the crowd, I realized that their grief over the loss of Teddy Woods was bringing to the surface an even deeper hurt. This wasn't just a funeral; it was also a gathering of wounded, long-suffering believers.

In response, I began to weep uncontrollably. I tried to cover my tears, fearing someone would see me and recognize that I barely knew Teddy Woods. I thought they might accuse me of grandstanding to gain acceptance and approval in the inner city—a recruiting ploy. Yet I couldn't hold the tears back. The grieving and groaning exceeded anything I had ever experienced. I have never been the same since then.

I had come in touch, for the first time, with the pain, struggle, despair, and anguish of the black people. Stunned by that experience, I felt a great desire to understand what I had observed. I also wanted to pursue what I had felt in my spirit. Although Boulder, the city where I live, is 98 percent white, I worked with black athletes and fellow coaches every day. I visited the homes of many black families during recruiting season every year. And I had a sense that God was calling me to a deeper understanding of their lives that would greatly influence me both personally and in my role as a leader of Promise Keepers.

So I began to question black people I had known for years. It amazed me that despite wide differences in their ages and the places where they had grown up, they all identified directly with the pain I had felt in the church that day. They told stories about dramatic experiences and everyday examples of the injustices they face as black Americans.

One black clergyman, for instance, told of a gang shooting in which an innocent 12-year-old boy had been killed. The boy and his family were active participants in his church. When the news of the boy's death got out, the pastor almost doubled over in pain, so great was his grief. Many black leaders called or wrote to offer prayers and condolences, some from great distances. But nearby white leaders made no effort at all to express concern. The pastor was left with the clear impression that they simply didn't care.

A good friend who is not a Christian told me plainly why he doesn't believe in the "white man's God." As a child in the South, he knew he was not welcome in the all-white church on the corner. He would stand outside, near a window, during services and listen to the preacher speak about love, all the time knowing there was no love in that church for him.

At one point, this same friend witnessed a Ku Klux Klan rally in which the speaker held up a monkey's skull and claimed it was an exact replica of a black man's head. Can you imagine the rage mixed with fear that my friend felt that night? Can you understand why that night remains vivid and powerful in his memory?

The night before C.U.'s second game of the 1993 football season, we were in Texas preparing to play Baylor the next afternoon. To help the guys relax, I had arranged for our traveling squad to watch the Whitaker-Chavez championship prizefight that evening. Chavez's record was 88-0. Whitaker, a black man, had fought half as many matches with only one loss.

Seventy of us gathered in a small room to watch the bout. Approximately half were black. I sat back and observed my players closely. Virtually all the black kids were pulling for Whitaker; the white kids seemed evenly divided between Whitaker and Chavez. The black players were clearly more animated, often cheering and jumping to their feet, while the white players were generally more subdued. I was intrigued by the difference in culture.

Whitaker appeared to be in control throughout the fight, and the TV announcers spoke of his big edge over and over. Even though both boxers were still standing when the bout ended after 12 rounds, the winner seemed clear. We were all sure Whitaker had given Chavez his first defeat.

There was a delay, however, in totaling the judges' scorecards. The TV commentators said, "Could they possibly award this fight to Chavez? Surely not."

A hush came over our room. You could sense that the black players began to fear the worst. And when the ring announcer said that the fight was a draw—no winner—there was no protest in our ranks. Everyone filed out of the room quietly. The feeling was clear in the eyes and body language of our black young men: Injustice again. The black fighter has to knock out his opponent to win—he will never get the benefit of a decision.

THE CALL TO UNITY

Why do I tell these stories, hoping you'll feel at least a little of what I feel? Why are the issues of racial and denominational reconciliation so important to Promise Keepers that we're asking you to make a commitment to them? Let me explain in two ways.

First, the issue is vital because the Bible reveals clearly that it's the will of Almighty God for His people to be united. Jesus said to the Father, "I pray also for those who will believe in me through their message, that all of them may be one, Father, just as you are in me and I am in you. . . . May they be brought to complete unity to let the world know that you sent me and have loved them even as you have loved me" (John 17:20-23).

The apostle Paul wrote, "For we were all baptized by one Spirit into one body" (1 Cor. 12:13).

When the New Testament church struggled with the threat of division between believing Jews and Gentiles—two racial groups that generally despised each other in that time and place—Paul wrote the following corrective in Ephesians 2:13–16:

> In Christ Jesus you who were once far away have been brought near through the blood of Christ. For he himself is our peace, who has made the two one and has destroyed the barrier, the dividing wall of hostility, by abolishing in his flesh the law with its commandments and regulations. His purpose was to create in himself one new man out of the two, thus making peace, and in this one body to reconcile both of them to God through the cross, by which he put to death their hostility.

If I understand those passages and others like them correctly, divisions should not exist among Christians. But we know that's not the case. We are divided along racial and denominational lines.

The second reason reconciliation is so important to Promise Keepers grows out of an incident that occurred at one of our first conferences, in 1991. "Only" about 4,000 of us were gathered that year, but we already had dreams of filling Folsom Field with 50,000 men in the near future. As I got up to address the men at the end of that conference, I looked out over the crowd, and I noticed that it was overwhelmingly white. The absence of men of color somehow hit me between the eyes, and in that moment, the Spirit of God clearly said to my spirit, "You can fill that stadium, but if men of other races aren't there, I won't be there, either."

That message, which has since been confirmed in various ways to all the leaders of Promise Keepers, was the beginning of our understanding that the building of bridges across the divisions that currently separate believers is an important part of why God called us into being as an organization. It may be our most difficult mission, but I'm convinced that it's essential.

What will happen if Promise Keepers begin to reach out across racial and denominational lines? One strong possibility is the outbreak of revival in America. You see, I believe racism and denominational divisions have done more than just about anything to hamper the church's witness to the world. So many people of color, like the friend I mentioned earlier, have been totally turned off to the God we proclaim by our obvious lack of love. Even nonbelieving white people know that Christians are supposed to love and that far too often we fail to do so. This is why I'm certain that revival can't take place until the church grows far more united in obedience to God's command.

On the other hand, I'm equally convinced that if we take this promise seriously and begin the process of reconciliation, incredible things are possible for the kingdom of God. Think back to the story of the early days of the church in Acts 2. The church was born on the Day of Pentecost, when people from many countries, cultures, and (no doubt) races heard the gospel in their own languages and believed in the Lord Jesus. Then, we read beginning in verse 42, those new Christians met regularly to eat together, to fellowship, to pray, and to worship God. Those who had possessions gave joyfully and sacrificially to meet the needs of those who lacked. And what was the result of this display of loving unity? The church "enjoy[ed] the favor of all the people. And the Lord added to their number daily those who were being saved" (v. 47).

Imagine how the world would respond to a church that was truly one in spirit. To be sure, we would face some opposition. Racism and sectarianism are Satan's strongholds, after all, some of his best tools for breeding hatred and undermining the work of the church, and he won't give up easily. But many thousands—if not millions—would be drawn to such a fellowship, such a demonstration of the power of God's love, just as they were 2,000 years ago.

Imagine what a united church could do with the gang problem in our country; with the need for young people in single-parent homes to have positive role models, heroes, and hopes for a better tomorrow; with the lack of educational and employment opportunities for certain segments of our society. I believe the kind of unity in the Body of Christ that we're talking about could unleash the fantastic potential God has given us to make a positive difference that no one else can possibly make. The unifying of godly people would be an undeniable witness of His grace.

Now, I don't mean to suggest that all cultural differences and denominational distinctives should disappear. But what I know is that Almighty God wants to bring Christian men together regardless of their ethnic origin, denominational background, or style of worship. There's only one criterion for this kind of unity: to love Jesus and be born of the Spirit of God. Can we look one another in the eye—black, white, red, brown, yellow, Baptist, Presbyterian, Assemblies of God, Catholic, and so on—and get together on this common ground: "We believe in salvation through Christ alone, and we have made Him the Lord of our lives"? Is that not the central, unifying reality of our existence? And if it is, can we not focus on that and call each other brother instead of always emphasizing our differences? Men, we have to get together on this!

THE SIN OF DIVISION

Perhaps you look at the issue of racism and denominational divisiveness and say, "That's not me! I don't hate anybody, and I don't take responsibility for the plight of people of color." Or, "I can't be responsible for what happened hundreds of years ago. I wasn't there." If that's the case, let me ask you to rethink the issue in a couple of ways.

First, take the time and make the effort to prayerfully examine your heart. In God's presence, ask yourself questions like these: "Do I truly not consider myself better than people different from myself—more intelligent, creative, honest, hard-working, moral, trustworthy? How would I feel if a family of another color sat next to me in church, invited my family to a picnic in a public park, or moved in next door? How would I react if my Sunday school teacher or my child's teacher were a person of another race? What if my child married someone from a different denomination?"

As you ask yourself such questions, keep in mind these words given by the Holy Spirit of God through the apostle John: "If anyone says, 'I love God,' yet hates his brother, he is a liar. For everyone who does not love his brother, whom he has seen, cannot love God, whom he has not seen. And he [God] has given us this command: Whoever loves God must also love his brother" (1 John 4:20-21).

Then, as you lay your heart open to God, deal with any traces of racism and division you find there according to 1 John 1:9, and ask Him to begin the process of changing your mind and heart.

Historically, the church has stood against a lot of other social evils, but we have not stood against prejudice and called it what it is: sin! We should feel conviction deep in our souls. The damage is incalculable. The toll is immeasurable. We should drop to our knees before Almighty God in repentance.

Because God reconciled us to Himself through His only Son, Jesus Christ, we must reconcile with our Christian brothers of different races, cultures, and denominations. We must break down the walls that separate us so that we might demonstrate the power of biblical unity based on what we have in common: our love for Jesus and our connectedness through Him. We will live for one purpose: to bring glory to the name of Jesus Christ and to fulfill the desires of God's heart.

FIRST STEPS

I don't know of any way to achieve this unity apart from Jesus Christ. Only His Spirit can break down the walls that separate Christians. Matthew 22:37-40 sums up our strategy: " 'Love the Lord your God with all your heart and with all your soul and with all your mind.' This is the first and greatest commandment. And the second is like it: 'Love your neighbor as yourself.' All the Law and the Prophets [i.e., the entire Old Testament] hang on these two commandments." Love God and love your neighbor. That's the bottom line. In the words of Paul,

> Let no debt remain outstanding, except the continuing debt to love one another, for he who loves his fellowman has fulfilled the law. The commandments, "Do not commit adultery," "Do not murder," "Do not steal," "Do not covet," and whatever other commandment there may

be, are summed up in this one rule: "Love your neighbor as yourself."
Love does no harm to its neighbor. Therefore love is the fulfillment of
the law. (Rom. 13:8-10)

Biblical love and unity do not come at an easy price. They require
us to lay down our lives for our friends (see John 15:13), to leave our
self-centeredness and enlarge our circle of understanding so we can
appreciate another's history and experiences. They demand that we
become good listeners and share the pain of those who have been hurt
by our sins in the past. They oblige us to seek forgiveness for the
racial oppression and sectarianism that continue to this day. They
require that we endure confrontations and crises until we establish
trust in one another.

This kind of love means that we come together in our common
poverty, weaknesses, and sins to receive God's riches, strength, and
grace—together. It means we allow God to replace our personal prejudices with His perspective. It compels us to accept the essential value
of every person, understanding that we need each other to be complete:

> But God has combined the members of the body and has given greater
> honor to the parts that lacked it, so that there should be no division in
> the body, but that its parts should have equal concern for each other. If
> one part suffers, every part suffers with it; if one part is honored, every
> part rejoices with it. (1 Cor. 12:24-26)

If our hearts are right before God and our motive is love, He will
show us the way. The plan I'm proposing starts with prayer, then calls
for genuine, real relationship with brothers of different ethnic and
denominational heritages.

1. Pray.

Can you imagine what might happen if every church in the United
States identified a point person to lead a prayer posse in that congregation? I challenge you to begin by making that a goal in your church
and to pray for the following:

First, pray that your pastor will see through the darkness of a
divided church to the light of a unified Body of Christ. Pray that he

will address the problem of division vigorously and lead his congregation in repentance.

Second, pray that the hearts in your congregation will soften. Pray that they will become educated about the sins of racism and sectarianism and begin to bear the burden of pain that their brothers and sisters have endured. Pray that this effort will be sustained and not a one-time venture.

Third, pray for your community to address the problems caused by racism. The inner cities and slums need resources to help lift them out of total apathy. We need to dissolve the gangs. All of this is possible because Jesus wants to do it.

Godly men must be impassioned with righteous determination to make amends. Society tries in vain. Government efforts are losing ground. Defeat swallows mankind's best ideas. May every church plead in unison for God's heart and God's solution to bring reconciliation. May our prayer warriors work overtime. Let the pulse of the Body of Christ quicken and not rest until we see change. And let it begin with you and me.

2. Pursue genuine relationships with Christian men of different races and denominations.

Our hearts will not break for our brethren until we enter into relationship with them. I suggest that you begin by establishing groups of men who are committed to living as promise keepers. Find at least two other guys from your church who share this vision. From there, look around and find a few brothers from different denominational and ethnic heritages with whom you can start to build a relationship of trust and honor. You might meet these men at a local Promise Keepers breakfast, at work, at the Y, or in your neighborhood as you and they are out walking your dogs or playing catch with your kids.

The men may be from one church or several. You may meet in groups at work, in a restaurant, in a church, or in a home. Keep the agenda simple. Share insight and wisdom from the pages of Scripture. Understand each other's pain and victories. And pray for one another.

Make a concerted effort to get below the surface in those relationships. Let me explain why that's so important. I know two guys, one black and one white, who are nearly inseparable. You can see them together on any given day. They work together. They laugh and clown around. They hug and embrace. They sing and harmonize. They claim to be best friends.

One day while I was with them, I asked the black man, "Have you ever told your best friend how you really feel about being black, about the pain and resentment, about the smoldering hostility for white people deep in your spirit?"

"No," he said.

"Is it there?" I asked.

"Yes," he answered.

Those two men had something good going. However, until a man hurts as his brother hurts, they don't really know each other. How can you pray for someone when you don't know his deepest pain? When you do know his pain, you have real relationship.

As one missionary said, "I don't know how to love the poor except one at a time." We can embrace that same wisdom in overcoming hostility and division in the body of Christ—one relationship at a time. But beware! If a man of another color or denomination doesn't trust you right away, remember that you may represent hundreds of years of oppression and mistrust to him. Stay with it. Keep trying; keep reaching out in love. Ask God to work in the hearts of everyone involved.

Micah 6:8 is a profound Scripture. This is what God requires of us: "To act justly and to love mercy and to walk humbly with your God." It sounds simple enough. However, when I looked into the verse, I discovered that it meant something entirely different from how it originally appeared to me. "Act justly" means to see the need in others and respond to it. To "love mercy" always triumphs over judgment. And to "walk humbly with your God" means that we agree with what God says as opposed to what man says.

God requires that we see the need in our brethren and respond. If we do, His very heart will go with us.*

---

* See also "Life Aboard the Fellow-Ship," page 239.

Help Me Understand

by Raleigh Washington, Glen Kehrein, and Claude V. King

Suppose you see a man in a convenience store with three preschool children who are wild and out of control. The father seems not to notice or care. He walks through the aisles collecting groceries while the kids terrorize the rest of the customers. While you're trying to pay for your gas, one of the older boys runs by you and nearly knocks you down.

But then suppose the man apologizes to you. "I'm sorry. My wife—their mother—died yesterday," he explains. "I'm still dazed by it all, and the kids seem to be more hyperactive than usual. I don't think they really understand why their mother isn't around."

Does that change your feelings and opinions toward him? Sure it does. Instead of wanting to lecture him or turn him in to social services for negligent parenting, you wish there were some way you could help. That bit of knowledge about his wife caused you to empathize with him. Suddenly you felt some of his pain and loss. Now you can also understand why he may have been slow to discipline the children.

In the same way, we need to seek knowledge about our brothers in order to relate empathetically to people from different denominations, traditions, races, social standings, or cultures.

RACISM AND DISCRIMINATION ARE NOT DEAD

An investigative television news show in 1995 broadcast a stunning destruction of the myth that discrimination is now rare. Two investigators were similar in every way—except that one was white and the other was black. The plan was simple: Both men would do everyday activities in a white community and see if they were treated differently. In a dozen instances—buying shoes or a car, applying for a job or an apartment—the young men were treated in nearly opposite ways. While the white man was welcomed, the black man was ignored or insulted. Such covert racism is seldom, if ever, experienced by whites, who sometimes view blacks as being "overly sensitive" about racism.

Without becoming sensitive to the experiences of another person, we can't possibly know how we might respond in similar circumstances. Being ignored, mistreated, or insulted *once* is a matter that can be overlooked. Experiencing that daily could easily lead to anger and even hate. Racism is painful. Constantly experiencing it can have a profound effect on a person, family, or group.

In 1992, following the Los Angeles riots, a paraphrase of Rodney King's plea became a coined phrase: "Why can't we all just get along?" It's a poignant question, and it's even more crucial when applied to the body of Christ. It's one matter when a sinful world can't get along, but it's much more serious when brothers and sisters in Christ can't get along. Some Christians might think, *If I'm doing okay, why should I worry or care about other Christians?* The answer is found in 1 Corinthians 12:21–26:

> The eye cannot say to the hand, "I don't need you!" And the head cannot say to the feet, "I don't need you!" On the contrary, those parts of the body that seem to be weaker are indispensable. . . . God has combined the members of the body . . . so that there should be no division in the body, but that its parts should have equal concern for each other. If one part suffers, every part suffers with it; if one part is honored, every part rejoices with it.

LACK OF KNOWLEDGE LIMITS UNDERSTANDING

The cultural isolation in which most of us live places us in different worlds. We may practice the out-of-sight, out-of-mind approach to caring about the body of Christ. If we can remain ignorant, we suppose, then maybe God won't hold us accountable. Another response could be a failure to recognize that we have separate histories, environments, and life experiences. The common expression that "we're all Americans" assumes we all experience life in more or less the same ways. We do not. A Christian who grew up in south-central Los Angeles will have very different experiences from one who grew up on a Nebraska farm. We must be intentional in developing sensitivity to the needs of other members of the body.

The moral revolution and the deterioration of family values in our world often tempt us to wish for the "good old days." Family life seemed so healthy back then—to some, but not to all. Those were also the days of Jim Crow laws, which dehumanized people and enforced racial segregation—in churches as well as in the rest of society. Those were the days of the Ku Klux Klan, which terrorized African Americans and others. Those were the days of sharecropping, where landowners often got rich at the expense of those who worked the farms. To return to those days would be a nightmare from the standpoint of racism.

For Americans of European background, Ellis Island evokes warm feelings of ancestors from the "old country." But it seems different to Hispanic immigrants who are struggling today for the same entrance to American citizenship. If we don't know a person's background or experiences, we won't understand his attitudes, actions, and beliefs. We won't know his pain and suffering, and the body of Christ will lack the health it could have.

JESUS LEARNED SENSITIVITY TO THE HUMAN CONDITION

When God sought to reconcile us to Himself, He became one of us in the person of Jesus. Jesus grew from a baby to adulthood and experienced what it's like to be a man. He is able to empathize with us because of His knowledge of our experiences.

While the ultimate purpose for Jesus' body was to be a sacrifice for our sins, Jesus also became flesh to identify with us. As a human being, He experienced the pain, struggles, and temptations of a man—yet without sin. He can identify with everything we face. We can feel the love of a God who is sensitive to our feelings and who has identified with our experiences.

Jesus modeled sensitivity for us. He became a friend of sinners and tax collectors. He chose to go through Samaria to meet the woman at the well. He took time to get to know people. Sometimes He even showed that He also felt their pain.

HELP ME UNDERSTAND

The principle of sensitivity requires that you enter into the experience of your brothers and sisters in Christ. If they're different from you, you need knowledge to empathize and understand. Read books and watch videos documenting other ethnic groups. Frequently ask, "Would you help me understand?"

We might like to believe we're completely free agents. We may believe the "American Dream"—that if you work hard enough, you can be anything you want to be. It's true that we can all make choices of how we respond to our surroundings. But we also are deeply influenced by our ethnic history and the models we've seen in those who have gone before us. Many have experienced pain as the result of sectarian strife, closing the door to understanding and sensitivity. Even though we might feel that others are living in the past, we can't understand without talking about experiences. Sensitivity—the gaining of knowledge to relate with empathy—requires that we actively reach out for understanding.

Most people want to be understood. Few believe the past can be changed or repaired by present actions. But they do want someone to hear their personal story and try to understand.

(Adapted from *Break Down the Walls* workbook by Raleigh Washington, Glen Kehrein, and Claude V. King [Chicago: Moody Press, 1997].)

Walking in Your Brother's Shoes

A Hispanic Perspective
by Jesse Miranda

HISPANIC DIVERSITY

Being culturally relevant to historical distinctives and cultural traits of Hispanics will help you as you begin building relationships. First, you need to understand some terms used for this group. Some use the term *Hispanic,* while others use the term *Latino.* The majority of the Hispanic community is from Latin America—especially Mexico. *Latino* refers to immigrants from Latin America. This term tends to exclude those from the Caribbean and from Spain. The term *Hispanic* is more inclusive, since all these people trace their roots to Spain.

It's also important to know Hispanics in terms of how long they've been in this country. There are the recent arrivals; some are resident and others are not. Then there are the assimilating Hispanics who have one or two generations of residency. And finally, many Hispanics have totally assimilated into mainstream America and have little in common with the recent arrivals. The important point here is to understand that there is great diversity even within the Hispanic population.

Another aspect of diversity among Hispanics is the national origin of their ancestors. Hispanics from Cuba are culturally different from Hispanics from Mexico or Puerto Rico, Hispanics from a South American country are different from those from Spain.

One way of better understanding Hispanics is to make some contrasts with those of the mainstream population. Although these are generalizations, they offer some insight into Hispanic life.

TASK VS. RELATIONSHIP

Anglo Americans think and talk in terms of "doing." Most Hispanics think in terms of "being." Anglos focus more on tasks, while Hispanics focus more on relationships. Take, for example, a conversation between people who have never met. An Anglo might introduce himself by saying, "Hi, I'm John Doe. I'm a lawyer from Beverly Hills." He sees his identity related to what he does (he's a lawyer) and what he has achieved (he lives in Beverly Hills).

A Hispanic might introduce himself by saying, "Hola, I am Juan, the son of Don José from the town of Morelos." He sees his identity related to who he is in relationship to others. He's a son (of Don José), and he comes from a community of people (the town of Morelos). His sense of identity comes from his roots.

METHODS OF COMMUNICATION

Suppose Jim, Amed, and José get together in an accountability group. They enjoy open discussions about their goals in life and confess their shortcomings to one another. Jim and Amed wonder, however, why José is reluctant to participate openly in the discussions. Jim, who is white, and Amed, an African American, don't understand that José's family circle is where he discusses his personal matters, and he's less experienced in open discussion with people outside his family.

Or suppose John (white) is planning a meeting, and he invites Juan (Hispanic) to attend:

John: "We have a meeting coming up at the end of the month. Are you coming?"

Juan: "Yes, I'll be there."

At the end of the month, Juan does not show up. John is disappointed and does not understand. John places high value on accuracy and truth, and he took Juan's words at face value.

Juan's values are placed on the relationship. He may or may not have intended to attend the meeting, but he wants to maintain John as a friend. Because he values the friendship, Juan gave John the "Hispanic polite yes." He didn't want to embarrass John or hurt his feelings by saying he wouldn't attend. The way to assure that Juan comes to the meeting would be to follow up and even perhaps pick him up for the meeting. These actions would emphasize the importance of the relationship.

An African-American Perspective
by Rodney L. Cooper

A few years ago, a researcher performed an experiment using carp and a glass plate. Several carp swam in a tank of clear water, with a large plate of glass dividing the aquarium's middle. The experiment consisted of some food being placed on the other side of the glass plate—food that was very desirable to the carp.

Every time the carp tried to reach the food, they didn't see the glass and so swam full speed into it, only to be stopped by the solid but invisible object. This went on for several days, with the carp finally "wising up"; they saw the food but stopped trying to reach it. After about a week, the glass plate was removed from the tank so that the food would now be accessible to the fish. An interesting phenomenon happened. Every time the carp would head for the food, they would stop just short of it and not get it. Although they were hungry and the glass plate had been removed, they still operated as if the glass were there. Their past experiences kept them from attaining what was now readily available.

THE POWER OF THE PAST

If a child grows up in a closed family system—a system marked by a pervading sense of unacceptability—he or she will be influenced in a notably negative way. Consider the likely outcomes in social relations, status, and security:

Social Relations

1. The world is seen as a hostile, unsociable, closed place.

2. Most people are considered unfriendly and uninterested in personal relationships.

3. The child begins to dislike and avoid close companionship with certain others.

Status

1. The world is seen as a competitive place full of prejudice and discrimination, with little opportunity.

2. Most people are perceived to be treated with unequal fairness and respect, and their strengths and personal worth go unnoticed by others.

3. The child feels little worth, and his strengths are unrecognized by others.

Security

1. The world is viewed as a harmful place that is unpredictable and full of worry and incertitude.

2. Most people are thought to be untrustworthy.

3. The child mistrusts the motives of others.

In American society, dominated by the Anglo-American majority, most members of minority races feel and often have been treated as though they have been raised in a closed family system. They believe the world is hostile and unsociable, a competitive place full of prejudice and discrimination. They believe that most people can't be trusted, and they act according to this closed-system viewpoint. In addition, many minority men have grown up in families dominated by a closed system. Thus, both society and their families of origin have given them a restricted and negative view of their world.

A Sense of Shame

As a counselor and psychologist, I have found that anybody, regardless of race, who comes from a closed system will have a profound sense of insecurity and inferiority—in essence, a sense of shame. If the family is in disarray, the schools are poor, and the neighborhood is unsafe, then everywhere the individual looks, he will see reasons not to trust or not to feel trustworthy. In contrast, if his childhood environment is stable and positive, the family whole and loving, the schools good, and the community stable and safe, he will believe in himself and have confidence.

I'm not saying that one cannot overcome a difficult childhood, but a mind-set is established in childhood about whether we can approach the world with confidence—a strong self-image—or with shame and doubt—a poor self-image.

Every man has an innate capacity for insecurity. But our experiences can expand and deepen that tendency to feel insecure. The experiences of black people as a whole—indeed, of most minorities—have ingrained a deepened sense of doubt, shame, and inferiority upon their minds. We feel shame for what we are. People feel guilt because they *did* something wrong, but people feel shame because they *are* something wrong.

Among black people, social shame has existed for a long time, tracing all the way back to the slave days in the early 1800s. Social shame is when one group is despised and rejected by another. Most minorities endure the stigma of skin color, an easy way for the majority culture to label the minority. And skin color is perhaps most obvious within the black race, since all minorities are being compared against the white-skin majority. The condition of being black in America means that one is likely to endure more wounds to one's self-esteem than others, and that the capacity for shame and doubt born of these wounds will be compounded and expanded by the black race's reputation for inferiority based upon past experiences.

Abandoning the Stereotypes

If you are a nonblack, your past family experiences have influenced your attitudes toward blacks. In many cases, nonblacks have not had direct contact with African Americans. If that is your case, you probably have picked up stereotypes from your family, friends, television, movies, and newspapers. The stereotypes help you classify a group of men you don't know. They also let you lump together people who are unique.

The solution to this unfair generalizing is to get to know African Americans by spending time with them in different settings. Research has shown that attitudes about other races do not change by legislation but by relationships. Only through the context of relationships will we be able to overcome the stereotypes that have kept us apart.

Generally speaking, this is a process that will take time. We must recognize that our cultural experiences are a part of who we are—not all of who we are. Every man shares common human experiences and feelings. We must also realize we are relating to an individual—not the total race—whose personal experiences make him one of a kind. Thus, we should treat each person as unique.

For reconciliation to occur between black men and white men, I offer the following dos and don'ts for nonblacks, especially my white brothers as they cross over to the black man's turf:

Dos

1. Do assume blacks have individual feelings, aspirations, and attitudes, just like any ethnic group. Sometimes there's a tendency on the part of whites to make generalizations or to say, "Well, you're an exception." No, I am me.

2. Do assume blacks have a heritage of which they are proud. Even though the history books don't record many of the accomplishments of blacks, there are actually many to celebrate. Recognize them and celebrate them.

3. Do assume blacks are angry. Everyday experiences remind the black man that he is not acceptable. Anger is an ever-present emotion in a black man.

4. Do recognize that whiteness/blackness is a real difference, but not the basis on which to determine behavior. It's true, people are different in skin color, but that's where we must stop. All

people have the same needs and desires to live a good life. We must not look at a person's behavior as indicative of an entire race but of that person only.

5. Do assume most blacks can handle whites' authentic behavior and feelings. Blacks value openness and authenticity. Do not try to "identify" by taking on mannerisms of the black person, but be yourself and be open to learn. Be authentic.

6. Do assume blacks want reconciliation. Blacks want harmony to exist in the body of Christ. Reconciliation means we value each other equally. Blacks desire this greatly.

7. Do assume that you may be part of the problem. Take time for self-reflection, and see if there are any negative attitudes or unhealthy stereotypes that could keep reconciliation from happening.

Don'ts

1. Don't assume color is unimportant in interpersonal relation-ships. Color has distinguished the black man as the scapegoat in our society. Just because it has not been an impediment to you does not mean it's not an issue.

2. Don't assume blacks will always welcome and appreciate inclusion in white society. Expect to be met with suspicion when you approach a black man. In years past, blacks have been included because of guilt and not on their terms. Sometimes blacks have felt included as an afterthought. So there may be resistance.

3. Don't assume white society is superior to black society. Instead, the two are different. For instance, many blacks are event-oriented rather than time-oriented. Event-oriented indi-viduals usually go somewhere with the attitude, "When we get started we start—and we end when we end." In contrast, a time-oriented individual begins and ends with time as the issue. Neither perspective is right or wrong; they're just different. However, if a black man is "late," he is seen as undependable

by the majority culture. Instead of judgment, we need acceptance of differences as simply being differences in cultural
behavior.

4. Don't assume blacks are oversensitive. Instead, blacks strongly
    support what they believe. That's how it should be—every
    man a strong advocate for his position. I have taught in a sem-
    inary where most of my students are white. I remember pre-
    senting a position on an issue with passion. I was not committed
    to the position, but I presented it with zeal to stimulate class
    discussion. No one asked a question for fear they would be
    shot down. I explained to the class that most blacks come
    across as advocates for their position. This gets things out on
    the table to discuss.

An Asian-American Perspective

by Bruce Fong

My first memory scar of racism happened while I was just a youngster
in California. On a hot Sacramento summer day, my parents dropped
off my brothers and me at a public pool. We stayed until closing time.
In the shower rooms, most people had already left. As my brothers and
I were putting our gear together, three much older white teens confronted us. The taunts, mockery, derision, and name-calling had an
awful effect on me. I was frozen in place. My knees turned to jelly. I
couldn't understand the reason for such verbal abuse. I thought we
were in for the beating of our lives. Then, there was a change. The boys
abruptly stopped their vicious barrage and melted away out of the
locker room. A presence behind me made me turn. There an adult
white male had his eyes fixed on the exit where those boys had disap-
peared. Without addressing us, he sternly declared, "Trash! They are
just trash." As our champion picked up his bag and left, my two
brothers and I followed close behind him.

I learned something that day. The world is populated by two kinds
of people: racists and champions. Racists take every opportunity to
live a life of hatred and abuse. They attempt to dominate others
through intimidation. Champions use the very same opportunities

and issues to help others. They use their position and values in life to aid those who are victims of racial hatred.

THE VALUE OF ASIAN-AMERICAN FRIENDSHIPS

The Asian-American experience includes its share of mistreatment. History records those difficult episodes. But it is not as volatile or painful as the history of African and Native Americans. Yet, as with other ethnic minorities, seeing America through Asian eyes may be a big step in the right direction for further reconciliation on a personal level.

Asian-American friendships can provide a helpful transition in the arena of racial reconciliation. If you are white or black, you may find that a friendship with an Asian American can be a valuable first step in cross-cultural relationships, a bridge to more difficult areas of reconciliation.

As you consider a friendship with an Asian American, keep in mind that programs and official functions or events will be limited in their effect. Something longer lasting requires not a single meeting or the creation of a new position, but a commitment to building a meaningful relationship. Friendships are a vital part of the Asian-American identity, though a depth of intimacy may be slow to develop in the early stages of these friendships.

Be sensitive to the cost to an Asian-American friend. Blacks who engage in reconciliation endeavors with whites are called "Oreos." Asian Americans are called "bananas"—yellow on the outside and white on the inside. Asians who are closer to their cultural roots call fellow Asians involved with reconciliation "jooksing." It is loosely translated as "bamboo." The derision is in the fact that bamboo is hollow on the inside. It has end caps but nothing in between—no culture, no traditions, no history. Those willing to pay the cost of being your friend will be friends of great value.

DIFFERENCES IN GENERATIONS

When I left the West Coast and moved to Texas to attend seminary, I was warned by several fellow Asian Americans about life in the South. I went to an early new-student reception and met many new people. One couple and I struck up a friendly conversation. After a number of pleasant topics, I was faced with an inquiry. With a distinctly southern drawl and innocent spirit, this fellow student's wife asked me, "Now, Bruce, tell me, what part of China are you from?"

I took advantage of the situation to inject a little humor mixed with some new information. I responded, "I'm from one of the far eastern provinces called California. And I was born in a village called Sacramento."

"Oh, Bruce, I am so embarrassed!" she said as we laughed together.

Asian Americans define their ethnic identity within the tension of two elements. One factor is their closeness to their cultural roots. The other is the inevitability of assimilation of the surrounding culture. The influence of these factors varies during life and according to individual experiences.

The closer an Asian American is to the generation of his forebears who immigrated to the United States, the more closely tied he is to his cultural roots. The further he is from those original immigrants, the more he will reflect American culture in speech, choices, and values. Thus, intentionally building a relationship with an Asian American should begin by understanding what generation he belongs to.

Most Asians find it awkward to be asked, "What are you?" or "Where do you come from?" It is more beneficial to be asked, "What generation are you?" This kind of intentional inquiry shows an understanding of the great tension experienced by Asians in this country. Expectations, stereotypes, and limitations by the majority white society are still common. In starting a relationship with an Asian American, you might ask questions like: "What country did your ancestors immigrate from? When did they immigrate?" or "What generation are you from the first immigrants to this country?"

The generational issues among Asians can perhaps be best understood by looking at their use of language. Those of the immigration generation are usually tied to their culture and Asian identity through their speech. Their mother tongue is their primary expression. Those of the second generation—that is, the first generation born in America—grow up bilingual. They speak their mother tongue at home, largely at the insistence of their parents. But they speak English at school, in the shops, with their friends, and at work. The third and subsequent generations use English as their primary language. Except for a few phrases, the mother tongue is not a daily practice. This is inevitable; it has little or nothing to do with one's loyalty to one's culture. Those outside the Asian realm who understand this phenomenon will be far more successful in building relationships with Asian Americans.

THE PAIN OF RACISM

Every ethnic minority group in America has experienced the pain and scars of racism. Many continue to receive fresh wounds today. The hurt from racism is more than an inconvenience in the day's schedule. It's more than a thoughtless or even a naïvely spoken word. Rather, it is a deep hurt that humiliates and strips a person of his human dignity. Every Asian group that has come to America has experienced the pain of rejection and isolation. Those experiences taint the context of trust and intimate relationships. An ethnic minority is either prepared for racial tension or suspicious that it is lurking behind a new face. Most of us have been hit too hard too many times to be caught unaware.

Sensitivity to an Asian American will require that you understand he has real hurts due to racial injustices and prejudices that have occurred in his life. Ignoring those or joking about them will keep you from a meaningful relationship. Take time to build trust and accept feelings as real and important.

VALUED FOR THEIR CONTRIBUTIONS, NOT QUOTAS

I desire to be valued as a contributing team member. A relationship is not gratifying if I am perceived as a token minority, but I can thrive as a contributing member of an organization, company, or ministry team. In the heart of every Asian American is the same passion that drives any person—the desire to be valued for his genuine contribution.

Tokenism compounds the problem of racial tension. If impersonal quotas become the basis of a relationship, reconciled relationships will seldom be achieved. Minorities are well versed in patronizing attitudes that feel safe once quotas are reached.

If you choose to build a friendship with an Asian American, do it because you anticipate he will make a valuable contribution to your life. Let him assume a position of influence in your life, and there will be mutual benefit.

American-born Asians are often gifted individuals. But they can be overlooked in churches that haven't taken the time to know, relate to, and value individual members of the body. Because of a humble spirit, many Asian Americans will not assert themselves. Without the rest of the body's encouragement, they may remain quietly on the sidelines when they could make significant contributions.

In the local church and in Christian organizations, actively discover Asian Americans who have the gifts and capabilities to serve in meaningful ways. This is not an advocacy for affirmative action, where quotas are the driving force, but a recognition of how God has gifted individuals by His Spirit to benefit the body of Christ as a whole. Find value in their service, and cheer them on to continued ministry.

A Native-American Perspective

by Huron Claus

In the early seventies, a book was published titled *Bury My Heart at Wounded Knee.* The words of the writer ripped out the hearts of readers as he unfolded the picture of the history of the Native-American people during the Indian Wars with the U.S. Government in the 1800s. Stories were told of many Indian tribes and the intentional efforts to diminish and even exterminate them and take their land. It was a book that stirred the soul of America.

A fire of anger toward the past was ignited in the hearts of our native youth in the early seventies. Almost one hundred years after these injustices and atrocities took place, a strong, militant voice known as AIM—the American Indian Movement—trumpeted through our land. Today there is a burning that still resides in the innermost parts of our people. If you look deep in the eyes of our Native-American people, you will see much pain, anger, bitterness, unforgiveness, and unsettledness.

LOOKING BACK AT OUR LEGACY

It has been estimated that before Columbus came to this land, approximately nine to twelve million indigenous peoples lived here. Today there are about 1.9 million Native Americans from 515 federally recognized tribes and about two hundred not yet officially recognized.

Native Americans inhabited the land from the east to the west and the north to the south. There were no land boundaries to the Native-American people. They understood it wasn't their possession to keep. In the minds of our people, we were given the stewardship by the Creator God to be the keepers of the earth. That was precisely what God called Adam to do in Genesis.

At the beginning of the nineteenth century, the native population plummeted below 250,000 due to diseases and the Indian Wars. What was once the home of the Native-American people was being possessed in the name of "Manifest Destiny," until today only 4 percent of all our country belongs to the various tribes.

As I read and hear about the history of my people, my heart is broken and tears well up inside me. I remember traveling through the Denver International Airport on my way to speak at a native men's meeting in Mission, South Dakota. I had just finished reading the chapter of *Bury My Heart at Wounded Knee* telling of the "Long Walk" of the Navajo people, and I began to cry uncontrollably. It was a journey forced by the U.S. government that starved and killed thousands of Navajo people. I have a Navajo friend who tells a story, passed down through his family, about that unforgettable walk. When the Navajos began the walk in the bitterly cold winter, they were given government-issued blankets. It was later discovered that those blankets were infested with smallpox and cholera. Thousands of Navajos died as a result. My dear friend has a beautiful Indian blanket that has been passed down as a memorial of what his people went through.

My heart breaks because I know that many of our people carry the weight of the past on themselves, and it has almost crushed them beyond hope. Only at the foot of the cross of Calvary have I found peace and rest regarding the past deeds done to my people. There I have seen Christ as our supreme example of someone crushed and rejected, bruised and despised. He cried out to the Father to forgive

His tormentors through the love and power of God. There I have
learned to bury my heart at Calvary.

THE ROAD OF RECONCILIATION

The theme of reconciliation has permeated the lifestyle and culture of
the Native-American people. The word that is often used in place of *reconciliation* is *unity*. There is a great desire to be in unity, or right relationship, with everything about them. Each of the 515 federally recognized Native-American tribes in the U.S. is as different in its ways of life
as the Germans are from the Chinese. Language is different. Styles of
worship can have varying implications. Customs are different. We are
not all the same, yet there's a thread of similarity that runs throughout
all tribes. One point of similarity is the importance of relationships.

RELATIONSHIP WITH MANKIND

The horizontal relationship of mankind is valued by the Native
American. He sees himself as part of the whole picture rather than
focusing on the individual. With this type of mind-set, our people can
be easily misunderstood. I have heard it said at times that we lack initiative or are lazy. In reality, because of our communal social structure,
it would be unheard of to promote oneself above others. Even in discussion, our people contemplate first before giving their opinion.
Often they offer their thoughts only after being asked. When talking
with a Native-American brother, he may not look you directly in your
eyes. This is a sign of respect, considering the relationship with others
more important than oneself. Relationship to others is essential to our
people.

RELATIONSHIP OF THE FAMILY/TRIBE

The family has a high priority among our people. Each family member
plays a vital role in the function of our society. You most likely are
familiar with the role of the chief or tribal chairman. In some tribes, the
clan's mother plays just as important a responsibility in tribal decisions as the chief. And elders are highly revered in honor of their wis-

dom and experience in life. To reach out to Native-American families and nations, the key is the elders. History has proved that when a Native-American elder chooses to enter relationships with outsiders, families often follow.

The tribe is also important. When you meet a Native-American brother, begin your conversation by asking him, "What tribe do you come from?" You have just communicated to him not only your interest in him ethnically as a Native American, but you also are giving him an opportunity to honor his heritage by telling about his tribe. Our people are proud of their tribal heritage. Each tribe has special leaders and chiefs. Each contributes in his unique way. It's important to know your tribe within native society. It reminds me of a time when a well-intentioned lady came to me and was excited to meet a Native American. She was telling me of her interest in our people since she was a youth. She went on to say that she had Native-American ancestry in her family line that she believed was from the "Chihuahua" tribe. I thought that very interesting!

As you develop a friendship with a Native American, you might begin by sincerely asking questions about the importance of relationships among his people. Share with him similar insights about your own relationships. Ask about his tribe and the history of his people. Listen to his pain, and share with him a painful time in your life that God brought you through. Describe what you have learned by it, and ask to pray with him in his pain. Prayer is a vital part of the Native-American culture.

BUILDING TRUST

Dr. Ralph Winter once said, "The Native-American people are one of the hardest people groups in the world to reach with the gospel of Jesus Christ." I believe he's right and that it is largely due to broken relationships and promises in the past. When sharing Christ with my own people, I often hear them say, "Christianity, that's the white man's religion. We have our own way of worship. We have the Native-American way." When I hear that kind of response, I understand the hurt they feel. I can even accept the hostility they demonstrate to me regarding the past. As a Christian Native American, I find the greatest challenge in my life is to be intentional in demonstrating to our people that Jesus Christ, God's Son, came to reconcile with all the people of the world—the Native-American people included.

Historically, more than three hundred treaties were made by the U.S. government with the Native-American tribes, and few were kept. When you begin to build a relationship with our people, build it on the "potential" or on the outcome of the relationship, not on the "plight" of the people. Stay away from the stereotypes of Native Americans. Acknowledge your ignorance about native peoples, but show a desire to understand them more. When you approach your friendship with that openness and sincerity, it encourages your Native-American brother to be open in return. Understand that relationships, actions, and time are much more important than words. Allow time for trust to be developed for greater levels of brotherhood.

White Christians are increasingly willing to come to Native Americans and confess the sins of the past and ask for forgiveness. Confession and repentance from the white man and forgiveness from the Native American have great potential for healing. But remember that words have proved to be shallow. Don't stop at words of confession just to ease a sense of guilt. Go on to relationships and actions. Show by your love and actions that the repentance is genuine. Value your Native-American brother and the contributions he may make to your life and faith. Move into a relationship where you both can live out reconciliation and unity in Christ.

A White Perspective

by Glen Kehrein

For people of color, race is a significant issue. But for the whites in the majority community, it's not. We think about it only when there's a problem. Even then, most whites don't understand what the big deal is. Much of today's racial insensitivity comes from ignorance rather than overt hostility. In brief, white folks just don't know—we don't understand.

As is the case in any country, most folks of the dominant culture interact little with the minority cultures. Even though legal segregation is past, racial and class separation is a reality. Many whites live in racial isolation and don't have much experience or knowledge of people of color. When racial issues become public, we may be sincerely shocked. But when such things "blow over," life returns to normal, and little thought is given to racial issues until the next incident.

GOD IS MOVING

Today, there's a significant change in this pattern. Many white men are beginning to leave their comfort zone and reach out for reconciliation. Why? God is moving their hearts. God seeks to bring an end to racism between brothers in Christ. He has already made it possible through Christ's death on the cross. Will men of color look beyond their pain, anger, and distrust and reach out, too? If you will, we can all join God in this vital work.

White guys, for the most part, don't see the depth of the issue. They don't relate to the pain of a minority, but some are trying. The response from the minority community is cool and cautious. I understand the reaction: "Here we go again. The white guy wants to do it, and I'm supposed to jump." But what if God is doing it? What if God is moving in men's hearts to reach out? I ask you to meet us halfway and lead us toward understanding.

Perhaps you've been at a Promise Keepers conference and have seen white men respond by the thousands to the call for reconciliation. Most have little understanding of what that means and know less about what to do back home. They live in suburbs and small towns that have become isolated, homogeneous communities. But God is opening up their hearts. How many are genuine? Only God knows, but I'm sure that many are genuinely seeking to obey God and seek reconciliation. One thing is for sure: God has brought reconciliation to the front burner.

OUR WAY WITH QUESTIONS

When white people reach out to establish relationships, we do that by asking questions—"Where do you work?" "Where do you live?"

"What did your father do?" "How long have you been married?" "What are your hobbies?" Often, people of color bristle, "Man, they are nosy!" "What do they want to know all that for?" or, if distrust is running deep, "What are they going to do to me with this information?" As a person who crosses subcultures often, I've seen this common dynamic. White men ask questions to get to know others; men of color shy away. But guess what? If I go to a party with a group of strangers who are white, I get the same questions. It's our ordinary way of social interaction and how we get to know each other. White folks don't have a clue that they are perceived as prying.

SUPERIORITY AND INFERIORITY

A great issue that exists between the races in this country is superiority and inferiority. This has deep, historic roots. Using the rationale of superiority, the white culture enslaved and dominated African Americans and Native Americans. We used perceived superiority to take land from indigenous peoples, both Mexican and Indian. It is deep in the fabric of this thing called racism. But today we find only radical groups standing for and espousing this philosophy. Nevertheless, it exists just below the surface in many whites, including Christians. I believe that whites are insensitive and minorities are hypersensitive to the existence of the superiority/inferiority dynamic.

Many whites have a strong, self-confident, and take-charge manner. They have found it's the fastest way to get a job done. When they bring that take-charge spirit to cross-cultural experiences, they usually do not stop to think about how domineering it appears to men of color. They also may have a sincere heart to help meet needs. With a spirit of generosity, they may give to meet a need without stopping to think about the feelings of the receivers. They may not be sensitive to respect, dignity, and interdependence issues. We can wind up hurting men of color through our ignorance and insensitivity.

These kinds of mistakes will happen. But reconciliation demands that we work through difficulties with commitment. When we open ourselves with sincerity, we can build sensitivity and break the back of racial alienation and division. When confronted with such experiences, people of color often do one of two things: (1) confront the whites and condemn their racism or (2) bury their feelings and say nothing.

The first response leaves whites bewildered and frustrated. It can eventually lead to anger: "No matter what I do, it's never enough!" The second response leaves a false sense of relationship and creates a distance that's not understood.

For bridge-building to work, people of color must be willing to speak the truth in love (see Eph. 4:15). Truth without love can be brutal, but love without truth is hypocrisy. Because whites are often "clueless" about how their actions are perceived by others, reconciliation demands sincere and loving honesty. Truthful and loving interaction produces understanding, clarifies misperceptions on both parts, and builds trust.

RACE FATIGUE

Failed attempts at cross-racial relationships produce a kind of race fatigue. Well-meaning white folks get quickly burned out because we're not appreciated and affirmed. We don't understand how deep the issues are. We know little about the history of minority groups and don't understand how their heritage affects them today. Our heritage often is not too significant. We conclude that our identity is "American." With that, we don't even think that our ancestors came by choice, seeking and getting a better way of life. When minority groups express that the "land of opportunity" and the "American dream" have not been their experiences, whites can't conceive of why not. It's not hateful or racist—it's just our perception of reality. Most of us determine "truth" through the grid of personal experience. Until our experiences teach us otherwise, we'll hold on to our perceptions as facts.

Many people of color say to me, "I get tired of educating white folks, especially when they don't want to be educated." I understand that. But I believe God is doing a new thing. Christian men's hearts are opening. We have much to teach each other, but it will take commitment with perseverance from both sides. The majority and minority Christian communities all could be justified to just quit and leave things the way they are. But God is calling us all to the table of brotherhood in Christ in unity and reconciliation. Will we respond to His call? Will we be faithful and pay the price? Will you men of color stay with us until we can get our education and sensitivity about people of color and start responding in new and meaningful ways? We pray that you will. We need your help.

(Adapted from *Break Down the Walls* workbook by Raleigh Washington, Glen Kehrein, and Claude V. King [Chicago: Moody Press, 1997].)

Taking the
Next Step

by Phillip Porter and Gordon England

Why in the world did Promise Keepers select "racial and denominational barriers" when it focused on Christian unity? The primary reason is our sense that the Lord led us to embrace this truth. We must be obedient.

Alone we can't change much; you can't, either. But together, with a million other brothers—committed Promise Keepers—we can influence a nation. We can demonstrate that what history, the political process, and the legal system could not do, faith, obedience, repentance, and unity in Jesus Christ can change.

The body of Christ is different from the culture in general. The world system is not designed to conform to the will of God. As citizens of all races, we should hope for respect, dignity, and opportunity for one another. But the body of Christ is called to a higher standard—not mere tolerance, but love such as Christ has for you.

Consider this: Whoever loves God must also love his brother (see 1 John 4:19–21). The Bible is clear about that. What does it mean? We might say that it is impossible truly to love Jesus Christ more than we love the man we love the least! Now, that's a sobering thought.

Perhaps our own journey will encourage you. Both of us are in ministry in the Denver area, Phil as a bishop in his denomination and chairman of the board for Promise Keepers, Gordon as pastor and Promise Keepers staff member. However, we'd never met prior to a planning meeting for a Concert of Prayer. During our time of discussion, Phil, a black man, was asked to give his testimony. He told about coming to southern Colorado to take a job as a social worker in 1959. He was fresh out of Phillips University in Oklahoma with a letter confirming his job. But his employer was shocked when he arrived. The agency was unaware that Phillips had any black students. "There's no job here for you!" he was told. Too hurt and ashamed to return to Oklahoma, Phil took a bus to Denver, where he got a job as a cook in order to provide for his family.

Gordon, who is white, had known many blacks but had never met a person of Phil's stature who, in abject honesty, had divulged such pain, yet with a loving spirit. When Phil finished his testimony, it seemed only appropriate for Gordon to apologize for that wrong and to ask for forgiveness on behalf of those from Gordon's race who had sinned against Phil. The meeting ended with tears and prayer, and the forging of a brotherhood had begun.

Does it really matter whether Christian men are seeking unity? We think the importance is clear from Jesus' prayer in John 17: Those who are His must be one, even as God the Father and Jesus the Son are one. It is this unity, Jesus said, that will show the world the reality of God's love.

As someone has said, the idea of unity is to create a salad, not a stew. God has made a world of people different from one another, even within denominational and ethnic groups. Gender, age, personality, ability, physical characteristics, appearance, talent, and interests are but a few of the specific points of diversity.

Some people say they don't see color. But unless they're blind, they're probably trying to be nice and say race is not an issue. In either case, they're wrong. For example, the authors of this chapter, Phil Porter and Gordon England, are different racially. Both are okay, both are unique, but clearly they are not the same. Yet each adds flavor to the body of Christ. Lettuce, tomatoes, cucumbers, and bell peppers are all different in appearance, taste, and texture, but all are good together in a salad. If this is hard to accept, run all your food through the blender for a month and you'll get the point.

Okay, then, what do we do? If we're convinced that God desires unity among all believers, each of us needs to reach out to brothers who are of different denominational or ethnic backgrounds. How do we go about this? We suggest four things.

1. Relationships with brothers begin in the heart.

Reaching out begins with conviction by God's Spirit about sin in our attitudes and behavior. Sin is not ethnically specific. We all have probably, at some time, experienced hate, bad attitudes, or even just the emotional scum of feeling somehow better than another. That needs to be dealt with. Recognize it. Admit it. Confess it to the Lord. Then confess it to any we have specifically sinned against.

Gordon didn't have to ask for Phil's forgiveness that day they met. Gordon didn't personally offend Phil thirty years earlier. However, Gordon recognized the pain of that experience, and in the interest of building a bridge and helping to heal the hurt of his new friend, he bore the burden of Phil's pain and asked for forgiveness. That act was the beginning of their fellowship. It was an act of humility that opened the door to healing and relationship.

Repentance is an active choice we can each make. We can choose to acknowledge the reality of historic sin and the ongoing existence of prejudice in every ethnic group. The fact that others are also "to blame" does not lessen our responsibility to hear from the Lord and to deal, as He convicts us, with our part. For example, I (Gordon) was raised in a home that had little classic bigotry, but during the past fifty years, I've heard innumerable ethnic jokes. A small percentage were clever and funny, but the vast majority had a demeaning, derogatory, and hurtful twist.

What could possibly motivate men to repeat those jokes? There are plenty of other good stories available. I must admit—perhaps you will also—that if you degrade another person or group, you take yourself off the hook to treat them well. But that's certainly not the Golden Rule—treating others as you'd want to be treated.

As a young black man of about fifteen growing up in Enid, Oklahoma, I (Phillip) remember an experience that taught me about forgiveness. My father and I had gone into a grocery store some distance from the "Negro" district, as it was called then. As my dad bent down to look at an item on a bottom shelf, a man came up behind him and kicked him—a solid boot! Dad was a good-sized man, and I was already well developed and a successful boxer. When Dad was kicked, I was shocked but waited to see what he would do. He straightened up slowly and deliberately, then turned toward the assailant, who blurted out that he had wanted to "kick his butt" for a long time. I could feel myself getting angry. I was ready to square off with the guy. After all, my dad and I were both there; we could put a hurt on this guy.

But Dad, a "tent-making" pastor, looked the guy straight on with strength and poise and said, "As long as you're a white man and I'm a black man, don't you ever do that again." Then he turned to me and said, "No! We're going," and we walked out together to the car. There Dad told me that guys like that didn't see us as people. They were ignorant and afraid. We could be angry and bitter, or we could forgive them because they didn't know what they were doing. We could leave that hurt with God. He would take the offense and leave us free in our spirit. Over my years as a pastor, I've often reflected on the same words of forgiveness our Savior spoke concerning His tormentors.

The result of repentance, apology, forgiveness requested, and forgiveness granted is a reconciled relationship.

2. Relationship is a process.

The process of building a relationship across old barriers is a "going deeper" kind of experience. It moves from the surface, the generalizations, to the specific; from the comfortable, good feelings of initial obedience to understanding and, through understanding, to the pain of the other. To accept a trip into another's pain willingly seems masochistic or stupid. However, it is a precursor to blessing. Just as the apostle Paul called us to be identified with the suffering of Christ, he also promised that we will share in His glory.

To develop a truly open, reconciled relationship—be it with a man of a different race, your wife, a child, or any other person—is to be personally and spiritually enlarged. This is the basis of the interdependency of the body of Christ. Conversely, in isolation we are incomplete. We are joined to the Head, Jesus Christ, but we are missing body parts.

Several years ago, a friend of Gordon's suffered a stroke that left him paralyzed on the left side. He said it was as if he had lost his arm and leg—in fact maybe worse, because he still had to carry them around but they would not function. Through bold, tenacious discipline in therapy and the prayers of family and the church, however, he was restored to nearly full function. The pleasure and excitement to this man of effectively "adding an arm and a leg" was thrilling.

Reconciliation can bring us the same kind of joy as we experience all the parts of Christ's body. Jesus modeled this when "for the joy set before him [He] endured the cross" (Heb. 12:2).

Can you be a bridge builder? Many Promise Keepers are currently asking that question. The answer is that you can have a part. If your spirit is saying "Yes!" you fit the first category of bridge builders—those who demonstrate a heart for others.

If you aren't sure how to start, you might begin with a Promise Keepers event—perhaps a breakfast—where you can meet men of different denominations and cultures in your community.

Some of the men from my (Gordon's) suburban, largely white church meet with a group from a couple of inner-city churches. This has become meaningful to our guys and, I hope, also to the men from the inner city. At one of the early Saturday-morning sessions, we were still introducing ourselves, talking of our families or our jobs. Then a man named John from our group quietly and honestly said, "I'm trying to learn some new skills and get back into the job market." He had been out of work since defense-industry cutbacks eliminated his job. When he said he was unemployed, every inner-city guy turned toward him. It seemed there were surprise and immediate support for him—surprise that a sharp, professional-looking white guy could be unemployed, and support because even though this guy didn't have a job, he still would get up early and drive into the city to show he had a heart to be a bridge builder.

The process of building relationships will also be aided if you or others in your group already have cross-cultural experience. This may have been through a job, the military, athletics, or a college roommate. The value of this exposure is not that it makes you a cultural expert, but it probably showed you that others don't see you the same way you see yourself or your cultural tradition. It informs you of others and of the inaccuracies of your perceptions.

Traveling and living in other places also facilitate bridge building. Just being where things are different or seeing situations through fresh eyes will increase a person's willingness to accept different ways of doing things. (We all tend to think that if our way isn't the only way, at least it's the best way.)

When we change our perspective, we open ourselves to the possibility that our world may have been too small. We realize that our prejudice was unfounded or at least not well founded. To lead in bridge building, we need to be open to learning and expanding our horizons.

The ability to speak a second language will also help in bridge building. Language and culture are not the same, but many nuances of culture are reflected in the idioms of the language. This is another key to expanded perspective. It may be a tool, too, for direct and meaningful communication in another person's native tongue.

Yes, you can be a bridge builder if you have a heart for others. And it will help if you have experience cross-culturally, have traveled or lived in other places, are married to a person of a different ethnic background, or speak a second language. Jesus was a bridge builder from heaven to earth—He became a man, spoke our language, and is calling for Himself a bride out of every tongue, nation, and tribe.

3. Develop a plan.

The cliché that says, "People don't plan to fail, they just fail to plan" is true with groups as well as individuals. Planning is essential in groups, because without a plan, it's impossible to share the vision and get people to become involved.

Prayer is the single most important part of the plan. Activists would say, "Never mind, let the elderly women pray. We need to be involved!" But we say, "Not so fast." People have been trying to fix through natural means a problem that started in sin. Separation and alienation go clear back to Genesis 3.

Prayer and reconciliation are the two greatest needs of the church. The lack of prayer robs us of the power of God. The absence of reconciliation robs the church of the power of unity! To break down the barriers of historic sin, both the sin of racism and the sin of resentment, we need God's power. So start the plan with prayer. Pray first for passion and commitment, then pray for conviction and repentance.

This initial step will make you ready to start involving others of differing backgrounds. It's probably best for your group to reach out to one other group. Caution! Don't go any further until you start to build relationships. Don't set an agenda other than that you want to establish a relationship based in the Lord Jesus Christ and with a goal of being reconciled to Christian brothers. Do not set an activity agenda or a five-year plan—yet.

Make it your pattern to do things *with* one another, not for, to, or in spite of one another. The early period of relationship building needs to be for getting acquainted, building trust, and letting personal bonding occur. As Christian man to Christian man, start praying together. Pray for each other and for one another's families. Pray for direction in the shared relationship.

Also, have some fun! Eat together, go to a ball game, or whatever. The relationship needs to be real and broad and touch several areas of life, not just church. When a sense of loyalty and interest is developing on both sides of the ethnic aisle, then it's time to start doing further planning. When what started as "oughta" turns to "wanta," you know you're on track.

What makes a relationship grow? Keeping at it. Phil observes about Gordon that "he keeps comin' at ya" and doesn't give up. That tenacity works both ways. Just recently, when we had been apart for about three weeks due to travel and business in our churches, Phil called Gordon just to see how he was doing. No needs, no projects, no advice, just a brother affirming another out of mutual love.

Humor is a must! All guys will make mistakes, and it's wonderful to be able to lighten up a bit with each other. This is especially helpful when you're wrong. Phil laughs with Gordon (he could laugh at him often) when he blows it. It's easy to think you know how the other guy or all people of the other race feel. Your brother may realize that you're off base and don't have a clue. Humor can open up the conversation, kindly removing your foot from your mouth.

Prayer has been a vital part of our friendship. Prayer is a vulnerable activity. In sincerity, if you strip away all pretense before God, you can also be real with one another. We pray together about our kids, our churches, and Promise Keepers. It's not always convenient—we live across the city from one another. But when we pray together, the bond grows between us, and the motivation to pray for each other increases when we're apart.

Understanding will help break down fear or stereotyping. A great resource can be books on the subject of reconciliation. Tapes by key leaders are good discussion starters. Relaxed dialogue will allow individuals in both groups to gain insight. People in both groups will learn not only from the other group's insight, but also from hearing members of their own group speak.

If the opportunity affords itself, your new cross-racial group may choose to take on a project related to one of the churches or perhaps reaching out to help someone else. There is something very bonding about men working together. Often we let down our guard and become more vulnerable when laboring alongside someone else.

Keep the relationship-building issue on the front burner, but don't be in a hurry! Each person is starting at a different place of readiness. Plan periodic opportunities for new men to become involved, but reduce the walk-in, walk-out syndrome as much as possible.

4. Be ready to change and to give generously as you learn.
Reading the story of Zacchaeus in Luke 19, you wonder what Paul Harvey would say if he told the rest of the story! Zacchaeus was a sinner according to both the crowd around him and Jesus. His scam was exploiting his countrymen for personal gain. As if Roman rule wasn't bad enough for a Jewish businessman, here was a turncoat who would collect all he could get from the victimized subject, give the government only what he had to, and pocket the rest.

Zacchaeus was rich, but he must have been empty inside. Somehow he overheard the truth about this prophet Jesus. His curiosity was so intense that he did a most unusual thing. This short but fully grown man climbed up a tree! Little boys climb trees when at play. Put it in our terms—a collection agent pulls his Lexus over to the curb, jumps up to grab a branch, and still in his three-piece suit, pulls himself up so he can look over the crowd surrounding a street preacher as it moves down the avenue toward him.

It didn't take a lot of preaching on Jesus' part, perhaps none, to convince Zacchaeus of his need. Maybe it was the truth that another person had told him about this Jesus and His call for mercy and justice. That truth may have been like the statement of Billy Graham for us that racism is the greatest sin of our land. Anyway, he was ready to respond. He had a change of heart. From his personal greed, he addressed others' needs.

The poor—do you care about them? Do you see them as a nuisance and maybe even like nonpeople? Zacchaeus gave 50 percent of what he had! Give us a break! Did you notice that the tax collector didn't even stop to see if he could get an IRS deduction? For some of us, that's not a change of heart, that's a cardiac arrest! Then he paid restitution for the wrong he had done. He was speaking about individual people he had ripped off. He knew who they were and what he had taken. He doubtless had two sets of books.

How does that fit the modern American scene? We submit that the ripoff we can all identify is the lack of access to the economic mainstream for inner-city minorities. We're not talking about charity, welfare, or the dole. But what would happen if every Christian man who had the power or opportunity would take a man outside the economic loop and pull him in? Mentor, help, affirm, guide, and in every way possible ensure that the one who had been denied an opportunity got a chance to succeed? Do you think that person would also be interested in knowing our Jesus?

This "Zacchaean" pattern of sin to repentance, greed to need, and restitution for wrong puts substance to the words of James 2:18: "I will show you my faith by what I do."

Rather than try to rationalize or skirt around it, a man of integrity will say, "Yes, I see it. I'll repent in my heart, ask God for forgiveness, and ask for forgiveness from my ethnic brother."

Forgiveness is an unconditional choice! And it's God's call to those who have been offended; they can decide to be obedient to the Lord Jesus and forgive. This forgiveness is not based on preconditions. It's also not based on assumed future favor. It doesn't even depend on the offending party's desire to be reconciled, but rather on the offended party's desire to live openly before the Lord and not be burdened with the weight of unresolved sin or the sin of resentment.

That's what it's all about. Take the risk! Step out in prayer and faith, and see what God will do as you obey and the body of Christ is unified.

 **In the Life**

# of One Community

Modesto, California, is a city of fewer than two hundred thousand that has grown around an agricultural base of almonds, grapes, and alfalfa. Though folks seem reluctant to put a name to it, something big is happening. "Names sometimes limit us," a Modesto church worker explained. "They give us the impression we have arrived at our goals. We don't want to make that mistake. This is a beginning. We want people to continue to strive rather than celebrate a premature victory."

Amid the almond blossoms and walnut groves, surrounded by vineyards, orchards, and fields, a new crop is growing. Seeds of reconciliation, watered by faith and tended in unity, promise to bring forth a new harvest of Christian renewal.

In June 1996, five thousand men from the Modesto area traveled seventy miles to attend the Promise Keepers conference in Oakland, California. Led by their pastors, these five thousand men from myriad churches and a variety of ethnic backgrounds chose to lay aside their denominational identities and affiliate themselves with a greater body, a body that expresses the unity they are working to achieve. Most of their contingent came to Oakland sporting T-shirts that proclaimed the spirit of the movement now taking place. The off-white shirts carried a brightly colored logo that read, "The Church of Modesto."

And what is "The Church of Modesto"? It's nothing more and nothing less than men and women breaking down the walls of race and crashing through denominational barriers to seek the face of God. It's people making conscious efforts to disregard economic standing and pray for and with one another. It's a group of believers standing together as a part of the united body of the Lord Jesus Christ. Although they don't meet in a single building, they have agreed to meet with the single purpose of glorifying God.

What brought the community of Modesto to this place of renewal and promise? In January 1994, at the invitation of David Seifert, pastor of Big Valley Grace Community Church and president of the Greater Modesto Area Ministerial Association (GMMA), fifty-three pastors joined together to attend a prayer summit. At a coastal mountain retreat, these leaders spent four days fasting, praying, and seeking God's will.

"There was often a competitive spirit between pastors up until that point," says Pastor Wade Estes of First Baptist, Modesto. "I don't know about other communities, but I would guess we were pretty much the same. There was some ill will between members and former members of congregations. It wasn't necessarily that anyone was speaking badly about another. It was more like, 'You do your thing, and I'll do mine.'"

Many pastors came to the prayer summit with their own individual agendas. But on the final day, the group broke up into smaller units to answer the question, "What does God want us to do?" Each returned with the same conclusion: Meet with Him regularly and pray.

To some, the idea seemed almost frightening. "With our busy schedules, who has time to meet apart from his own church every week to pray with a group of pastors?" Nevertheless, the group entered into a covenant, agreeing to meet each Wednesday at high noon for prayer and accountability. In the first year, the men met fifty of fifty-two weeks, taking time off only during the Christmas holidays. A second prayer summit the following year brought more than seventy pastors, and the group's numbers continued to climb.

Today, it's not at all unusual for one hundred men of God to meet for the regular Wednesday prayer session. Visitors come from throughout the area, hoping to see something they can take back to their own communities, and members rarely miss a meeting. As Pastor Seifert put it, "If the men are in town, they know where they need to be."

What does a GMMA meeting look like? The pastors enter the meeting hall one, two, or three at a time, shaking hands and exchanging the normal pleasantries. At precisely 12:00, a worship leader's solo voice sings out in praise and is immediately joined by the entire assembly in a chorus of "There's Something About That Name."

Another pastor opens the session in prayer: "Lord, we relinquish all other thoughts right now. We put everything else aside for this moment. Though we've been working for You today, maybe we haven't really stopped to worship You. We focus in right now; nothing else is worthy of our attention. You are everything."

Clearly, it's the intent of the "Associate Pastors of the Church of Modesto" (as they call themselves) to seek the face of God. In the process, they put aside minor doctrinal differences and make concerted efforts to achieve an ethnic diversity that mirrors the city's demographics. They model a lifestyle of reconciliation for their flocks.

But what of the congregations? Have the efforts of their pastors filtered through to the men and women of the greater Modesto area?

Yes! In the spring of 1996, more than fifteen hundred men, women, and children met at the railroad tracks in Modesto as an outward sign of reconciliation. "The tracks," according to Wade Estes, "were long seen as dividing the city along ethnic and economic lines. They were viewed as a spiritual barrier the Christian community needed to overcome." A ribbon running some length of the tracks symbolized the division among both the churches and the people of Modesto. After the occasion was dedicated with prayer, the ribbon was cut and Christians from both sides of town crossed over their own spiritual barrier—to unite in fellowship. The believers then walked to a nearby church and held a community service.

Possibly the greatest evidence of God's work in the hearts of Modesto's people occurred during the heat of the summer. On July 7, more than eight thousand people braved the early evening heat to attend a rally targeted at chipping away racial and denominational walls. Backing up traffic for several miles, Christian families streamed to Johansen High School's football field to worship and hear Thomas Trask, general superintendent of the Assemblies of God, speak to the packed stadium.

Bearing a name borrowed from the 1996 Promise Keepers theme, "Break Down the Walls," the rally focused attention on diversity, rather than division. Shepherds challenged their flocks to celebrate the common bond shared through faith in Jesus Christ. Pastors greeted the assembly in several languages, including English, Spanish, Cambodian, and Hindi.

Acknowledging the efforts of the congregations to see beyond home-church boundaries, leaders asked their people to look ahead and contemplate the existence of God's church in an even broader scope, beyond Modesto and San Joaquin County and outside the state of California.

That evening, The Church of Modesto also took an offering, not for their rally and not for the needs of the local community, but for two predominantly black churches among those burned in the recent arson fires plaguing the South. More than $25,000 came from the heart of this congregation to help rebuild facilities in Corinth and Kassuth, Mississippi.

If tentative plans are any indication, the future looks bright for The Church of Modesto. While some worry that the path to diversity can go too far and fear trading a truthful presentation of the gospel for ecumenical harmony, that appears extremely unlikely to the GMMA members. "First and foremost, we profess salvation through faith in the resurrected Christ," declares Pastor Charlie Crane of Greater True Light Baptist Church. "That isn't negotiable."

Has revival come to Modesto, California? No one there makes that claim. This is by no means a completed work, they insist. But many pray for God to bring revival to their city, and they desire to lay a solid foundation for that day.

Still, in many ways, one might contend that revival is already stirring in this valley town. After all, when you get right down to it, it's not the stadium events or large rallies that indicate the heart of

Christian Modesto. It's the smaller, more individual happenings—men seeking to glorify God through one-on-one relationships beyond racial and denominational lines and families fulfilling their neighbors' needs out of love for their Savior. It's Pastor Krueger of Grace Lutheran Church noticing that another congregation's piano is out of tune and making a gift of having that piano tuned.

It's summed up by the banner adorning the front of Dry Creek Evangelical Free Church that reads, "The Church within the Church of Modesto."

(Adapted from G. Ron Darbee, "Walls Came Down in Modesto" *New Man,* vol. 3, no. 8 [November/December 1996]: 36-40. Used by permission.)

A MAN AND HIS WORLD

A Promise Keeper is committed to influencing his world, being obedient to the Great Commandment (see Mark 12:30–31) and the Great Commission (see Matt. 28:19–20).

The Greatest
Power Ever Known

by Bill Bright

Two gifted attorneys had great professional animosity, even hatred, for one another. Even though they were distinguished members of the same firm, they were constantly criticizing and making life miserable for each other.

Then one of them came to Christ through our ministry, and some months later he asked me for counsel. "I have hated and criticized my partner for years," he said, "and he has been equally antagonistic toward me. But now that I'm a Christian, I don't feel right about continuing our warfare. What do I do?"

"Why not ask your partner to forgive you and tell him you love him?" I suggested.

"I could never do that!" he said. "That would be hypocritical! I don't love him. How could I tell him I love him when I don't?"

That lawyer had put his finger squarely on one of the great challenges of the Christian life. On the one hand, everybody wants to be loved. Most psychologists agree that man's greatest need is to love and be loved. No barrier can withstand the mighty force of love. On the other hand, however, so many people never experience love. And many people don't know how to express it—especially to those with whom they're in conflict. But early in my walk with God, I made an exciting spiritual discovery that has enriched my life and the lives of tens of thousands of others. By learning and applying these truths, you, too, can discover the life-changing power of love. It is a principle I call "How to Love by Faith."

FIVE TRUTHS ABOUT LOVE

There are three Greek words translated into the one English word *love: eros,* which suggests sensual desire and does not appear in the New Testament; *phileo,* which is used for friendship or love of one's friends or relatives and conveys a sense of loving someone because he is worthy of love; and *agape,* which is God's supernatural, unconditional love for you revealed supremely through our Lord's death on the cross for your sins. It is the supernatural love He wants to produce in you and through you to others by His Holy Spirit. *Agape* love is given because of the character of the person loving rather than because of the worthiness of the object of that love. Sometimes it is love "in spite of" rather than "because of."

How does this kind of love express itself? The apostle Paul gave us an excellent description:

> Love is patient, love is kind. It does not envy, it does not boast, it is not proud. It is not rude, it is not self-seeking, it is not easily angered, it keeps no record of wrongs. Love does not delight in evil but rejoices with the truth. It always protects, always trusts, always hopes, always perseveres. Love never fails. (1 Cor. 13:4–8)

Later Paul admonished, "Let love be your greatest aim" (1 Cor. 14:1, TLB). There are five vital truths about love that will help you understand the basis for loving by faith.

1. God loves you unconditionally.
God loves with *agape,* the love described in 1 Corinthians 13. His love is not based on performance. Christ loves you so much that while you were yet a sinner, He died for you (see Rom. 5:8).

The parable of the prodigal son illustrates God's continuing unconditional love for His children. A man's younger son asked his father for his share of the family estate, packed up his belongings, and took a trip to a distant land, where he wasted all his money on parties and prostitutes. About the time that his money was gone, a great famine swept over the land, and he began to starve. He finally came to his senses and realized his father's hired men at least had food to eat. So he decided to return home, admit he had sinned, and ask for a job.

While he was on the road and still a long distance away, his father saw him and was filled with loving pity. He ran to his son, embraced him, and kissed him. Just as the son started to make his confession, his father interrupted to instruct the servants to prepare a celebration! His lost child had repented and come home, and he was lovingly restored to full status as a son.

Even when you are disobedient like the prodigal son, God continues to love you, waiting for you to respond to His love and forgiveness.

Just how much does He love you? Jesus once prayed to the Father, "... so that the world will know you sent me and will understand *that you love them as much as you love me*" (John 17:23, TLB, emphasis added). Think of it! God loves you as much as He loves His only begotten Son, the Lord Jesus. What a staggering, overwhelming truth to comprehend! In fact, such love is beyond our ability to grasp with the mind, but it is not beyond our ability to experience with our hearts.

2. You are commanded to love.

On one occasion, a teacher of the law came to Jesus and asked, "Of all the commandments, which is the most important?"

Jesus replied, "'Love the Lord your God with all your heart and with all your soul and with all your mind and with all your strength.' The second is this: 'Love your neighbor as yourself.' There is no commandment greater than these" (Mark 12:28–31).

Jesus also said, "There is a saying, 'Love your *friends* and hate your enemies.' But I say: Love your *enemies!* Pray for those who *persecute* you! In that way you will be acting as true sons of your Father in heaven. . . . If you love only those who love you, what good is that? Even scoundrels do that much" (Matt. 5:43–46, TLB).

When Christians begin to act like Christians and love God, their neighbors, their enemies, and especially their Christian brothers—regardless of color, race, or class—we will see in our time, as in the first century, a great transformation in the whole of society. People will marvel when they observe our love in the same way people marveled when they observed those first-century believers, saying, "How they love one another" (see Acts 2:44–47).

At one time in my Christian life, I was troubled over the command to love God and others so completely. How could I ever measure up to such a high standard? Two important considerations have helped me a great deal. First, I found the assurance in the Bible that God has already given us what we need: "We know how dearly God loves us, and we feel this warm love everywhere within us because God has given us the Holy Spirit to fill our hearts with his love" (Rom. 5:5, TLB).

Second, by meditating on the attributes of God and the wonderful things He has done and is doing for me, I find my love for Him growing. I love Him because He first loved me.

As for loving others, when we are vitally yoked to Christ and walking in the Spirit, loving God with all our hearts, souls, and minds, we will fulfill His command to love others as ourselves. The apostle Paul explained just how wise this command is:

If you love your neighbor as much as you love yourself you will not want to harm or cheat him, or kill him or steal from him. And you won't sin with his wife or want what is his, or do anything else the Ten Commandments say is wrong. All ten are wrapped up in this one, to love your neighbor as you love yourself. Love does no wrong to anyone. That's why it fully satisfies all of God's requirements. It is the only law you need. (Rom. 13:9–10, TLB)

Love is also a sure sign of our discipleship. "All men will know that you are my disciples, if you love one another," Jesus said (John 13:35). Our doctrine should be sound. Our faith should be strong. But neither is a sign or testimony to the world of our discipleship. Only love is.

3. You cannot love in your own strength.

Just as surely as "those who are in the flesh cannot please God," so in your own strength you cannot love as you ought. How many times have you resolved to love someone? How often have you tried to manufacture some kind of positive, loving emotion toward another person for whom you felt nothing? It's impossible, isn't it?

By nature, people are not patient and kind. We are jealous, envious, and boastful. We are proud, haughty, selfish, and rude, and we demand our own way. We could never love others the way God loves us!

4. You can love with God's love.
It was God's kind of love that brought you to Christ. It is this kind of love that is able to sustain and encourage you each day. Through His love in you, you can bring others to Christ and minister to fellow believers as God has commanded.

How does this love enter your life? It becomes yours the moment you receive Jesus Christ and the Holy Spirit comes to indwell you. The Scripture says the "fruit of the Spirit is love" (Gal. 5:22). In other words, when you are controlled by the Spirit, one of the ways His presence is demonstrated is by an outpouring of *agape* love in your life.

Now, this may all sound good in theory, but how do you make God's love a practical reality in your experience? By resolutions? By self-imposed discipline? No. The only way to do it is explained in my final point.

5. You love by faith.
Everything about the Christian life is based on faith. You love by faith just as you received Christ by faith, just as you are filled with the Holy Spirit by faith, and just as you walk by faith.

But if the fruit of the Spirit is love, as we just saw, you may logically ask, "Isn't it enough to be filled with the Spirit?" That's true from God's point of view, but it will not always be true in your actual experience.

Many Christians have loved with God's love without consciously or specifically claiming it by faith. Yet, without being aware of the fact, they were, indeed, loving by faith. Hebrews 11:6 reminds us that "without faith it is impossible to please God." Clearly, then, there is no demonstration of God's love where there is no faith.

How, then, do we love by faith in a practical way? It works like this:

We know God has commanded us to love. We also know He promised in 1 John 5:14–15 that if we ask anything according to His will, He hears and will answer us. So we ask according to His command (His will), and then we receive His love by faith according to His promise, knowing His promises are always true. Let me illustrate how this happens.

In one case, I was having trouble loving a fellow staff member. I wanted to love him, and I knew I was commanded to do so. But because of certain inconsistencies and personality differences, I found it difficult. Then the Lord reminded me of 1 Peter 5:7: "Let him have all your worries and cares, for he is always thinking about you and watching everything that concerns you" (TLB). So I decided to give the problem to Him and love the man by faith—to act lovingly toward him regardless of my feelings, depending on God's love and strength within.

An hour later, I received a letter from that very man, who had no possible way of knowing what I had just decided. In fact, his letter had been written the day before. The Lord had foreseen the change in me. This friend and I met that afternoon and had the most wonderful time of prayer and fellowship we had ever experienced together.

One evening in Chicago, I spoke to a crowded room of more than thirteen hundred college students. They seemed to hang on every word as I explained how to love by faith. Early the next morning, a young woman with sparkling eyes and face aglow came up to me and said, "My life changed last night. For many years I have hated my parents. I haven't seen them since I was seventeen, and now I am twenty-two. I left home as a result of a quarrel five years ago and haven't written or talked to them since, though they have tried repeatedly to contact and encourage me to return home. I determined that I would never see them again.

"A few months ago, I became a Christian. Last night you told me how to love my parents, and I could hardly wait to get out of that meeting and call them. I now really love them with God's kind of love, and I can hardly wait to see them!"

Remember the lawyer whose story began this chapter? After he protested that he couldn't love his critical partner, I explained how God commands His children to love even their enemies and that we love His way as a choice of the will, which we exercise by faith. I read to him the part of 1 Corinthians 13 quoted above. "You will note," I said, "that each of these descriptions of love is not an expression of the emotions but of the will."

Together we knelt to pray, and my friend asked God's forgiveness for his critical attitude toward his law partner and claimed God's love for him by faith.

Early the next morning, my friend walked into his partner's office and announced, "Something wonderful has happened to me. I've become a Christian, and I've come to ask you to forgive me for all I've done to hurt you in the past and to tell you that I love you."

The partner was so surprised and convicted of his own sin that he, too, asked for forgiveness and said, "I would like to become a Christian. Would you show me what I need to do?"

Other examples are endless. God has an infinite supply of His divine, supernatural *agape* love for each of us. It is for us to claim, to grow on, to spread to others, and thus to reach hundreds and thousands of others for Christ.

God's love is the greatest power in the universe. It changed the course of history. It can change our world today. It can revolutionize your family, your neighborhood, your workplace, and your church. Nothing—absolutely nothing—can overcome it.

I encourage you to make a list of everyone whom you do not like and begin today to love them by faith. Include those people who have hurt you in the past. Pray for them. Ask for eyes to see them as Christ sees them. Act lovingly toward them no matter how you feel. We don't love people because they deserve to be loved—we love them because Christ commands it and empowers us to do so. Your relationships will change as God's love in you overflows to others. Further, you will be a channel of God's own life and power into this needy world, and loving by faith, you will please your loving Master. The greatest force in the world is love!

# In Search of

the Good Samaritan

by Don Bartlette

In 1932, when I came into the world, two people welcomed me. They happened to be Native-American people and they happened to be poor. And because they were Native American and poor, my mother and father were not welcome in that small North Dakota village. So they lived up in the hills in a one-room log cabin.

My father helped my mother to deliver me. He was a tall man, a strong man, an athlete, a hunter. He longed for a son to share his life with. As he looked at my newborn face, my father put me down and turned away from me in anger. It was obvious that I was different, that I was malformed. My father noticed first that I had only half a nose, hanging on the left side of my face. Then my father noticed I had no upper lip. And when my father looked for the third time, he noticed a huge hole in the top of my mouth.

My mother and father had wanted many children, and when I was born, they needed a church. In that small community of seventeen hundred people, there were seven churches. My grandmother ran to town for help. And not one of these seven churches would come into the hills to help my family and me. So my grandmother found a doctor, a white doctor. He did not like our people. He knew we were poor and could not afford to pay him, but he was a church member and felt an obligation to come.

When he looked at me, the doctor threw up his hands and whispered to my mother, "Send him away. We don't want him in our town. He'll never talk. He'll never learn. Send him away now."

My father, a proud man, did not want a handicapped child and he began even then running away into a world we now call alcoholism—a world from which he never returned. But my mother was a beautiful Native-American woman, a woman who valued life—all life. My mother clasped me to herself, wanting me. She would never send me away.

When the doctor went back down into the community, he told the people that I was a freak Indian baby. When they heard I was handicapped, they came up in the hills, walked into our one-room log cabin and tore me away from my mother. Not wanting a child like me in their community, they sent me away to another community where the people wouldn't have me either. So they put me in a hospital.

Another doctor came to examine me, this time a man of compassion. He took the left part of my nose, pulled it over to the right side of my face, giving me a very flat nose for the first seventeen years of my life. He pulled my upper lip together, but didn't know what to do with the cavern in the top of my mouth. Then he sent me back to live with my mother and father.

For nine years, I wasn't allowed in the community. I wasn't allowed in a church. I wasn't allowed in a school. I wasn't allowed to have friends. For nine years, I grew up in a world of isolation, loneliness, hunger, and poverty. For nine years, I lived in a world of alcoholism, a one-room shack of child abuse.

My mother tried to protect me. She did her best to nourish me. Then the doctors found the hole in my heart. I developed problems in my legs and became even more handicapped. One day I felt a pain in my stomach—hunger. As a young Indian child, I went down into that small white community and found an isolated area at the dump ground where I saw people throwing away food. Out of extreme hunger, I picked up the food and pushed it down the hole in the roof of my mouth. The pain and hunger went away momentarily.

I began regular visits to the dump ground, and I found more: clothing, magazines, and newspapers. I wanted to learn. I wanted to read.

I wanted to understand. I wanted to be in school. But I was not allowed in school because of my disability—and because I happened to be Native American.

One day, when my mother came to the dump ground looking for me, she found me playing with the rats. Outraged, she took me to a parochial school that rejected me, so she took me directly to the public school. The children gathered around me, looking at me, laughing, and pointing at my flat nose. They called me names like "smelly Indian," taking me by my hair and hitting me. When one of the children spit all over my face, I ran into the school and the first-grade teacher locked me in a closet. The second-grade teacher would not allow me in her classroom. The third-grade teacher told the children not to play with me because I was mentally retarded. All three of these teachers went to church.

And when the children thought that I could not understand—and they knew I could not talk—they took me up into the hills. They tied me to a tree with my hands behind my back and hit me in the face repeatedly until the blood ran down on my shirt. They ran back to the school, laughing. They never told anybody what they had done to me. Nobody knew where I was until late that night when an old man—a homeless person—found me, untied the rope, and set me free.

And as I ran home that night, my alcoholic father was there. When he saw the blood on my shirt, my father went into a rage and began to beat me. He threw me against a wall and kicked me. Finally, I broke away from him and ran from my home to a small community near the Canadian border. There I broke into homes and churches and was labeled a juvenile delinquent.

The police found me and put me in jail. And—what I could not talk about for thirty-five years—two policemen took me by the hair that night, removed my clothing, and added sexual abuse to my hurt.

I began to hate my handicap. I began to hate my Native-American heritage. I began to hate white people. And as I remained in that jail, unable to speak, not one church came to the jail in my defense.

They sent me back home to my parents. My body was covered with bruises on the outside, but because I could not talk, I couldn't tell my parents about the bruises within. Being an angry man, a man of frustration, my father once again began to beat me with a large leather belt. Something inside me snapped. I could take it no longer. When my father fell asleep from the alcohol, I crawled over to the wall and took down my father's rifle. Thankfully, my mother saw what was happening and ran to knock the rifle out of my hand.

I was twelve years old at this point, and by God's grace, my life began to change. One person in that white community decided to take a risk. I don't mean to be offensive, but she was not the pastor of a church. She was not chairman of a board. She went to one of the seven churches, but unlike all of the others, she valued Native-American people. She valued handicapped people. She valued poor people.

She was a wealthy woman, a prominent member of that community. When she heard I could not talk and found out we were living in a one-room shack in poverty, she came into my life to help me. I'll never forget her. She was the first person ever to put her hand on mine without hurting me. She was the first white person to invite me into her home, give me food, clothe and shelter me. She showed me love when I didn't even know the meaning of the word.

When she saw me unable to chew my food, she put her hand in my mouth and taught me how to move my tongue. She taught me how to eat, how to read, and how to write. It was this woman who taught me all about personal grooming and personal hygiene. She taught me how to work and hired me to wash her car so I could make some money to buy my own clothing and toothpaste.

She took me back to the public school and they made fun of her, calling her an Indian lover. They told her not to bring me into her church, but it was this woman who first showed me a Bible. She encouraged me, challenged me, taught me, motivated me, accepted me, affirmed me, empowered me, and *loved* me. Year after year.

One night, she had me run home to visit my parents. They had just made some macaroni to eat. For the first time in front of my parents, I put the macaroni inside my teeth and began to chew. My parents realized for the first time how much this woman had taught me. They asked her if she could help even more.

She made arrangements for me to go to a large hospital in North Dakota where they gave me a new nose and a new upper lip. They also gave me new teeth. I was placed in a special program for handicapped children, where, with her help, I learned how to speak in the manner I now speak.

She went back to the community where I was born and prepared them for the change in me. It was through her efforts that I was able to get into the public schools. And with her help, Don Bartlette became the first Native-American handicapped student ever to graduate valedictorian of his high-school class!

With my new speech, I asked this woman why she cared about me. She opened the Word of God and began telling me about Jesus Christ. She told me I had a heavenly Father who loved me, whose Son came on earth and died for me.

I couldn't understand that as a teenager, but the white woman gave me a Bible of my own to read. When I was learning about the Bible, a man from our parochial church came into the hills. In front of my mother and me, he struck a match and burned the Bible that had been given to me.

And at that point, I decided I would never go into a church for the rest of my life. I went to a university and became a social worker, counselor, and educator. As I began working around the country, I began to hide my handicap and to run away from my heritage for fear of rejection.

Twenty-nine years ago, after I had hurt many, many white people, after I had kept the hate inside and shared it with people outside, after I had fought the church, I met another white woman. And as she came into my world, she met the white woman from my childhood.

My wife-to-be knew about survival. She valued people. She valued handicapped people. She valued minority people. She valued poor people. And, like the white woman in my childhood, she told me about Jesus Christ. Through the help of my wife, I took a risk and went to church. I could hardly believe what took place in that small congregation. The men welcomed me—hugging me, holding me, and accepting me. They taught me about the Word of God, invited me into their homes, and fellowshipped with me.

Through the ministry of the men in that church, I opened my heart and became a born-again believer in Jesus Christ! That was twenty-four years ago. My wife knew about the hurt and the hate buried inside me. Through her help and the help of that small evangelical church in Minnesota, I was encouraged to read the Word of God and to begin living a legacy of reconciliation.

With the love of Jesus in my heart and empowered by the Word of God, I went back to that small, white community where I was born. I went back to the seven churches. I went back to the teachers. I went back to the two policemen, the children—now adults—who had tied me to a tree. I went back to my father. I began forgiving them all. And as Christ loved me, I am free to let Him love through me.

The Great Commission

by Luis Palau

Lord, I promise to help fulfill the Great Commission in my world for Your glory.

It's a gutsy commitment to make, no question about it. It's not one to make lightly, flippantly, or without counting the cost.

But now is the time to re-evangelize America! And we men should lead the way—in our families, our churches, and our communities. I can think of no greater thrill than obeying the Lord in this area of personal involvement in and commitment to evangelism.

PEOPLE ARE SEARCHING

A few weeks ago, a successful businessman came to a Bible study I was leading. As I spoke about having the assurance of eternal life through faith in Jesus Christ, I noticed he had tears in his eyes.

On the way out, this man and I talked about the companies he owns. When the elevator stopped at the floor occupied by his investment company, he commented, "I have insurance, but no assurance."

Before parting, this gentleman agreed to have lunch with me. The next day, while we dined and talked, he understood at last that salvation is a gift from God, not something he needed to work hard to earn.

Right there in the restaurant, the man bowed his head, opened his heart, and prayed to receive Jesus as Savior. The transformation in his life was instantaneous. He finally had eternal life—and he knew it!

NO GREATER THRILL

Leading people to Christ is exciting! The miracle of winning someone to faith in Christ surpasses any thrill this world has to offer.

Have you had that experience yet?

If not, I urge you to consider the Lord's Great Commission anew as you continue reading this chapter.

God is calling you to be a Promise Keeper, a man of integrity. You know that. But have you grasped that the Lord is calling you to be a godly man who—as much as anything else—is committed to influencing his family, friends, neighbors, work associates, countrymen, and others around the world for Jesus Christ?

Incredible? Idealistic? Impossible? Listen to what the Lord Jesus said:

> All authority in heaven and on earth has been given to me. Therefore go and make disciples of all nations, baptizing them in the name of the Father and of the Son and of the Holy Spirit, and teaching them to obey everything I have commanded you. And surely I am with you always, to the very end of the age. (Matt. 28:18–20)

"Well, Luis," you may say, "I agree, the Lord does want us to help fulfill His Great Commission in our generation. It's just that, um, I suspect He's thinking more of using you than using me. After all, I certainly don't have the gift of evangelism."

Cut!

I don't see anything in the Great Commission about gifting or talent or ability or personality or even opportunity.

The Lord is clear: "You . . . and you . . . and you, I'm calling all of you men to go, make disciples."

It's not a matter of gift, it's a matter of obedience.

Lord, I promise to help fulfill Your Great Commission.
Will you?
It's not a matter of gift, it's a matter of heart.

HEART FOR THE WORLD

Thousands of godly men have helped fulfill the Great Commission throughout the world during the closing centuries of this millennium. How can we be like them?

I've studied that question and found the answer has little to do with method or technique. Some have preached before the masses, some in churches. Some have presented the gospel in small groups, mostly one-on-one. Most have used a combination of approaches. But that isn't what made them effective fishers of men.

What I've found is that the great "fishers of men" (Matt. 4:19) over the years all have shared ten distinctives that gave them a tremendous heart for the world. Both Scripture and church history speak to the importance of these distinctives that should shape every Christian man's heart and life:

- passion for those apart from Christ
- Christ-centered message
- holiness in every area of life
- vision to reach the great cities
- boldness to try new methods
- willingness to endure criticism
- commitment to a local church
- love for the whole body of Christ
- sacrificial financial giving
- seriousness about private prayer
- faithfulness to the end

Sounds like a Promise Keeper, doesn't it?

Unfortunately, today, the first distinctive listed above is sorely missing in our churches. So many lack any measure of concern for those who have not yet trusted Christ as Savior.

How's your heart? How can we sit around while so many press forward all that much closer to an eternity without Christ? For heaven's sake—if nothing else!—we must do something.

Almost all of us get nervous about witnessing. At least I do, even after all these years. But when we willingly obey the Lord, He uses us.

A WILLING HEART

Today, before another hour goes by, *let's look to the Lord and say, "Yes, I am willing to help fulfill Your Great Commission."* That's prerequisite to all else. Unless we're willing to say yes to the Lord in *every* area, there's no use pretending we're a Promise Keeper in any area of life, wouldn't you agree?

A PROFOUND MESSAGE

Second, *let's begin to take pride in the good news of Jesus Christ.* Like the apostle Paul, let's affirm, "I am not ashamed of the gospel." Why? "Because it is the power of God for the salvation of everyone who believes" (Rom. 1:16).

It's sick what pride the world takes in its debauchery and sin. As Promise Keepers, shouldn't we be all the more proud of the liberating, life-changing gospel of Christ?

What is the gospel? It's "For God so loved the world that he gave his one and only Son, that whoever believes in him shall not perish but have eternal life" (John 3:16).

The gospel is "that Christ died for our sins according to the Scriptures, that he was buried, that he was raised on the third day according to the Scriptures, and that he appeared to Peter, and then to the Twelve," and then to the five hundred (1 Cor. 15:3–6).

It's no more than those great truths, no less. It's simple enough for a child to understand, profound enough to amaze the most brilliant theologians.

Are we proud enough to share this good news with others?

A WORLD OF CONFUSION

Third, *let's gain a better understanding of those outside Christ.* To me, the word that best describes our society today is confusion. According to the latest Gallup polls, an astounding eight out of ten Americans claim to be Christians. But ask the average American to define what he or she means and you'll be in for a surprise. Here are some of the most popular myths about what makes someone a Christian:

- being born in America
- thinking positively
- living a good life
- attending church
- giving to others
- receiving a sacrament
- believing in God
- talking about Jesus
- praying
- reading the Bible

Those are all good things, but they're not good enough! Let's take God at His Word and not believe everything men tell us. Just because someone says he is a Christian doesn't mean he's right.

A MESSAGE FOR ALL MEN

Fourth, *let's remember the gospel isn't just for "nice" people.* When God calls us to become Promise Keepers, He is not calling us to shun those whose values, beliefs, and actions are diametrically opposed to ours (see 1 Cor. 5:9–10).

Moments before Westley Allan Dodd was executed by hanging at Washington State Penitentiary in 1993, the convicted serial child killer was given the customary opportunity for last words. Here was a man who had viciously abused and mutilated three young boys, a man who said he'd do it again, a man who said there was no hope he'd ever be released from the hideous darkness within his soul.

His final words came as a shock. "I was wrong when I said there was no hope, no peace," Dodd said from the gallows. "There is hope. There is peace. I have found both in the Lord Jesus Christ."

According to a reporter who witnessed the execution, the father of two of the boys murdered by Dodd "hissed quietly" when Dodd invoked Jesus Christ's name.

No one can fault this father for the hiss of contempt and skepticism. Until the last hours of his life, Dodd had shown no signs of remorse. If we're honest, we Promise Keepers will admit to the same skepticism when we hear that a Dodd or a General Noriega or, twenty years ago, a Charles Colson has turned to Jesus and found forgiveness. Though we proclaim otherwise—".Everyone who calls on the name of the Lord will be saved" (Rom. 10:13)—do we ever act as though the gospel is really only for nice people?

In reality, it's much harder for nice people to find salvation than it is for bad people. C. S. Lewis wrote: "There is even, when you come to think it over, a reason why nasty people might be expected to turn to Christ in greater numbers than nice ones. That was what people objected to about Christ during his life on earth: he seemed to attract 'such awful people.'"

Take Zacchaeus, for example. Jesus' encounter with that tax-gathering cheat was the context for His statement that the "Son of Man came to seek and to save what was lost" (Luke 19:10). When Jesus was invited to the home of Simon the Pharisee, "a woman who had lived a sinful life" wet His feet with her tears, wiped them with her hair, and poured perfume on them. Simon expected Jesus, if He were a prophet, to rebuke this woman of ill repute. Instead, Jesus said to her, "Your sins are forgiven" (Luke 7:37, 48; see 36–48).

Another tax collector, Levi, invited Jesus to a banquet at his home. The Pharisees complained to Jesus' disciples, "Why do you eat and drink with tax collectors and 'sinners'?"

Jesus answered, "It is not the healthy who need a doctor, but the sick. I have not come to call the righteous, but sinners to repentance" (Luke 5:29–32).

Scripture is filled with "who would have thought?" conversions, including a fair number of skeptics. Saul of Tarsus was "a blasphemer and a persecutor and a violent man" (1 Tim. 1:13). Ananias wondered if such a man could ever be changed by grace, let alone overnight. But even "the worst of sinners" was shown mercy. In this context, the apostle Paul could write, "Here is a trustworthy saying that deserves full acceptance: Christ Jesus came into the world to save sinners—of whom I am the worst" (1 Tim. 1:15).

If it seems that grace is being pushed to the limit in rescuing child killers, drug traffickers, and those who vigorously oppose us, we haven't begun to fathom God's ocean of grace and mercy. Nor have we peered long enough into our own hearts.

Years ago, I met a Methodist minister who worked in the inner city of Bristol, England. Asked what he did there, he replied, "I minister to the last, the least, the lonely, and the lost." That was precisely the mission of Jesus.

How often we hear the testimony, "If God can save me, He can save anybody." Yes, He can and does. Together, let's ask God to save the not-so-nice people we meet in our neighborhoods, schools, workplaces, and marketplaces.

A LOST WORLD AROUND US

As well, *let's embark on out-and-out evangelism here in America, before it's too late.* In a 1993 *Time* magazine cover story on "Kids, Sex & Values," a high-school teacher in New York City said teenagers' lives are "empty, and their view of the future fatalistic." One nineteen-year-old said, "I believe in God. If he wants something bad to happen to me, it will happen. Anyway, by the time I get AIDS I think they'll have a cure."

Lakewood, California, was shaken not long ago by the teen sex scandal of the "Spur Posse," whose boastful members tallied their conquests of adolescent girls. As alarming as their behavior, however, was the "boys will be boys" condoning by some parents. The director of research at the University of Minnesota's adolescent-health-training program told *Newsweek* magazine, "What we see is what's in the society at large."

What else does society hold? Some 1.6 million elective abortions last year. More than a million out-of-wedlock births. Broken families. Brutal violence on the streets and in the media. Drug addiction.

America needs Promise Keepers committed to evangelism like never before. Billy Graham once said, "It's either back to the Bible or back to the jungle." The jungle truly is creeping up on the United States. Theologian Carl F. H. Henry put it this way: "The barbarians are coming." Dr. Henry could see that without a wave of evangelization that converts hundreds of thousands of people to Jesus Christ, barbarians are going to take over the land—not foreigners, but our own unrepentant children and grandchildren.

The problem is in the heart, not just the outward behavior. God says, "The heart is deceitful above all things, and desperately wicked" (Jer. 17:9, KJV). What's needed is not more good advice but the good news—"the power of God for the salvation of everyone who believes."

Political campaigns, family counseling, and education do nothing about the inner condition of human depravity. Unless there's a change of heart, nothing has happened to change a person. And unless millions of hearts are changed, little has happened to change America.

The United States today is similar to eighteenth-century England, which also was in a disastrous moral condition. The slave trade was at its worst. A barbarous prison system entertained the public with outdoor hangings. Gambling was a national obsession—one historian said England was a vast casino. Drinking gin dominated English men and boys. False rumors manipulated the financial markets.

Likewise, the national church and its pulpit were in decay. Zeal for Christ was considered highly dangerous. Twenty percent of the clergy were dismissed, victims of an anti-Puritan purge. Bishop George Berkeley wrote at the time, "It is to be feared that the age of monsters is not far off."

The stage was set for John and Charles Wesley, George Whitefield, and the young men at Oxford known as the Holy Club. They made what we would call today a mission statement. It said, "We want to reform the nation, particularly the church, and to spread scriptural holiness over the land." And beginning with that small group of committed men, evangelistic action changed the nation, perhaps sparing England the kind of revolution that bloodied France.

God alone knows what awaits an unrepentant America. Yes, it is time to re-evangelize America. Only the gospel gets at the root of the problems destroying the nation:

A spirit of despondency. Many people have lost hope. They need a positive message of God's love, of what Christ can do for broken families, the lonely, the addicted, the dying.

A spirit of separatism. We've got to get over this business of being hyphenated Americans. My passport doesn't say Hispanic-American. It says citizen of the United States of America. As discussed in the preceding chapter, Christ alone can bring reconciliation—a deep, sincere love for people.

A spirit of impurity. We have lost our sense of what is proper and honorable. Now we're talking to eight-year-old girls and boys about condoms and "safe sex." Have we no shame? America needs a restored spirit of holiness. We need it in the church; we each need it in our own soul.

A spirit of guilt. What America needs most is forgiveness preceded by repentance. God is ready to forgive. He will forgive young women who have had abortions. He will forgive adulterers and fornicators and practicing homosexuals. He will forgive murderers and rapists and embezzlers. He will forgive the self-righteous and hypocrites. He forgives all of us sinners the instant we believe Him with a repentant heart.

That message—that God forgives sinners and offers everyone the chance to start over—has transformed millions of lives all across the Americas in the past twenty-five years. Evangelicals, many of them illiterate, have stood on street corners of the so-called Third World preaching John 3:16 and 1 Corinthians 15:3–5 and testifying of God's grace. Millions of Latinos have said, "That's the gospel? I want to know this God and live for Him."

But in the United States, we evangelical men have acquired a reputation as harsh, unloving, bitter people, with no sensitivity or compassion for those who have failed. We're known for what we're against, not what we're for. If we Promise Keepers will stand and, with pride in Jesus Christ, proclaim His gospel in all its purity, I think we'll find many willing to be converted to true Christianity.

Evangelism is good news. More than ever, that's what America—and the world—needs.

A WORLD TO WIN

Finally, *let's gain a new vision of helping fulfill the Great Commission in our generation.* When you think about those who have never committed their lives to Jesus Christ, who comes to mind? Write down the names of at least five people you'd like to see trust Christ. Begin praying daily for their salvation. Ask God to draw at least one of them to Himself before the end of the year.

Then think about the crowds you see in the cities—at the airports, in the streets, everywhere. How do you feel when you think about them?

Scripture tells us that when Jesus saw the crowds, "he had compassion on them, because they were harassed and helpless, like sheep without a shepherd" (Matt. 9:36). We need to ask God to move our hearts with the same compassion that moves His.

Two of the greatest dangers we face as Promise Keepers are cynicism and a cool detachment: "So more than three billion people don't know Christ. That's too bad." We must not forget the actual people—including those we know and love—behind that number who live "without hope and without God in the world" (Eph. 2:12).

The Lord pointed out the urgency of helping fulfill the Great Commission by reminding His disciples, "The harvest is plentiful but the workers are few" (Matt. 9:37). We must sense the urgency of our time. How long must people wait before they hear the gospel? How many more generations must pass before some parts of the world hear the message for the first time?

It's exciting to see the tremendous harvest being reaped in most of the so-called Third World today. Several nations in Latin America, Africa, and Asia could become 51 percent Christian within ten or fifteen years. Right now the doors are open as perhaps never before. Mass communications have made it possible to reach even "closed" countries with the message of life. All of this is before us now, but it could pass in such a short time.

Our task is urgent. That's why Jesus commanded His disciples, "Ask the Lord of the harvest, therefore, to send out workers into his harvest field" (Matt. 9:38). Our Bibles end the chapter right there, but don't stop reading! In the next five verses, the Lord gave His disciples authority and sent them out into the harvest. The twelve became an answer to their own prayer!

To finish the task, we must have the authority of God that comes from a holy life. Paul told Timothy, "God did not give us a spirit of timidity, but a spirit of power, of love and of self-discipline" (2 Tim. 1:7). I like to think of that as holy boldness.

The unfinished task of winning the world to Christ is enormous. Are you willing to gain a compassion for the unsaved and a sense of urgency in reaching them for Christ? Are you available to serve God with holy boldness as a Promise Keeper? Let's press on to finish the task set before us.

7 In the Life
of One Man

The two had nothing in common, except the work they shared at a large manufacturing plant thirty-two years ago. In fact, their prospects for friendship were grim. Sean was a hard worker, good at his job on the late shift. Karl was a cocky young student engineer new to the company. And yet, the Lord placed them next to each other on the job, stretching both of their comfort zones.

Sean—affectionately known as "the preacher" at the plant—attended seminary during his off-work hours. Karl greeted this bit of information with scorn. Outspoken on almost every subject, he shared his pride in being a clear-thinking, committed atheist. Their only hope for civility was that they respected each other's work, despite the awkward silences between them.

Karl noted that he found the Bible to be a "good, moral book of fairy tales" and needled Sean about his seminary study. "I didn't think that could even be a legitimate academic discipline," he says. Finally, Sean could stand Karl's arrogant sarcasm no longer. On the way home from work one night, he found himself praying, "Lord, You're going to have to save Karl, or I'm going to kill him." In that moment of transparency before the Lord, Sean suddenly realized that his relationship with Karl could be the only thing that stood between Karl and eternal damnation.

Sobered by this truth, Sean reached out to Karl in a tangible way. They began to ride to work together, making the ride time a perfect opportunity for Sean to discuss his faith. He became a real friend to Karl and patiently answered all his questions. "He was never antagonistic even when I was," remembers Karl. "I was impressed by his consistency. He opened up the fantastic depth of the Scriptures to me and showed me prophecies fulfilled." Karl's contempt began to turn to wonder as he discovered something very alive and powerful drawing his interest.

At this same time, Karl's wife, Catherine, was drawn to a neighborhood mom who seemed to be raising some extraordinary children. Catherine, like Karl, also prided herself for her skepticism. Ironically, her newfound friend Mary happened to be a strong Christian. As their friendship grew, Catherine began to pepper Mary with the same cynical questions that Karl threw at Sean. Sometimes, Karl and Catherine conspired to ask the same question of their friends separately, in an effort to trip them up or find the hole in their argument. But their plan faltered in the light of the truth of God's Word. Not only were Sean and Mary's answers consistent, but they were often supported by identical Scripture passages. While Catherine and Karl looked for reasons not to believe in God, they found confirmation after confirmation of the truth in the testimony of their friends.

It was a logical progression for them, with no emotion attached. "We just reached the point where we couldn't *not* believe that the Bible was really true. We were astounded by our conviction that Jesus died for us—even us," Karl recalls, "and He would have given His life, even if we had been the only ones to be so saved."

In time, Catherine and Karl began attending church and accepted Christ as their Savior and Lord. Never one to go halfway in anything, Karl pursued his faith with the same energy he had previously devoted to atheism. He studied Scripture; his faith grew; and the Lord eventually led him into full-time ministry. He began a formal program to train others in the same step-by-step friendship evangelism that had won him and Catherine to the Lord.

Sean went on to become a pastor. Mary still serves the Lord in the context of her family. And all learned firsthand how persistent, caring friendship can change a life forever!

APPENDICES

Promise Keepers

Purpose Statement

Promise Keepers is a Christ-centered ministry dedicated to uniting men through vital relationships to become godly influences in their world.

Statement of Faith

1. We believe that there is one God eternally existing in three persons: the Father, the Son, and the Holy Spirit.

2. We believe that the Bible is God's written revelation to man and that it is verbally inspired, authoritative, and without error in the original manuscripts.

3. We believe in the deity of Jesus Christ, His virgin birth, sinless life, miracles, death on the cross to provide for our redemption, bodily resurrection and ascension into heaven, present ministry of intercession for us, and His return to earth in power and glory.

4. We believe in the personality and deity of the Holy Spirit, that He performs the miracle of new birth in an unbeliever and indwells believers, enabling them to live a godly life.

5. We believe that man was created in the image of God but, because of sin, was alienated from God. Only through faith, trusting in Christ alone for salvation, which was made possible by His death and resurrection, can that alienation be removed.

Eight Biblical Principles for Reconciliation and Unity

1. **Call:** All Christians are called to a ministry of reconciliation and are commanded to be reconciled with our brothers across racial, cultural, and denominational barriers.

2. **Commitment to Relationship:** Love by God and adopted into His family, we are called to committed love relationships with our brothers.

3. **Intentionality:** Experiencing a committed relationship with our brothers requires purposeful, positive, and planned activities that facilitate reconciliation and right relationships.

4. **Sincerity:** We must be willing to be vulnerable and express our feelings, attitudes, differences, and perceptions, with the goal of resolution and building trust.

5. **Sensitivity:** We must seek knowledge about our brothers in order to relate empathetically to people from different denominations, traditions, races, social standings, or cultures.

6. **Sacrifice:** We must be willing to give up an established status or position and accept a lesser position in order to facilitate reconciling relationships.

7. **Empowerment:** Through prayer, personal brokenness, repentance, and forgiveness, we remove barriers and are freed to experience the power of the Holy Spirit in reconciling relationships.

8. **Interdependence:** As we recognize our differences, we also realize that God has placed us as members in the body of Christ where we need and depend on the contributions of each member.

Life Aboard
the Fellow-Ship

by Max Lucado

God has enlisted us in His navy and placed us on His ship. The boat has one purpose—to carry us safely to the other shore.

This is no cruise ship; it's a battleship. We aren't called to a life of leisure; we are called to a life of service. Each of us has a different task. Some, concerned with those who are drowning, are snatching people from the water. Others are occupied with the enemy, so they man the cannons of prayer and worship. Still others devote themselves to the crew, feeding and training the crew members.

Though different, we are the same. Each can tell of a personal encounter with the Captain, for each has received a personal call. He found us among the shanties of the seaport and invited us to follow Him. Our faith was born at the sight of His fondness, and so we went.

We each followed Him across the gangplank of His grace onto the same boat. There is one Captain and one destination. Though the battle is fierce, the boat is safe, for our Captain is God. The ship will not sink. For that, there is no concern.

There is concern, however, regarding the disharmony of the crew. When we first boarded, we assumed the crew was made up of others like us. But as we've wandered these decks, we've encountered curious converts with curious appearances. Some wear uniforms we've never seen, sporting styles we've never witnessed. "Why do you look the way you do?" we ask them.

"Funny," they reply, "we were about to ask the same of you."

The variety of dress is not nearly as disturbing as the plethora of opinions. There is a group, for example, who clusters every morning for serious study. They promote rigid discipline and somber expressions. "Serving the Captain is serious business," they explain. It's no coincidence that they tend to congregate around the stern.

There is another regiment deeply devoted to prayer. Not only do they believe in prayer, they believe in prayer by kneeling. For that reason you always know where to locate them; they are at the bow of the ship.

And then there are a few who staunchly believe real wine should be used in the Lord's Supper. You'll find them on the port side.

Still another group has positioned themselves near the engine. They spend hours examining the nuts and bolts of the boat. They've been known to go below deck and not come up for days. They are occasionally criticized by those who linger on the top deck, feeling the wind in their hair and the sun on their face. "It's not what you learn," those topside argue. "It's what you feel that matters."

And, oh, how we tend to cluster.

Some think once you're on the boat, you can't get off. Others say you'd be foolish to go overboard, but the choice is yours.

Some believe you volunteer for service; others believe you were destined for the service before the ship was even built.

Some predict a storm of great tribulation will strike before we dock; others say it won't hit until we are safely ashore.

There are those who speak to the Captain in a personal language. There are those who think such languages are extinct.

There are those who think the officers should wear robes, there are those who think there should be no officers at all, and there are those who think we are all officers and should all wear robes.

And, oh, how we tend to cluster.

And then there is the issue of the weekly meeting at which the Captain is thanked and His words are read. All agree on its importance, but few agree on its nature. Some want it loud, others quiet. Some want ritual, others spontaneity. Some want to celebrate so they can meditate; others meditate so they can celebrate. Some want a meeting for those who've gone overboard. Others want to reach those overboard but without going overboard and neglecting those on board.

And, oh, how we tend to cluster.

The consequence is a rocky boat. There is trouble on deck. Fights have broken out. Sailors have refused to speak to each other. There have even been times when one group refused to acknowledge the presence of others on the ship. Most tragically, some adrift at sea have chosen not to board the boat because of the quarreling of the sailors.

"What can we do?" we'd like to ask the Captain. "How can there be harmony on the ship?" We don't have to go far to find the answer.

On the last night of His life, Jesus prayed a prayer that stands as a citadel for all Christians:

> I pray for these followers, but I am also praying for all those who will
> believe in me because of their teaching. Father, I pray that they can be
> one. As you are in me and I am in you, I pray that they can also be one
> in us. Then the world will believe that you sent me (John 17:20, NCV).

How precious are these words. Jesus, knowing the end is near, prays one final time for His followers. Striking, isn't it, that He prayed not for their success, their safety, or their happiness.

He prayed for their unity. He prayed that they would love each other.

As He prayed for them, He also prayed for "those who will believe because of their teaching." That means us! In His last prayer, Jesus prayed that you and I be one.

Of all the lessons we can draw from this verse, don't miss the most important. Unity matters to God. The Father does not want His kids to squabble. Disunity disturbs Him. Why: Because "all people will know that you are my followers if you love each other" (John 13:35). Unity creates belief. How will the world believe that Jesus was sent by God? Not if we agree with each other. Not if we solve every controversy. Not if we are unanimous on each vote. Not if we never make a doctrinal error. But if we love one another.

Biblical Unity and Biblical Truth: A Necessary Tension

by Glenn Wagner

For he himself is our peace, who has made the two one and has destroyed the barrier, the dividing wall of hostility. (Eph. 2:14)

Unity—a beautiful word, a powerful ideal, a biblical concept. Regrettably, through the years, confusion has developed in the church over it, and what was meant to be a glorious reality has become an elusive, fleeting, and divisive dream. On one extreme stand those who are determined to achieve unity at any cost; on the other, those who claim that any pursuit of unity comes at the expense of truth. Truth and unity have come to be viewed by many as antithetical— you can align with one or the other, but not with both. Promise Keepers believes Scripture teaches that this is a false dichotomy and that the Word of God commands us, and the love of God compels us, to pursue both.[1]

While regional splits have always existed within the church, from its founding and for the first one thousand years, there was but one recognized church. When errors of teaching were discovered, they were addressed, and various church councils were called to deal with doctrinal disputes over important issues such as the nature of God and the deity of Christ. The first major division took place in A.D. 1054, resulting in the Eastern Orthodox and the Roman Catholic churches. A little more than five hundred years later, another fracture occurred,

242

leading to the creation of the Protestant church. Protestantism, in turn, has experienced the formation of myriad denominations and sects, each intending in its own way to maintain the purity of the gospel and to uphold biblical Christianity.

Since its inception, with varying degrees of intensity, the issue of unity has been an ongoing matter of discussion within the church. In the late 1800s and early 1900s, the controversy began to focus on what has been called the Ecumenical Movement. Intending a broad-based reunification, the movement was plagued by one major difficulty: the idea that church unity should be achieved "at any cost"—to the extent of sacrificing the essential truths of the Word of God. Opposition arose from individuals, churches, and denominations committed to the defense and proclamation of the truth, generally dividing the church into what have come to be known as "liberal" and "conservative" camps. This division persists in our day, with those on one side of the issue perceived as willing to pursue love apart from truth, compromising the integrity of the gospel message, and those on the other side viewed as defending the truth of God's Word at the expense of love, often leading to coldness, arrogance, and pride.

In view of this history, and in spite of the difficulties involved, Promise Keepers believes the Lord is calling Christian men to denominational reconciliation in our day. The ministry has, therefore, sought to find a common ground upon which all Christians can unite—one it believes to be entirely biblical and consistent with the will of Christ for His church. Simply stated, Promise Keepers believes: *We must be committed to truth, and we must also be committed to unity.*

Theologians call it an antinomy—two truths that at times seem to be in conflict, but nonetheless are equally true. In obedience to God and His Word, we do not believe one should be sacrificed for the other. Each is vital to accomplishing God's purposes. We believe He calls us to pursue both. Therefore, while Promise Keepers desires to call men of all Christian denominations together in biblical unity, that unity must be based on the historically essential truths of Christianity.

Doctrine—right belief—is the core and essence of Promise Keepers. Everything we do is guided and informed by biblical doctrine. Realizing that any doctrinal stand has the potential to divide, the ministry nonetheless believes that such a stand is not inconsistent with the love of Christ. Indeed, Promise Keepers seeks to reflect Christ as He embodies the truth and love of God. While recognizing that our ultimate unity has been accomplished by our Lord through His death on the cross, we believe the sectarianism that characterizes the church is hurting the cause of Christ. We feel compelled, therefore, to call believers together according to our highest common denominators— faith in Christ and the truth of God's Word. Our pursuit of unity, then, is based on a core theology of historic doctrines of the church, which is represented by our statement of faith.

At a time when surveys indicate that up to 42 percent of those who call themselves evangelical Christians believe that there is no such thing as absolute truth,[2] Promise Keepers takes the stand that the Bible is the inspired, inerrant, infallible Word of God (2 Tim. 3:16). Although some are troubled by the subject of inerrancy, we believe that everything hinges upon it. If God, who is without error, is not able to reveal Himself through the written Word in an inerrant fashion, how can we trust His revelation through His Living Word, Jesus Christ? If we believe the Bible has errors, we place ourselves above it, determining for ourselves what is and is not truth. But if the Bible is the infallible revelation of Almighty God, then we must place ourselves under it, even though our understanding may be incomplete.

Nor do we believe that it is enough just to call men to worship God. The Word of God says we are to worship Him in spirit and in truth (John 4:24). We do not want men to have their emotions merely stirred by Christian music or to worship the experience of worship. Our desire is for the men who attend Promise Keepers conferences to worship the true and living God of the universe, the One who created all things and is sovereign over all. Our question for every man is, are you worshiping some vague idea of God or the God revealed in the Bible who eternally exists in three persons—the Father, Son, and Holy Spirit? *This* is the God we believe in and the One we want men to meet.

Some just want to lift up Jesus, believing that in so doing, all men will be drawn to Him. But this will only happen if the *authentic, biblical* Jesus is exalted (Gal. 1:6–9). Only a clear understanding of God's Word will lead men to exalt the Jesus who is God of very God; the Jesus who took on human flesh, was born of a virgin, lived a sinless life, and died on the cross, making atonement for our sins; the Jesus who was buried, rose again on the third day, was seen by many witnesses, has ascended on high, sits at the right hand of God the Father, and intercedes for us; the Jesus who is going to return in power and great glory to judge the world. *This* is the Jesus we are exalting and teaching.

Men need to understand the person and work of the Holy Spirit. He has birthed us anew in Christ and has come to fill us with power to live a godly life (Acts 1:8). He is not simply some impersonal "force" that men can call upon to fulfill every whim, but He is the third Person of the Trinity who indwells believers, enabling them to walk in obedience and holiness and in the Word and will of the Father (John 16:13). *This* is the Holy Spirit we want men to understand and experience.

An alarming percentage of those who claim to be born again believe they can get to heaven by good works. However, the Bible tells us that salvation is not by works, but by faith in Jesus Christ *alone:* "For it is by grace you have been saved, through faith—and this not from yourselves, it is the gift of God—not by works, so that no one can boast" (Eph. 2:8–9). Salvation is by grace alone, through faith alone in Christ alone. When we stand before Almighty God, and He says, "Why should I let you into My perfect heaven?" the only answer is, "Because I have trusted in Your Son, Jesus Christ, who paid the penalty for my sin on the cross at Calvary."

The above five tenets form the core beliefs in our statement of faith. We believe they provide a firm biblical foundation upon which Christians can join together and live out the unity called for in John 17:22–23, where Jesus prayed to the Father, "I have given them the glory that you gave me, that they may be one as we are one. . . . May they be brought to complete unity to let the world know that you sent me and have loved them even as you have loved me."

With the apostle Paul, we implore all men who share a common faith in the biblical Jesus to "live a life worthy of the calling you have received. Be completely humble and gentle; be patient, bearing with one another in love. Make every effort to keep the unity of the Spirit through the bond of peace" (Eph. 4:1–3). For too long now, the church has allowed its differences to divide it, preventing it from ministering effectively and from displaying the glory God intended for it. As a consequence, the church has lost its "saltiness."

Is it not terrible to realize that by overemphasizing our differences, we have actually served to hinder the Father's answer to our Lord's prayer for oneness in the church as well as our witness to the lost? If, after all, Christians can't love and embrace one another, expressing the oneness that is already ours in Christ, the world will rightfully question the validity and the value of our faith. "By this all men will know that you are my disciples, if you love one another, " Jesus proclaimed (John 13:35). Furthermore, as Jesus' prayer in John 17 indicates, while division and divisiveness are natural in this life, there's something *supernatural* about unity that even the ungodly can recognize. When Christians merely display the love of Christ to each other, the world knows that God sent Jesus, and He receives the glory due His name. Biblical unity, then, is one of the most powerful testimonies that exists to the reality of God.

"How good and pleasant it is when brothers live together in unity!" (Ps. 133:1). At Promise Keepers, we are not preoccupied with a man's denominational label, nor do we wish to see all church distinctives disappear. Rather, we are committed to calling Christian men to reach beyond labels and to enter into vital relationship with each other based on our common faith in Jesus Christ. Through loving relationships, we can demonstrate to a hopelessly divisive world that, by God's grace, men can live peacefully together in spite of their differences. This way, we can also know if a man holds to the core doctrines of God's Word. If he does, we are brothers in Christ. If not, we may be used by God to lead him to the knowledge of the truth. As it has been said, "In essentials, unity. In nonessentials, liberty. In all things, charity."

Many are grateful for and committed to their denominational affiliation and heritage—and rightfully so. But while it is vital to fight for truth, the day has come when we must not allow ourselves to be separated by sectarian labels and secondary issues. At a time when only approximately 10 percent of the world's five billion people are professing Christians, and when Christianity is under attack on virtually every side, it is imperative for us to reach out to one another in love and unity. While respecting our differences, we must come together in relationship, ensuring that each man is trusting in the finished work of Christ for his salvation, thereby receiving God's gift of eternal life and becoming a fellow member of God's family. To continue down the road (or roads) we have been traveling is to court further divisiveness, disunity, loss of witness, and disaster.

Finally, it is truth—the truth of Christ—to which we call all men, and it is in this truth that we can find biblical unity—unity in truth. When we stand before Jesus in the Judgment Day, we believe those who strive for this ideal will hear the words, "Well done, good and faithful servant." For our Savior's sake, for His glory, and that the world will know that God sent Him, we can do no less.

As fellow members of His church, we need each other "so that the body of Christ may be built up until we all reach unity in the faith and in the knowledge of the Son of God and become mature, attaining to the whole measure of the fullness of Christ" (Eph. 4:12–13).

Authors

Don Bartlette—International speaking ministry; major presentation title *Macaroni at Midnight*; film testimonies *Believing for the Best in You* and *When Nobody Loves You*; social worker, counselor, and educator; involved with the National Association for Native-American Children of Alcoholics, Christian Home Educator of Ohio, and Children's Harbor in Alabama.

Ron Blue—Managing Partner of Ronald Blue & Co., a fee-only financial planning firm; author of seven books on personal finance including *Master Your Money*; Board of Directors of Campus Crusade for Christ International, Family Research Council, MISH (Medical Institute for Sexual Health), and Promise Keepers.

Wellington Boone—Founder of Wellington Boone Ministries; pastor for more than twenty years; outreach to African-American and urban communities based on prayer, reconciliation, and unity; Executive Board Member for Evangelical Council for Financial Accountability; National Board Member for March for Jesus.

Bill Bright—Founded the Campus Crusade for Christ international ministry in 1951, now with thirteen thousand full-time staff and more than one hundred thousand trained volunteers in 161 countries, serving inner cities, prisons, families, the military, executives, athletes, women and men; his booklet *The Four Spiritual Laws* distributed to more than a billion and a half worldwide.

Huron Claus—CEO/Executive Vice President, CHIEF, Inc. (Christian Hope Indian Eskimo Fellowship), dedicated to discipling and equipping Native-American church leadership; Board of Trustees, InterAct Ministries International; Board of Directors, Flagstaff mission to the Navajos; Advisory Committee, International Bible Society; Board of Directors, Promise Keepers.

Rodney L. Cooper—Professor of Leadership and Counseling and Director of the Masters of Leadership program, Denver Seminary; former National Director of Educational Ministries at Promise Keepers; author of four key books, including *We Stand Together, Reconciling Men of Color*, and the newly released *Shoulder to Shoulder: The Journey from Isolation to Brotherhood*; conference speaker and consultant.

Ken Davis—President, Dynamic Communications; author of seven books including *Fire Up Your Life, How to Live with Your Parents without Losing Your Mind*, and *Jumper Fables*, which won the CBA Gold Medallion Award; seminar teacher and motivational speaker.

James Dobson—Founder and president of Focus on the Family, a nonprofit evangelical organization dedicated to the preservation of the home; author of numerous books, including *Parenting Isn't for Cowards, Straight Talk, Love Must Be Tough, Life on the Edge, and When God Doesn't Make Sense*; a licensed psychologist in the state of California and a licensed marriage, family, and child therapist in the state of Colorado; formerly an assistant professor of pediatrics at the University of Southern California, School of Medicine; host of international radio broadcast *Focus on the Family*, heard on more than two thousand stations worldwide.

Gordon England—National Director of Evangelism for Promise Keepers and manager, International Expansion for the movement; served as a missionary in the Philippines for nine years before going on to serve as a pastor in the Denver area; member of the faculty at Asian Theological Seminary (Philippines), University of the Philippines, Febias College of the Bible (Philippines), Denver Seminary, University of Denver, and Rockmont College (Colorado); recognized as a public speaker, effective in motivation and evangelism through his work with HIS Ministries (multicultural issues) and as a board member for Concerts of Prayer/Colorado Prayer Network.

Bruce Fong—Professor of Homiletics, Bible, and Pastoral Ministries at Multnomah Biblical Seminary; author of *Racial Equality in the Church*; conference and retreat speaker; cofounder and pastor of Clear Creek Community Church.

Jack Hayford—Senior Pastor, The Church on the Way, the First Foursquare Church of Van Nuys, California; board or key committee member to several Christian organizations including National Religious Broadcasters, Pentecostal/Charismatic Churches of North America, and Promise Keepers; author of more than two dozen books including *Worship His Majesty* and *The Key to Everything*; composer of nearly five hundred songs, hymns, and other musical works, including the widely sung chorus "Majesty."

Howard Hendricks—Chairman, Center of Christian Leadership, Dallas Theological Seminary, Dallas, Texas; pastor for fourteen years; author of eleven books and producer of five films; former chaplain for the Dallas Cowboys.

Glen Kehrein—Graduate of Moody Bible Institute and Wheaton College; active at the Rock of Our Salvation Evangelical Free Church; works closely with urban ministries as teacher and elder in church; awarded Doctor of Peacemaking degree from Westminster College (Pennsylvania); coauthored *Breaking Down the Walls* with Raleigh Washington.

Greg Laurie—Evangelist and president of Harvest Crusades, Inc.; pastor and founder of Harvest Christian Fellowship; author of several books including *Every Day with Jesus, The New Believer's Bible*, and *The God of the Second Chance*; Board of Directors of the Billy Graham Evangelistic Association.

Crawford Loritts—Associate Director, U.S. Ministries, Campus Crusade for Christ; author of *A Passionate Commitment: Recapturing*

Your Sense of Purpose and *Never Walk Away;* cofounder of Oak Cliff Bible Fellowship in Dallas, Texas; international conference and seminar speaker; 1997 cochair of the Nation Congress on the Urban Family.

Max Lucado—Minister of the Oak Hills Church in San Antonio, Texas; speaks daily on his national radio program, *UpWords;* author of numerous best-selling books, including *Just Like Jesus, In the Grip of Grace, When God Whispers Your Name, He Still Moves Stones, No Wonder They Call Him the Savior,* and *Six Hours One Friday.*

John Maxwell—Founder of INJOY, Inc., INJOY Stewardship Services, INJOY Management Services, and EQUIP; pastor and evangelist; author of twenty books including *Becoming a Person of Influence, Breakthrough Parenting,* and *The Winning Attitude.*

Bill McCartney—Founder, Promise Keepers; former football coach of University of Colorado; named Kodak Coach of the Year, Bear Bryant Coach of the Year, Walter Camp Foundation Coach of the Year, UPI Coach of the Year, and three-time Big Eight Conference Coach of the Year; well-known speaker and author of several books, including *From Ashes to Glory* and *Sold Out.*

Jesse Miranda—Professor, Azusa Pacific University; well-known educator, author, and speaker, particularly with a heart for the Hispanic community.

Gary Oliver—Clinical Director, Southwest Counseling Associates, Littleton, Colorado; advanced degrees include Ph.D., M.Div,. Th.M., and M.A.; twenty-five years as a Christian counselor; author of *Real Men Have Feelings Too* and other books; host of national radio program *Confident Living.*

Luis Palau—Founder of Luis Palau Evangelistisic Association; evangelist to twelve million people in sixty-five nations face-to-face, plus hundreds of millions via radio and television broadcasts; host of *Luis Palau Responde* and *Cruzada* Spanish radio programs and *Luis Palau*

Responds, a two-minute daily radio program; author of forty-one books and booklets in English and Spanish, including *God Is Relevant* and *The Only Hope Left for America*.

Phillip Porter—Chairman of the Board of Promise Keepers since 1994; founder and pastor of All Nations Pentecostal Center Church of God in Christ in Aurora, Colorado; host of a Denver radio show called *It's Prayer Time*; author of *Let the Walls Fall Down* and the newly released *On the Path to Purity*.

Dale Schlafer—Senior Pastor at South Evangelical Presbyterian Fellowship of Littleton, Colorado, for twenty-two years; served an integral role in developing and overseeing "Stand in the Gap—A Sacred Assembly of Men" and "Clergy '96—Fan into Flame"; holds a B.A. from Westminster College and an M.Div. from Princeton Theological Seminary; pastored churches in New Jersey and Colorado as well as acting as founder and Chairman of the Board of Mile High Ministries, a suburban inner-city partnership for building the church.

Gary Smalley—President, Today's Family; popular speaker and author on family issues; hosts a national television program that airs nationally; has a wide background in psychology including an M.A. from Bethel Seminary in Minnesota, doctoral studies at California Coast University, and mentoring by other experienced psychologists in many areas of marriage and family issues.

Joseph Stowell—President of Moody Bible Institute of Chicago since 1987; radio personality on Moody's *Proclaim!* and *Moody Presents* broadcasts; pastor for sixteen years prior to coming to Moody; author of fourteen books including *Far from Home*, *Shepherding the Church*, and *Following Christ*.

Glenn Wagner—Senior Pastor of Calvary Church; national and international speaking and training ministry; former Promise Keepers Board of Directors member and Vice President; author of *The Heart of a Godly Man*, *The Awesome Power of Shared Beliefs*, and *Strategies for Successful Marriage*.

Raleigh Washington—Vice President of Reconciliation for Promise Keepers; founder and senior pastor of Rock of Our Salvation Evangelical Free Church in Chicago; served as a Lieutenant Colonel in the U.S. Army; coauthor of *Breaking Down Walls: A Model of Reconciliation in an Age of Racial Strife*; awarded two honorary doctoral degrees; featured speaker on missions, urban focus, and racial reconciliation.

Additional Book Resources

For information on how to become more involved with Promise Keepers, call 1-800-888-7595.

PROMISE #1

Laurie, Greg. *Discipleship*. Eugene: Harvest House, 1993.
Peel, William. *What God Does When Men Pray*. Colorado Springs: NavPress, 1994.
Wagner, Glenn. *The Heart of a Godly Man*. Chicago: Moody Press, 1997.

PROMISE #2

Gorsuch, Geoff and Dan Schaffer. *Brothers! Calling Men into Vital Relationships*. Denver: Promise Keepers, 1993.

PROMISE #3

Blue, Ron. *Master Your Money*. Grand Rapids: Zondervan, 1997.
————. *Money Talks and So Can We*. Grand Rapids: Zondervan, 1999.
Horner, Bob and Dave Sunde. *Character under Construction*. Nashville: Thomas Nelson, 1999.
Wilkinson, Bruce. *Victory over Temptation*. Eugene: Harvest House, 1997.

PROMISE #4

Shipp, Glover. *Marriage Is a Covenant, Not a Contract.* Joplin, Mo.: College Press, 1995.

Wagner, Glenn. *Strategies of a Successful Marriage.* Colorado Springs: NavPress, 1994.

White, Joe. *What Kids Wish Parents Knew about Parenting.* West Monroe, La.: Howard Publishing, 1998.

PROMISE #5

Colson, Charles. *The Body.* Dallas: Word, 1992.

Hayford, Jack. *The Key to Everything.* Orlando: Creation House, 1993.

London, H. B. Jr. and Neil B. Wiseman. *Pastors at Risk.* Wheaton, Ill.: Victor, 1993.

PROMISE #6

Garlington, Joseph. *Right or Reconciled.* Shippensburg, Pa.: Destiny Image, 1998.

Perkins, Spencer and Chris Rice. *More than Equals.* Downers Grove, Ill.: InterVarsity, 1993.

Washington, Raleigh and Glen Kehrein. *Breaking Down the Walls.* Chicago: Moody, 1993.

PROMISE #7

Aldrich, Joseph C. *Life-Style Evangelism: Crossing Traditional Boundaries to Reach the Unbelieving World.* Portland, Oreg.: Multnomah, 1983.

Bright, Bill. *Witnessing.* Nashville: Thomas Nelson, 1993.

Palau, Luis. *Say Yes!* Portland, Oreg.: Multnomah, 1991.

OTHER BOOKS

McCartney, Bill. *Sold Out.* Nashville: Thomas Nelson, 1997.

Maxwell, John. *The 21 Irrefutable Laws of Leadership: Follow Them and People Will Follow You.* Nashville: Thomas Nelson, 1998.

Stowell, Joseph. *Following Christ.* Grand Rapids: Zondervan, 1996.

Weber, Stu. *Tender Warrior.* Portland, Oreg.: Multnomah, 1993.

Endnotes

A Mandate for Mentoring—Howard Hendricks

1. Pierre Mornell, *Passive Men, Wild Women* (New York: Ballantine, 1979), 1.

Black-and-White Living in a Gray World—Dr. Gary J. Oliver

1. Dietrich Bonhoeffer, *Psalms: The Prayer Book of the Bible* (Minneapolis: Augsburg, 1970), 64–65.

2. Charles Swindoll, *The Quest for Character* (Portland, Oreg.: Multnomah, 1987), 19–20.

The Priority of Fathering—Dr. James Dobson

1. James Dobson, *What Wives Wish Their Husbands Knew About Women* (Wheaton, Ill.: Tyndale, 1975), 157–58.

2. Reprinted by permission from *American Girl*, a magazine for all girls published by Girl Scouts of the U.S.A.

Honoring and Praying for Your Pastor—Dale Schlafer

1. E. M. Bounds, *A Treasury of Prayer—The Best of E. M. Bounds* (Minneapolis: Bethany House, 1961), 172–73.

2. John Maxwell, in a letter to church leaders, quoting A. M. Hills in *Pentecostal Light*.

"Church" Means "People"—Jesse Miranda

1. Wes Roberts, *Support Your Local Pastor: Practical Ways to Encourage Your Minister* (Colorado Springs, Colo.: NavPress, 1995).

Biblical Unity and Biblical Truth—Glenn Wagner

1. Ps. 119:9, 160; Ps. 133; John 4:24; 10:16; 17:17–23; Acts 2:1, 42; 20:29–31; Rom. 12:4-5; 15:4–7; 1 Cor. 1:10; 12:12–13; 2 Cor. 13:11; Gal. 3:26–28; Eph. 2:14–18; 4:1–16; Phil. 1:27; 2:1–5; 2 Tim. 2:15; 3:16; 1 Pet. 3:8; 1 John 4.

2. George Barna, *Virtual America: The Barna Report 1994–95* (Ventura, Calif.: Regal Books, 1994).